THE IDEAS OF
NIKOLAI BUKHARIN

THE IDEAS OF
NIKOLAI BUKHARIN

Edited and Introduced
By
A. KEMP-WELCH

CLARENDON PRESS · OXFORD
1992

Oxford University Press, Walton Street, Oxford OX2 6DP

Oxford New York Toronto
Delhi Bombay Calcutta Madras Karachi
Petaling Jaya Singapore Hong Kong Tokyo
Nairobi Dar es Salaam Cape Town
Melbourne Auckland
and associated companies in
Berlin Ibadan

Oxford is a trade mark of Oxford University Press

Published in the United Sates
by Oxford University Press, New York

British Library Cataloguing in Publication Data
Data available

Library of Congress Cataloging in Publication Data
The Ideas of Nikolai Bukharin/edited and introduced by A. Kemp-Welch.
p. cm.
Includes bibliographical references and index.
1. Bukharin, Nikolai Ivanovich, 1888–1938—Influence. 2. Soviet
Union—History—1917–1936. 3. Communists—Soviet Union—Biography.
4. Soviet Union—History—1925–1953. I. Kemp-Welch, A.
DK268.B76134 1992 947.084'092—dc20 91–43393
ISBN 0–19–827866–7

Typeset by Best-set Typesetter Ltd., Hong Kong
Printed and bound in
Great Britain by Bookcraft (Bath) Ltd.
Midsomer Norton, Avon

Contents

Contributors

ANNA DI BIAGIO: Professor of History, University of Florence

JOHN BIGGART: Lecturer in Russian Studies, University of East Anglia

V. P. DANILOV: Professor of History, Soviet Academy of Sciences, Moscow

PETER FERDINAND: Senior Research Fellow, Chatham House, London

NEIL HARDING: Professor of Politics, University College, Swansea

A. KEMP-WELCH: Lecturer in Politics, University of Nottingham

ROBERT LEWIS: Senior Lecturer in Economic History, University of Exeter

ALEC NOVE: Emeritus Professor of Economics, University of Glasgow

The editor and contributors wish to acknowledge generous grants from the Ford and Nuffield Foundations.

I

Introduction

A. Kemp-Welch

> The rehabilitation of Bukharin may come—who can tell? If
> it ever does, it will be a sure sign that real and substantial
> changes have taken place in the essential nature of the
> Soviet system of rule.[1]

IN the late 1980s, the Soviet leadership embarked upon a
radical review of the legacy of Stalinism: an overcentralized
state, an inefficient command economy, an oppressive censorship, and prohibition of genuine discussion within the Party.
In recognition of his contribution to an understanding of all
these subjects, Nikolai Ivanovich Bukharin was restored to the
Academy. The official notice of his scholarly rehabilitation
described him as an 'outstanding Party figure and eminent
academic in the field of social sciences whose name was
criminally blackened during the years of the J. V. Stalin personality cult'.[2] The fifty-year ban on reading his works was
lifted when the 'Chief Administration for Protection of State
Secrets in Print' decided to return his numerous books and
pamphlets to the shelves of public libraries.[3] Interest in his
personality was fostered through memoirs;[4] he was adopted by
a nation-wide co-operative movement, which began to award
Bukharin prizes.[5] Eventually, Gorbachev commenced a cautious
process of political rehabilitation.[6]

---

[1] L. Schapiro, 'Bukharin's Way', *New York Review of Books*, 7 Feb. 1974; repr.
in L. Schapiro, *Russian Studies* (London, 1986), 290–301.

[2] Resolution of the Soviet Academy of Sciences, *Izvestiya*, 10 May 1988.

[3] *Izvestiya*, 3 Apr. 1988.

[4] *Ogonek*, 48 (1987), 26–71; A. Larina in *Znamya*, 10–12 (1988), and
Nezabyvaemoe (Moscow, 1989); *Moskovskie novosti*, 25 Sept., 9 Oct. 1988; 29 Jan.
1989.

[5] Statement by the Bukharin Discussion Club: V. F. Pisigin, 'My vidim pered
soboi put' . . .' (Naberezhnye Chelny, Mar. 1989). First winners included S.
Cohen and O. Latsis (*Izvestiya*, 16 Mar. 1989).

[6] For instance, by reprinting his last open statement as a member of the

Bukharin had never held, nor sought, the top Party post. Although a Central Committee member for twenty years, ten of them in the Politburo, editor of *Pravda* continuously from 1917 to 1929, apart from a brief interlude in the Civil War, and a leading speaker at every Party and Comintern Congress in the 1920s,[7] his real importance lay elsewhere. As Heitman explains:

> For Bukharin, the struggle for Communism had to be waged not only on the barricades, but also in the minds of men, and it was to this latter task that he devoted his major effort. Possessed of a keen mind, perhaps second only to that of Trotsky, amazing erudition unmatched by any other Party leader, and a facile pen, he was regarded in his day as the ablest and most versatile thinker in the Party by communist and non-communist alike.[8]

His intellectual eminence was confirmed during the 1920s through a 'school' of young theoreticians[9] gathered around him at the Communist Academy, the Institute of Red Professors, and the Institute of Marx–Engels–Lenin.[10] They shared his conviction that, in the long run, Marxism would be able to provide the answers to all questions, including those of science and culture. When answers had been found, they expected that the uncommitted, formerly bourgeois, intelligentsia would voluntarily turn to Marxism, much as they expected the peasants would turn to agricultural co-operatives, once they were persuaded of the benefits which they would receive. Consequently, they were most reluctant to advocate coercion, since this was likely to be counter-productive. Towards literature, for instance, Bukharin proposed a policy of *laissez-faire*, expressed in the 1925 Party resolution, which, while favouring the proletarian groups on political principle

leadership: N. I. Bukharin, 'Politicheskoye zaveshchanie Lenina', ('Lenin's Political Testament', *Kommunist*, 2 (1988), 21–35.
[7] Sketches of his career include: L. K. Shkarenkov, 'Istoricheskie portreti. Nikolay Ivanovich Bukharin', *Voprosy istorii*, 7 (1988), 59–78; I.E. Gorelov and A. Osipov, 'Nikolay Ivanovich Bukharin', *Agitator*, 5 (1988), 21–5.
[8] S. Heitman, Introduction to *Put' k sotsializmu v Rossii: Izbrannye proizvedeniya N. I. Bukharina* (New York, 1967).
[9] P. Ferdinand, 'The Bukharin Group of Political Theoreticians: Their Ideas and their Importance to the Soviet Union in the 1920s', D.Phil. dissertation (Oxford, 1984), and Ch. 3 in this volume.
[10] An intellectual history of these institutions remains to be written.

(against a counter-memorandum from Trotsky), did not allow the state to assist them in imposing their hegemony.[11] While accepting that a class-based approach to culture was valid, Bukharin did not try to lay down a rigid, personal interpretation. His stance contrasted sharply with that of Stalin.[12]

Bukharin had made his mark on Bolshevism before the Revolution. He influenced Lenin's thinking on crucial questions such as the role of the state in a future socialist society, and contributed new and original interpretations of the international economy. His early work, on imperialism, argued that finance capital served to unify almost all sectors into centralized organizations, so as to form a military–reactionary clique.[13] Thus, democratic and liberal tendencies were thrust aside by modern imperialism, which always had a great need for dictatorship.[14] Bukharin characterized imperialism by its most radical new development: state intervention in the country's economy and the consequent 'militarization' of everyday life. As the state apparatus became ever more gigantic, 'Thus emerges the finished type of the contemporary imperialist robber state, the iron organization, which, with its tenacious, raking claws embraces the living body of society. This is the New Leviathan, beside which the fantasy of Thomas Hobbes looks like a child's toy.'[15] Looking back on the war in *Economics of the Transition Period* (1920), Bukharin made the point yet more sharply: the imperialist states, by throwing tens of millions of people on to the historical stage, had placed the analysis of state power on the top of the theoretical and practical agendas: 'The life of a state organization that had become all-embracing—not the life of society but that of the state—moved to the forefront. In his *Leviathan*, old Hobbes wrote that there is no power to compare with that of the state, but his

---

[11] Central Party Archives, cited by A. F. Yermakov, *Obogashchenie metoda sotsialisticheskogo realizma* (Moscow, 1967), 376–7.

[12] See A. Kemp-Welch, *Stalin and the Literary Intelligentsia, 1928–39* (London and New York, 1991), ch. 8.

[13] N. I. Bukharin, 'K teorii imperialisticheskogo gosudarstva' (1915); trans. as 'Toward a Theory of the Imperialist State', in N. I. Bukharin, *Selected Writings on the State and the Transition to Socialism*, ed. R. B. Day (New York, 1982), 6–37.

[14] Ibid. 14–5.

[15] Ibid. 31.

Leviathan would seem like a puppy compared to the monstrous force displayed by the state apparatus of finance capital.'[16]

Bukharin did not return to Leviathan, the coercive theory of the state, until 1928–9. During the interim he developed a quite different notion of state power, based on consent. Here he was again an innovative thinker in the Marxist tradition, though arguably less so than Gramsci.[17] The argument now became that the classical Marxist–Leninists had focused too narrowly upon the state as a coercive instrument—a Leviathan—and gave insufficient attention to the intellectual and cultural aspects of political power. Gramsci's famous definition considerably expands the analysis: 'The state is the entire complex of practical and theoretical activities with which the ruling class not only justifies and maintains its dominance, but manages to win the active consent of those over whom it rules.'[18] Hence leadership is based not on force alone but on *hegemony*: intellectual and moral leadership, as opposed to dictatorship and domination. *Support* has to be sought in civil society in order to supplement force as an instrument of political rule. The state is 'hegemony protected by the armour of coercion'.

For Bukharin the introduction of the New Economic Policy (NEP) in 1921 was not a 'retreat', pending further 'advances' to socialism, but a belated and final recognition that 'War Communism' (1918–20) had not been an advance at all.[19] As V. P. Danilov shows in Chapter 4, he thereafter criticized left-wing extremism on the basis of personal experience. After 1921, no one was quicker to point out the dangers of a return to state violence and voluntarism, or more fearful of its consequences. Bukharin now wished to replace the argument of

[16] N. I. Bukharin, *Ekonomika perekhodnogo perioda*, i (Moscow, 1920); excerpted in Bukharin, *Selected Writings*, 42. His flowery footnote is: 'Thomas Hobbes, *Moral and Political Works* (London, 1750) "Non est potestas super terram quae comparetur ei", Job 41: 33 (King James); 41: 25 (Hebrew); 41: 24 (Vulg.)' (ibid. 84).

[17] See E. Hobsbawm, 'Gramsci and Political Theory', *Marxism Today* (1977), 205–13.

[18] A. Gramsci, *Selections from the Prison Notebooks*, ed. Q. Hoare and G. Smith (London, 1971), 224

[19] See M. Lewin 'Models in Soviet History', in *Political Undercurrents in Soviet Economic Debates: From Bukharin to the Modern Reformers* (London, 1975), ch. 4.

force with the force of argument. He believed in 'winning over' the uncommitted by peaceful means. Thus in *The Path to Socialism and the Worker–Peasant Alliance* (1925) he declared, 'It is now necessary to outgrow command-administrative methods. We need a decisive, complete, and unconditional switch to methods of persuasion.'[20]

Though it suited Bukharin quite well, the turn to persuasion was not purely temperamental. It reflected an anxiety which Lenin shared, at least on his deathbed, that Soviet society would be swallowed up by the state. Like Lenin, he sought remedies in the rotation of officials, fixed terms of office, and schemes for accountability that would help to fight the scourge of bureaucracy. But he went much further. While Lenin had been concerned to check the bureaucrats (*chinovniki*), Bukharin realized, as Neil Harding shows in Chapter 5, that this would not be enough. The Soviet state could not be self-confirmed: it needed to be surrounded by a vast network of relatively autonomous associations. Bukharin thus called for the formation of 'hundreds and thousands of small and large rapidly expanding voluntary societies, circles and associations'.[21] Society was not to be a passive recipient of orders 'from above', but a genuine partner with other associations, not dominated by state powers of veto and appointment. One cannot help noting how contemporary this idea seems!

Underlying this radically new notion of the 'listening state' was a theory of culture, partly borrowed from Bogdanov. In the 1917 edition of *Tektologiya* Bogdanov offered a warning that a successful revolution might result in the subjugation of the proletariat to 'some new social class'. Bukharin took this further and admitted that 'even in the most revolutionary parties like our own communist party (and there is no point in concealing this) there is a definite élite of leaders who are to a significant extent migrants from another class'.[22] In such circumstances,

---

[20] N. I. Bukharin, *Put' k sotsializmu i raboche-krest'yanskiy soyuz* (Moscow and Leningrad, 1925; 4th edn., 1927); repr. in N. I. Bukharin, *Izbrannye proizvedeniya*, ed. G. L. Smirnov (Moscow, 1988), 146–230.

[21] N. I. Bukharin, 'Zadachi vypusknika-Sverdlovtsa', *Zapiski Kommunisticheskogo universiteta imeni Ya. M. Sverdlova*, ii (Moscow, 1924), 255–9.

[22] N. I. Bukharin, *Proletarskaya revolyutsiya i kul'tura* (Petrograd, 1923), 24. See Ch. 7 below.

the enforced reliance of the proletariat upon a specialized intelligentsia, required to take the lead in carrying out a vast range of tasks in the new state, 'brings with it a great danger: the danger of degeneration of the proletarian state and of the proletarian party'.[23] To avert this outcome, Bukharin proposed a 'cultural revolution', described by John Biggart in this volume, which was to be educational in the broadest sense: developing proletarian cadres with 'solid communist–proletariat outlooks', training them in Marxist theory and American efficiency, and replacing a humanitarian with a technical bias in education. Just as in his earlier analysis of imperialism, so now reviewing prospects of the proletarian state, Bukharin saw technology as the key. Chapter 8 will describe his attempts, in political defeat, to carry this programme through.

From the outset, we must note that Bukharin's favoured policy of evolution, rather than a 'third revolution' which he so much feared, required the maintenance of balance and proportion in economics and social policy, and self-limitation by the political authorities. Bukharin's programme assumed the toleration of economic, social, and cultural pluralism in the context of political monopoly. Was this a plausible assumption?[24] Did it not underestimate the likelihood of erosion: might Bolshevism, faced with a backward society, dissolve 'like a grain of salt cast into a muddy pool'?[25] Alternatively might not the Party tire of compromise, and launch out again in order to extend its monopoly? Bukharin was obsessed with the second danger—the return to coercion—which he attributed, in many virulent speeches, to the Left Opposition.[26] The Trotskyites, in turn, were equally obsessed and accused Bukharin and his supporters of 'defeatism', charges which were later taken up by Stalin, and his supporters, and put Bukharin's policies under great strain. As the chapter by Peter Ferdinand shows, he and his followers were forced to retreat on key issues,

---

[23] Ibid. 79.

[24] Considered more fully in A. Kemp-Welch, '"NEP in Culture" and its Enemies', *Journal of Contemporary History* (July 1978), 449–65.

[25] See A. M. Gor'ky, *O russkom krest'yanstve* (Berlin, 1922).

[26] See E. H. Carr, *A History of Soviet Russia: Socialism in One Country, 1924–1926* (3 vols.; London, 1958–64), ii, pt. III.

including the use of force, perhaps wrongly believing that this was 'temporary'. Eventually, Bukharin realized that the incipient Stalinism, rather than the Left, was the main danger. As he put it to Kamenev in June 1928, 'Your differences with us are incomparably less than those we all have with Stalin.'[27] Having woken up belatedly, Bukharin and his allies fought hard within the Party's upper echelons against Stalin for about a year. Their defeat is discussed in Chapter 9.

THE DEBATE ABOUT BUKHARIN

The Carr–Deutscher school gave little space to Stalin's defeated rivals, other than Trotsky.[28] From the late 1940s it concentrated on what the country had achieved and on the top leaders themselves. The business of a historian was to record events, not to consider what had not occurred.[29] While Carr's chapter on 'Personalities' in his monumental *History* includes a lucid and perceptive portrait of Bukharin, as a Bolshevik theoretician and comrade of Lenin, it concludes that he was a political non-entity, a light-weight, 'weak, amiable and keen-witted, yet caught up in the turmoil of events beyond his moral stature'.[30]

Bukharin was first taken seriously by 'Sovietology' in two studies published at Harvard in 1960. In one, Alexander Erlich reviewed the debate between economists of Left and Right during the 1920s. On the Left, Preobrazhensky argued that socialism could be achieved through a period of 'primitive accumulation', involving expropriation of peasants' produce by the state. On the Right, Bukharin advocated the maintenance of a policy of equilibrium between town and countryside and a slower rate of industrialization. But, while Bukharin is praised as 'undoubtedly the best-educated economist not only of his

[27] Bukharin–Kamenev Conversation, Trotsky Archives, Houghton Library, Harvard University, T. 1897.
[28] T. Deutscher, 'Bukharinism vs. Trotskyism', *Monthly Review* (Apr. 1975), 48–56.
[29] The classic exchange is between Isaiah Berlin, 'Historical Inevitability', republished in *Four Essays on Liberty* (Oxford, 1969), and E. H. Carr, 'Causation in History', in *What is History?* (London, 1961).
[30] Carr, *Socialism in One Country*, i. 173.

group but of the whole Party as well', his ideas are spoiled by a 'penchant for enthusiastic and rash generalization'.[31] However, Erlich insists on the contemporaneity of Bukharin's contribution. Noting Khrushchev's damning of economic reformers for 'Bukharinism' and insisting 'There is certainly no going back to the late twenties', he concludes that 'it is equally incontrovertible that ideas which reverberated through the Soviet Union three decades ago and which since then have been blackened, denigrated and pronounced dead time and again are now playing their part in one of the most significant developments of our time'.[32]

The other study, still unsurpassed, was Robert Daniels's account of communist opposition within the Bolshevik Party. He, too, noted the relevance of the past: 'Soviet attitudes toward the history of the Party and especially of the Opposition deserve to be carefully watched: they are potentially significant as indications of any change in the dogmatism of the official "mentality". Yet, Party historians have made only small progress towards a firmly objective view.'[33] Daniels shows how Bukharin emerged as 'the leading spokesman for a determined, though still behind-the-scenes, faction', defending NEP (1921–8/9) against Stalinist policies, particularly towards the peasantry.[34] Yet the Right made many blunders, above all by failing to put the great debate about the future of the Soviet Union and the Revolution before the country. 'Hemmed in by their orthodoxy and their respect for Party unity,' they fought *in camera*, while only a public contest, risking a split in the Party and loss of power, could have prevailed over incipient Stalinism.[35] Had Party loyalty blinded them to actual possibilities? Or was it cowardice, enabling them to see public or party opinion only as a subject for manipulation, not as a court of appeal? In any case, their fall removed the last obstacle to Stalin's attainment of supreme power.

[31] A. Erlich, *The Soviet Industrialization Debate, 1924–1928* (Cambridge, Mass., 1960), 23.

[32] Ibid. 187.

[33] R. V. Daniels, *The Conscience of the Revolution: Communist Opposition in Soviet Russia, 1917–1929* (Cambridge, Mass., 1960), pp. vii–viii.

[34] Ibid., ch. 13, 'The Right Opposition'.

[35] Ibid. 362.

For Sidney Heitman, Bukharin's thought is an intriguing meld of orthodoxy and originality, 'filling the ideological gap between the death of Lenin and the rise of Stalin'.[36] It does not simply reiterate the Leninist legacy, but rather tries to carry that forward, thereby achieving a synthesis of orthodox Marxist social theory and Bolshevik revolutionary experience. Before the Revolution, Bukharin had argued, on classical Marxist lines, that the steady accumulation and centralization of capital led to the concentration of ownership in a few powerful hands. Eventually, he predicted, the anarchy of capitalist production would be replaced by 'organized state capitalism'. This could be defeated in advanced economies by a proletarian seizure of power. But, where workers remained a minority, in semi-capitalist or colonial countries, the peasant masses were the potential revolutionary force.[37] It followed that, in Soviet Russia, private ownership of land and small-scale enterprise could only be eliminated gradually, through economic incentives and persuasion. Any attempt to force the pace would disturb the social equilibrium and rupture the 'worker–peasant alliance' (*smychka*). Bukharin is thus a 'seeking Marxist' who does not shrink from ideological innovations, even ones shifting the *locus* of revolutionary potential from the most advanced capitalist states to the most backward. But he does retain the Leninist assumption that minority action by a revolutionary party could hurry history along.

The first biography of Bukharin was published in 1973.[38] Cohen's magnificent study suggested that Bukharin had developed a new theory of the path to socialism. He came to accept the (Menshevik) argument that the Russian Revolution had been premature, in the sense that the political attainment of power by, or in the name of, an advanced proletariat had taken place ahead of social and economic circumstances which should have been its determinants. Bukharin considered this unorthodoxy unavoidable. However, it had the most regrettable consequences. Bolshevism was surrounded and isolated in a

---

[36] S. Heitman, 'Between Lenin and Stalin: Nikolai Bukharin', in L. Labedz (ed.), *Revisionism: Essays on the History of Marxist Ideas* (London, 1962), 89.

[37] Ibid. 81–8.

[38] S. F. Cohen, *Bukharin and the Bolshevik Revolution: A Political Biography, 1888–1938* (New York, 1973; 2nd edn., Oxford, 1980).

hostile country. Hence the need for NEP, a policy of compromise with society, introduced 'seriously and for a long
time'. There could be no return to force. Only within a context
of consent, social peace, economic interchange, and harmonious interdependence of sectors would the peasantry
'grow into' socialism. As they become richer (Bukharin echoed
Guizot's advice of 'enrichissez-vous'), the state could tax their
profit ('surplus' and invest it in light industry. Consumer
goods would be manufactured first, as an incentive for the
peasantry, whose expanded productivity would provide investment for heavy industry.[39] In short, there was a Bukharinite
'alternative' to the Stalinist developmental approach.

The claim was contested from the outset. E. H. Carr referred
to 'the inherent impossibility in NEP conditions of inducing the
peasant to part with his grain'.[40] He argued that, by early 1928,
'all the principal leaders from Stalin downwards' had come to
recognize this fact and decided on forced requisitioning, in
which they all took part. 'Only Bukharin stayed behind in
Moscow.' He thus appeared to flinch at the 'vital turning-point
in Soviet history'. According to Carr, the grain-collecting
campaign was, '*in the short term*, a brilliant success' (emphasis
added). However, one would be inclined to reply, as did
Bukharin, that this emergency measure mortgaged the future:
peasants so exploited would revert to subsistence farming,
their reduced sowing making shortfalls certain the next year.
Greater, perhaps permanent, use of force would then become
necessary. Thus Stalin's 'Urals–Siberian method'[41] was a
problem rather than a solution. Carr also objected to the
presentation of Bukharin as 'a lost political leader', noting

a desire, especially strong among American liberals, to believe that
nice men make good political leaders. Cynical observation may throw
doubt on this conclusion. In our own century, Lloyd George and
Franklin Roosevelt were superb political leaders, but perhaps not very
nice men. George McGovern and Edmund Muskie are exceedingly
nice people, imbued with humane ideals and unimpeachable prin-

[39] Ibid., ch. 5, 'Rethinking Bolshevism'.
[40] E. H. Carr, 'The Legend of Bukharin', *Times Literary Supplement*, 20 Sept.
1974, 989–91.
[41] For the background, see J. Hughes, *Stalin, Siberia and the Crisis of the New
Economic Policy* (Cambridge, 1991), 97–122.

ciples. But if a biographer of one or other of them fifty years hence seeks to depict his hero as a lost political leader, frustrated only by the devilish machinations of the wicked Richard Nixon, he will be seriously distorting history. And this is what has happened to Mr Cohen over Bukharin.[42]

To this Cohen replied that there was no such claim. His thesis did not depend upon alleged political skills, but on the ideas that Bukharin had developed from Lenin's last articles: a strategy for the attainment of socialism which amounted to a 'viable programmatic alternative in the 1920s'.[43] Consequently, he maintained, the Stalinist outcome was not predetermined.

Cohen's interpretation was also challenged by Richard Day. Recalling Lenin's comment that Bukharin 'has never learned, and I think never fully understood, dialectics', he adds that for one Marxist to accuse another of misunderstanding dialectics 'is roughly the equivalent of one engineer accusing another of not understanding calculus'.[44] Day's Bukharin consistently misinterpreted Lenin's late thinking, putting an 'evolutionary interpretation' on the last articles, 'with the purpose of eliminating dialectics entirely from the theory of the NEP'.[45] Of course, we know that Bukharin did follow Lenin's earlier differentation of the peasantry, in *New Economic Developments in Russian Peasant Life*,[46] between rich, middle, and poor. In 1917 Lenin had turned this to revolutionary advantage by encouraging the middle peasantry to change positions, with most of them moving downwards. This strategy was, in the end, adopted by Stalin. But Bukharin's idea of NEP was to pull up, through incentives and education, those of the lowest peasantry who were most amenable to socialist ideas. Admittedly, there was statistical uncertainty, particularly concerning the distribution and movement of the 'floating' middle group, which led to the charge that the kulak element was getting richer and stronger, and one does look in vain for

[42] Carr, *Times Literary Supplement*, 20 Sept. 1974.
[43] Cohen, Introduction to *Bukharin and the Bolshevik Revolution* (2nd edn.).
[44] R. B. Day, Introduction to Bukharin, *Selected Writings*, p. xxxvii.
[45] Ibid., p. 1.
[46] On the background to this text, first published in 1923, see N. Harding, *Lenin's Political Thought; i. Theory and Practice in the Democratic Revolution* (London and New York, 1977), 25–8.

　　　　　　　　A. Kemp-Welch

substantive empirical analyses by Bukharin of the peasantry. However, it is surely absurd for Day to suggest that 'The theory of peaceful, evolutionary growth issued directly in the worst excesses of Stalinism'.[47]

We are also told that 'Bukharin bears an enormous historical responsibility for the onset of forced collectivization'.[48] Alec Nove strongly disagrees with Day below. Of course, Bukharin is no American liberal: the peasantry could not have a legalized party, since Bukharin frankly admitted most of them would vote for it. Bolshevik rule in Bukharin's view represented the rightful dominance of the working class within a worker–peasant alliance which nothing should be allowed to rupture. Under NEP, market competition between the industrial sector and 'private traders' (*chastniki*) would continue. The state would eventually win through fiscal pressures, and through the attractiveness of economies of scale which only social-ized industry could achieve. Usury, speculation, and petty trading would be gradually displaced by 'credit co-operatives and efficient shops'.[49] Coercion would not be necessary. As several of our contributors notice, Bukharin's opposition to the 'primitive socialist accumulation' of the 'ideologists of Trotskyism' found its fullest expression in his 'Notes of an Economist' (1928). There we learn that economic policy re-quires flexibility The tyranny of an 'omnipotent plan' had to be avoided; there were the dangers of miscalculation, and there would always be unpredictable elements. 'Control figures' were merely 'tentative'. A 'plan' without proportionality between sectors was 'capitulation in face of petit bourgeois spontaneity', as practised by 'Trotskyist ventriloquists, those gardeners would dig up plants "to make them grow faster"'.[50] Targets must be realistic: 'it is impossible to build a present-day factory with future bricks.' Yet the onset of central planning carried with it the terrible danger of 'bureaucratic degeneration,

---

[47] Day, Introduction to Bukharin, *Selected Writings*, p. liv.

[48] Ibid., p. lv.

[49] See also A. Nove, 'Some Observations on Bukharin and his Ideas', in C. Abramsky (ed.), *Essays in Honour of E. H. Carr* (London, 1974), 194–8.

[50] N. I. Bukharin, 'Zametki ekonomista (K nachalu novogo khozyaystvennogo goda)', *Pravda*, 30 Sept. 1928; trans. in Bukharin, *Selected Writings*, 308–9.

total indifference to the interests of the masses, their well-being, material and cultural interests'. Degeneration would seep through the 'pores of our gigantic apparatus', staffed by cynical officials, 'at your service', willing to produce 'any kind of plan, even to work out a super industrialist plan, only to laugh at us tomorrow in their own "closed circle" and walk hand in hand with our opponents on the day afterwards'.[51] Here was an accurate prophecy of Stalinism.

THE QUESTION OF REHABILITATION

The Russian definition of rehabilitation has a legal aspect which goes beyond its Western usage. Both languages emphasize retrospective re-establishment of a person's reputation and reinstatement to a previous position or privileges. In ordinary English this sometimes extends to successful re-education of offenders and simple restoration of health. But Soviet parlance, since Stalin, adds an assumption of original innocence. Rehabilitation thus restores rights unjustly or unlawfully removed. Paradoxically, the process is not judicial or juridical; it is done by a court but not law-governed. Consequently, the restoration of rights can seem *ad hoc* or arbitrary. When concerned with ordinary citizens, pragmatic considerations are paramount, such as financial benefits to the first batches of returnees from the labour camps in the mid-1950s. To these millions, rehabilitation meant a pension and the right to work, residence permits, and legal entitlements. It meant the ending of criminal status and the return to full membership of civil society, both for the ex-convicts and for their families, which had usually been treated as guilty with them.[52] When applied to the famous, however, most notably to victims of Stalin's show trials such as Bukharin, rehabilitation could not be so simple, partly because it is posthumous. To an outside observer the whole procedure appears to have an apologetic character, unduly influenced by contemporary politics.

---

[51] Ibid. 328–9.
[52] For the background to earlier rehabilitations, see A. van Goudoever, *The Limits of Destalinization in the Soviet Union: Political Rehabilitations in the Soviet Union since Stalin*, trans. F. Hijkoop (London, 1986).

Stalin's successors investigated some of the murkier aspects of the previous regime. Special commissions looked at the mysterious murder of Kirov,[53] the decimation of the military leadership in 1937, and the show trials, above all that which sentenced Bukharin to death for terrorism and espionage. A further team, chaired by P. N. Pospelov, studied 'Stalin's cult of the individual and its consequences'. According to Roy Medvedev, Pospelov's report faced problems boldly and 'made no attempt to evade the issue of Stalin's many abuses of his power',[54] but it was consigned, along with all the other research, to archives. Indirect evidence suggests that Bukharin's case had been discussed in the Party Presidium. Thus the next edition of the *Great Soviet Encyclopaedia* had a much briefer entry than its 1940 predecessor, omitting any mention of Bukharin's 'attempted assassination of Lenin' in 1918 or alleged attempts on Stalin.[55] Moreover, Tukhachevsky and other members of the former High Command were rehabilitated. This destroyed a key charge against Bukharin that they had mutually plotted with Nazi Germany. But Bukharin's own rehabilitation, which had been recommended by a special commission, was rejected. In retirement, Khrushchev blamed foreign Communists, two of whom had flown to Moscow for the discussion.[56] This alibi, which he later regretted,[57] is not particularly convincing; their view could hardly have prevailed against Soviet determination to proceed. When, in March 1961, investigation of Bukharin's case resumed behind the scenes, Bukharin's widow was called before the Central Control Commission. She revealed the existence of the 'Last Testament' he had made her memorize shortly before his arrest. Again, nothing came of the review, save that a Conference of Historians in December 1962 heard Pospelov state 'of course,

---

[53] The case is still open; see A. Yakovlev, *Pravda*, 28 Jan. 1991, 1, 3.

[54] R. Medvedev, *Khrushchev* (Oxford, 1982), 83–4.

[55] *Bol'shaya sovetskaya entsiklopediya*, xl (Moscow, 1955), 668–9.

[56] S. F. Cohen, *Rethinking the Soviet Experience: Politics and History since 1917* (Oxford, 1986), 81. The visitors were M. Thorez and H. Pollitt.

[57] 'We indefinitely postponed the rehabilitation of Bukharin, Zinoviev, Rykov and the rest. I can see now that our decision was a mistake. It would have been better to tell everything. Murder will always out. You can't keep things like that a secret for long' (*Khrushchev Remembers*, trans. S. Talbott (London, 1971), 318–19).

neither Bukharin nor Rykov was a spy or a terrorist'.[58] No further official statement was issued for fifteen years.

Reasons for such reticence are not hard to find. During and after Khrushchev's fall a major political struggle took place between advocates and opponents of reform. The argument was less about personal responsibility for past crimes, which all leaders shared in some degree, than over evaluation of the political and economic legacy of Stalinism. To reformers, the historical record provided a powerful case for condemnation of inherited institutions. As Moshe Lewin noted later, 'It was astonishing to discover how many ideas of Bukharin's anti-Stalinist program of 1928/9 were adopted by current reformers as their own, and how much of their critique of past practices followed his strictures and prophecies.'[59] Anti-reformers, denigrating NEP as a 'model', past or future, rejected Bukharin. Under their regime, from 1964, it seemed more likely that Stalin would be rehabilitated.

Faced with an impasse at home, Bukharin's son Larin eventually wrote to the Italian Communist leader Enrico Berlinguer.[60] In response, an appeal for Bukharin's rehabilitation was circulated widely amongst the European intelligentsia and was forwarded to the Soviet Union.[61] Their letter to Brezhnev remained unanswered. But the Italian Communist Party proceeded independently, devoting a conference to Bukharin's career.[62] It considered that Bukharin, 'neither a model nor a myth', occupied an ideological space left empty since the 1920s. Delegates hailed Bukharin as the champion of rational economics and genuine internationalism, and called for 'the complete restoration of Bukharin to the history of the Soviet Union and the Communist movement'.[63]

---

[58] P. N. Pospelov, *Vsesoyuznoe soveshchanie o merakh uluchsheniya podgotovki nauchno-pedagogicheskikh kadrov po istoricheskim naukam, 18–21 dekabrya 1962 g.* (Moscow, 1964), 298.

[59] Lewin, *Political Undercurrents*, p. xi.

[60] Larin's letter, dated 12 Mar. 1978—the fortieth anniversary of the death sentence—was published in *La repubblica* (Rome), 22 June 1978.

[61] The letter and numerous other statements from around the world are assembled in 'Dossier on Bukharin' (Betrand Russell Peace Foundation, Nottingham). For the background, see K. Coates, *The Case of Nikolai Bukharin* (Nottingham, 1978).

[62] *Bucharin tra rivoluzione e riforme* (Istituto Gramsci; Rome, 1982).

[63] *L'Unità*, 28, 30 June 1980.

Before this occurred, however, there was an unexpected prelude. A conference observer, the Director of the Institute of Marx–Engels–Mao Zedong Thought in Beijing, returned home sufficiently inspired to assemble a team of thirty or forty scholars for translation and analysis of Bukharin's works. From his later paper,[64] one can see the main preoccupations:

There is a Chinese proverb: 'A country can be conquered on horse-back, but it cannot be ruled in the same way.' This means that political power can be gained through military violence, but a country cannot be administered by it. This should be a self-evident truth. However, in the countries led by Communist parties, particularly because of the impact of Stalinism, the state system tends to emerge from the womb of the years of the revolutionary war and cannot free itself from the influence of military measures.[65]

Su argued that enactment of virtual war measures in political, economic, and social life had brought about disastrous and destructive consequences in China, especially during the 'cultural revolution'. Similarly, the Russian Civil War had a fatal impact or the Bolsheviks' conception of socialism. This formative experience was taken by Su as a starting-point for analysing differences between Lenin and his follower Bukharin, on the one hand, and Stalin, on the other. He concluded that Bukharin offered a radical critique of Stalinist and Maoist industrialization policies and terror. It was soon shown in Tiananmen Square how apt such comparisons could be.

The guilty verdict in Bukharin's case stood for fifty years. But on 4 February 1988 the Soviet Supreme Court dismissed it,[66] declaring that the confession of an accused could only be accepted by a court when supported by other kinds of evidence. The judge in charge explained that Bukharin's rehabilitation came after vast labours by dozens of researchers, running to hundreds of volumes and many thousands of

---

[64] Su Shaozhi, 'Bukharin on the Dangers of Leviathan: Thoughts on the Totalitarian State (Written on the Occasion of Bukharin's Rehabilitation)', unpublished typescript (Oxford, Sept. 1988). A copy is placed in the Russian library, St Antony's College.

[65] Ibid. 4.

[66] See *Pravda*, 9 Feb. 1988.

documents.[67] Clearly the judicial act was intended to be irreversible.

Academic rehabilitation was pressed by Russia's foremost scholar of the peasantry. In a pioneering article,[68] V. P. Danilov distinguished between three 'variants' of the first five-year plan—two which remained within the NEP framework, in the sense of retaining and utilizing existing economic mechanisms, including the market, advocated by Bukharin, Rykov and supporters and by the planners themselves, while a third version, the Stalinist, destroyed it. Danilov emphasized the contributions of other eminent economists, also being rehabilitated, such as Bazarov, Kondratiev, and Chayanov, whose sophisticated concepts and methods of planning were contrasted with the Stalinist leap into the unknown.[69] On the centenary of Bukharin's birth, Danilov published an account of Bukharin's role in the inner-Party struggles of 1928–9, and reissued the 'Notes of an Economist' with extensive annotation.[70] A round table at the Institute of Economics of the Soviet Academy of Sciences discussed the NEP and markets, peasant production and finance, and openly political problems, including the fates of Bukharin and of Trotskyism.[71] A. A. Belykh argued, convincingly, that the views of Left and Right (including Bukharin's) were far more compatible both than the participants themselves perceived and than Stalinist historiography claimed.[72]

Full political rehabilitation was also discussed. First came a political short biography,[73] cautiously welcomed by the press as an 'objective reconstruction'. But, though *Pravda* noted that Lenin's criticisms of Bukharin should not be taken literally or dogmatically, as Stalin had done, it concluded rather tamely

---

[67] M. M. Marov, *Izvestiya*, 7 Feb. 1988.

[68] V. P. Danilov, 'Fenomen pervykh pyatiletok', *Gorizont*, 5 (1988), 28–38.

[69] Discussed by Danilov in Ch. 4 below.

[70] V. P. Danilov and S. A. Krasil'nikov, 'K 100-letiyu so dnya rozhdeniya N. I. Bukharina', *EKO* (Novosibirsk), 8 (1988), 45–86.

[71] *Voprosy ekonomiki*, 9 (1988), 94–105.

[72] A. A. Belykh, 'Voprosy kolichestvennogo analiza v ekonomicheskikh rabotakh N. I. Bukharina', *Ekonomika i matematicheskie metodi*, 24: 5 (Moscow, 1988), 983–91; 'A. A. Bogdanov's Theory of Equilibrium', *Soviet Studies*, 42 (July 1990), 571–82.

[73] I. E. Gorelov, *Nikolay Bukharin* (Moscow, 1988).

that 'Bukharin's ideas and his views on many issues developed
over time and reflected the changes in actual reality and social
practice.'[74] The first *Selected Works* (1988) similarly skirted
around issues of greatest political saliency, concentrating
almost exclusively on Bukharin's exposition and defence of
NEP, indication perhaps of where the contemporary political
interests lay. Here, though, his 'liberal' image was not un-
varnished: one of his scurrilous attacks upon the Left was
included.[75] Gradually, his legacy began to be uncovered
on such varied matters as the planning of science and technology,[76] the Comintern,[77] the theory of socialism,[78] and youth
problems.[79] Political debate was sharpened by a two-volume
biography of disgraced or executed former political leaders,
which began with a sketch of Bukharin's career.[80] A teaching
manual on history for higher schools drew distinctions between participants in Soviet debates at the end of the 1920s. It
identified: the so-called 'Right' alternative (Bukharin's group);
the so-called 'Left' alternative (Trotsky's group); the version of
'political pragmatists' (Stalin's group), and the developmental
targets, enshrined in the early drafts of the five-year plan.[81]
Finally, the Institute of Marxism–Leninism published a sym-
posium on Bukharin's politics.[82] Despite all his zig-zags and
oscillations, Bukharin is portrayed as a loyal Leninist,[83] devoted to attainment of a democratic society. This approach is
explicitly contrasted with Stalin's bureaucratic and 'command-
administrative' methods.[84]

[74] *Pravda*, 5 Feb. 1989.
[75] N. I. Bukharin, 'Zhelezhnaya kogorta revolyutsii' (1922), in N. I.
Bukharin, *Izbrannye proizvedeniya*, ed. G. L. Smirnov (Moscow, 1988), 34–8.
[76] N. I. Bukharin, *Metodologiya i planirovanie nauki i tekhniki* ed. P. B.
Volobuyev (Moscow, 1989).
[77] N. I. Bukharin *Komintern*, ed. F. I. Firsov (Moscow, 1989).
[78] N. I. Bukharin, *Problemy teorii i praktiki sotsializma*, ed. G. L. Smirnov
(Moscow, 1989).
[79] N. I. Bukharin, *K novomu pokoleniyu: Doklady, vystupleniya i stat'i
posvyashchennye problemam molodezhi* (Moscow, 1990).
[80] 'N. I. Bukharin, 1888–1938', in A. Proskurin (ed.), *Vozvrashchenie imena.
Kniga I.* (Moscow, 1989), 9–53.
[81] S. A. Krasil'nikov (ed.), *SSSR v 20–30-e gody: al'ternativy i realii*
(Novosibirsk, 1990), 6–15.
[82] V. V. Zhuravlev (ed.), *Bukharin: chelovek, politik, uchenyy* (Moscow, 1990).
[83] V. P. Naumov, 'Vozvrashchenie k pravde', in ibid. 44.
[84] Ibid. 56.

THE IDEAS OF BUKHARIN

The book which follows is arranged in three parts. Part One focuses on economics and the peasantry. Alec Nove notes that Bukharin was one of the few Bolsheviks familiar with 'bourgeois' economics. He wonders how coherent and consistent Bukharin's economic alternatives had become by the late 1920s, when he found himself embattled with Stalin, but argues that a Right Deviation did not really exist, since Bukharin continued to stand (for NEP) where Stalin himself had stood before swinging over to an ultra-Left direction. Unlike Nove, Peter Ferdinand perceives a growing coherence in Bukharin's thought over this period, leading to a greater willingness to accept state intervention, in order to speed up industrialization. As he points out, had Bukharin survived politically, his defence of NEP might not have been his last word on the subject. Part One ends with Danilov's chapter contrasting Bukharin's policies towards the peasantry with those of Chayanov.[85] The latter, whose utopia included Chernov and Kerensky as well as Lenin, had stated clearly that it would not make economic sense to sacrifice the peasantry to the rest of the economy. He believed that it was possible to combine a populist, quasi-Socialist–Revolutionary version of Lenin's co-operative plan for socialization, with the retention of private institutions. As Danilov shows, Bukharin also sought to square the circle, through co-operatives. Of course, the scale of present-day problems goes far beyond the scope of Bukharin's solutions. Danilov insists that Bukharin's answers, though stimulating and instructive, should not be fossilized as 'answers for all time'.

Part Two considers politics and international relations. Neil Harding develops the examination of Bukharin's sociology of the state. As an orthodox Marxist, Bukharin regarded political structures and methods of management as neutral: they could be evaluated only in the context of class purposes they served. Hence, Harding finds a 'fateful gap' in the analysis, which led Bukharin to disregard or denigrate the importance of constitutional safeguards for society such as the rule of law or sep-

---

[85] See A. V. Chayanov, *The Theory of the Peasant Economy*, introduction by T. Shanin (Manchester, 1989).

aration of powers. In consequence, the problems of actually
attaining political pluralism are not addressed. Anna di Biagio
outlines the principal foreign policy debates of the 1920s. She
contrasts the different solutions Stalin and Bukharin offered to
the problem of the continuing applicability of Lenin's theory of
imperialism. While Stalin maintained an absolute fidelity to
Lenin's formulæ, Bukharin attempted to adjust it to changing
international conditions, above all in Europe. Supposedly
revolutionary events, in Germany of 1923–4, raised questions
of the universality of Lenin's thesis, which could not be applied
'mechanically and point by point'. Since he forecast a resurgent
Germany setting out on an expansionist policy, Bukharin
thought the Soviet Union needed new security guarantees,
while, simultaneously, using the Comintern to exploit the
'contradictions' of capitalist society. However, di Biagio concludes, Bukharin's programme 'could not be ratified by the
Party' at the end of the 1920s because it rejected on principle
any attempt to rethink not just Stalin's 'Leninism' but, still
more, Lenin's 'Leninism'.

In Part Three, on culture and science, John Biggart argues
that Bukharin's theory of cultural revolution differed so significantly from Lenin's that Cohen's presentation of Bukharin
as the custodian of Lenin's legacy requires radical revision. He
also examines the influence upon Bolshevik social thought of
Bogdanov, from whom Bukharin adopted the idea that, under
capitalism, the intelligentsia, as the organizer and controller
of ideology, acted on behalf of the ruling class. Bukharin
extended the analysis in the form of a warning that it might
metamorphose into a ruling class even under the Soviet
regime. Biggart also notes Bukharin's emphasis on the technical
development of the working class, in and through the Party,
thus forming an 'iron cohort of the proletarian revolution'. As
Robert Lewis shows in Chapter 8, Bukharin was active in
putting science and technology to the service of the first five-
year plans. While always insisting that scientific research and
development should have a base independent of the economic
planning structure, he did not lose sight of the vital role of
individual initiative and inspiration in scientific discovery,
which could so easily be destroyed by 'backward, bureaucratic
bungling'.

Finally Chapter 9 considers the extent to which Bukharin was able to comprehend the phenomenon that removed him from the political stage. While admitting that his analysis remained embryonic, it suggests that Bukharin's account of Stalinism is perceptive on fundamental questions, such as the power of the state and the appropriate relationship between state and society. However, his understanding of the personality of Stalin himself is found wanting.

Despite the admiration which all authors express towards Bukharin as a man, and our sympathy for his fate, this is emphatically not a work of hagiography. Rather, removal of the terrible stigma of 'judicial guilt' under which his 'after-life' was lived has freed scholars from previous constraints. For all his mild nature, Bukharin had a tendency to intellectual extremism, taking deeply held beliefs beyond the point of prudence. This characterized his stance on the far left of the Party shortly after the Revolution. We know that he acknowledged this by 1921, calling the collapse of 'War Communism' (1918–20) 'the end of our illusions', but he also tended to overcompensate afterwards. No one subsequently played a greater role in discrediting the Party's Left Opposition. In mitigation one might mention the similarly misguided intensity of the Left's own attacks on Bukharin as a 'Rightist', wishing to capitulate to capitalism. It is unlikely that any detached observer would wish to defend either side in this deadly quarrel, which much facilitated the rise of Stalinism.

Bukharin was not a leader of stature, still less a statesman. He was, rather, an intellectual in politics, with the attractive and familiar weakness of his kind. He was categorical in thought, but prone to self-doubt; determined and forceful in opinion, but hesitant and often vacillating in action. Confident of his own intellectual powers, he could rarely shut himself off from arguments from the other side. His outlook thus anticipated the attempts to attain 'communism with a human face'.[86] He was a unique figure in the Politburo. As Moshe Lewin observed, in the mid-1970s, 'Bolshevism and Lenin could afford to use an intellectual of this kind in the revolutionary period, but he had no place in a Stalinist hierarchy, nor

---

[86] Cohen, *Rethinking the Soviet Experience*, 76–7.

A. Kemp-Welch

are any people of his type to be found in the post-Stalinist top rank.'[87] An intellectual in politics is always liable to become a victim, not least of his own virtues. We may wonder, with James Joll, whether 'men of intelligence or imagination, sensibility or originality, independence or scrupulousness, can in fact stand up to the strain of the ruthless machine politics of the twentieth century'.[88]

[87] M. Lewin, review article, *Journal of Modern History*, 47 (1975), 374.
[88] J. Joll, *Three intellectuals in Politics: Rathenau, Blum, Marinetti* (London, 1960).

PART I

ECONOMICS AND THE PEASANTRY

2

Bukharin as an Economist

Alec Nove

THIS chapter divides naturally into three parts: Bukharin before the Revolution; Bukharin in the 'War Communism' period; and finally Bukharin and the New Economic Policy (NEP). After 1929 there is, in my view, nothing for us to consider: Bukharin was defeated and could no longer speak freely or defend himself, though, of course, he was still active and wrote and spoke a great deal.

BEFORE THE REVOLUTION

First, let us consider *The Political Economy of the Rentier* (1914),[1] which was Bukharin's reaction to the Austrian school of economics, after attending lectures in Vienna. In defending Marx against Böhm-Bawerk, he naturally counterposed the labour theory of value to the marginal-utility theory, arguing that it reflected the shift of emphasis in 'bourgeois' theory from production to consumption, from entrepreneurs to rentiers (coupon-clippers). It cannot be said that this was a very original line to take, but the young Bukharin (let us remember that, being born in 1888, he was still in his twenties when he wrote it) none the less produced a well-argued attack. It is a pity he did not distinguish between the *marginal* and the *utility* aspect of the theory. After all, there is also marginal productivity, which, whatever else it does or does not do, refers to production and not to consumption. He might not have known that the labour theory of value was challenged long before Menger, Wieher, Jevons, or Böhm-Bawerk, by those who chose to emphasize the importance of evaluation of the product by its

---

[1] First published as N. I. Bukharin, *Politicheskaya ekonomika rant'e. Teoriya tsennosti i pribyli avstriyskoy shkoly* (Moscow, 1929); trans. as *The Economic Theory of the Leisure Class* (New York, 1927).

users. For example, let me quote Shtorkh (Storch), who was the first Academician–economist. In 1815, long before the alleged domination of the 'rentier', he wrote: 'Labour in industry is productive not *because*, as Adam Smith asserts, it produces value; it is productive *when* it produces value. It is not effort and swea as such that produce value, but the usefulness of the products'[2]

It is probable that Bukharin had never heard of Shtorkh, but his own contemporaries included three who endeavoured to combine Marxist labour theory with marginal utility: Bortkiewicz, Dmitriev, and Tugan-Baranovsky. The last of these was certainly known to Bukharin, since he criticized him directly (though the main criticism seems to have been directed at Tugan's alleged detachment of production from consumption). This is not the place to discuss Marx's value theory, but it is worth noting that Soviet theory and practice to this day suffer from what Petrakov and other contemporary economists call the cost-concept of price, or cost-plus prices (*zatratnaya konts*ptsiya tseny*). Two baskets of goods that share only the common characteristic of requiring the same quantity of labour to produce them (even if the labour is homogeneous), are not for that reason *worth* the same, unless the use-values they contain are related through *the market* to the effort required to produce them. Marx took the existence of the market for granted, and, like Bukharin, assumed that under socialism it would not exist. This, as we now know, left an unfortunate gap in the Marxist economic theory of socialism. The gap might have been more easily bridgeable if use-value, relative scarcity in relation to demand, had been incorporated in the theory from the first. (Of course Marx made the *existence* of use-value a pre-condition for a good to have value, but some things are more useful than others!) This could have been done without abandoning the notion of exploitation, which rests on the denial of the legitimacy of obtaining income from ownership of the means of production. This could be accompanied by legitimate criticism of the overconcentration of the 'Austrians'

---

[2] *Cours d'économie politique* (St Petersburg, 1815), trans. into Russian by Vernadsky in 1881.

on the marginal (incremental) and the purely subjective, as distinct from the objective conditions of production.

Let us turn to his better known work, *Imperialism and the World Economy* (1920).[3] It was certainly influenced by Hilferding's *Finance Capital* (1910), and in turn had some influence on Lenin's famous work *Imperialism* (1917). The originality of Bukharin's approach was that he pushed the concentration of capital to its ultimate limit, identifying what he believed to be a trend towards the unification of a given nation's capitalism into a kind of united supertrust, directly linked with the state and, therefore, in this sense state capitalism: 'the state becomes more and more the direct exploiter, organizing and directing production as a collective capitalist', it plans, it overcomes the 'anarchy' of the market, it becomes militarist, it fights imperialist wars with other state supertrusts over raw material supplies and export markets, oppresses colonial peoples and so on. It is 'the new Leviathan'. (Lenin did not go that far, insisting that monopoly capitalism does not exclude competition within each society.) Stephen Cohen, in his biography, noted that Bukharin used the terminology of Jack London's futurist nightmare, 'the iron heel of the militaristic state'.[4] The contemporary reader is struck not only by the unreality of the united supertrust model of the capitalist state, but also by the similarity of his terminology with that used by certain neo-Marxist critics in recent years to describe the *Soviet* system (see, for example, Bettelheim's works, and those of others who see the Soviet Union of the later-Stalin or Brezhnev period as state capitalist).[5]

Bukharin was involved in an argument with Rosa Luxemburg at this period, and here one has to say that he was in the right. The argument turned on Luxemburg's assertion that crises of overproduction compelled capitalists to find external markets, since the internal market was restricted by the low level of workers' wages, and so the system could only function if there was a non-capitalist country or sectors.[6] Bukharin pointed to a

[3] N. I. Bukharin, *Mirovoe khozyaystvo i imperializm* (Moscow, 1918) (written in 1915); trans. as *Imperialism and World Economy* (New York, 1929).

[4] S. F. Cohen, *Bukharin and the Bolshevik Revolution: A Political Biography, 1888–1938* (New York, 1973; 2nd edn., Oxford, 1980), 31.

[5] C. Bettelheim, *Les Luttes de classes en URSS* (Paris, 1977).

[6] R. Luxemburg, *Die Akkumulation des Kapitals* (Berlin, 1913); trans. as *The*

clear fallacy, which I will illustrate with an example of my own. Suppose British capitalists produce more cotton cloth than the impoverished British workers can consume and export cotton to (say) India. India pays for this by exporting tea to Britain. If terms of trade are made artificially favourable to Britain (as some suggested), then back in exchange for the value of the exported cloth comes a *greater* value of tea. The total value (however defined) of goods to be consumed in Britain is either unaffected by the export or actually goes up. The workers will surely drink the tea! Of course, Luxemburg's basic error was to take literally Marx's notion of absolute and relative immiserization—but Bukharin did not directly question this notion in his critique.

Bukharin was one of the few Bolsheviks who, before the Revolution, had been exposed to the study of 'bourgeois' economics. Unfortunately neither he nor any other Marxist of the period attempted to grapple seriously with the question of how a socialist economy might function. Barone's warnings[7] went unheeded. Bebel thought that socialist planning would be simple, child's play (*ein Kinderspiel*), but this was in the tradition inherited from Marx and Engels ('everything would be simple without the so-called value', to cite *Anti-Dühring*). Perhaps it is appropriate to cite here the view of A. Sergeyev, expressed in a Soviet discussion:

It is known that Marx and Engels held that socialism and commodity production were not only contradictory but incompatible. Lenin took this view too. Even today no one has the theoretical effrontery [*teoreticheskii naglo ti*] to assert that Lenin was the creator of the theory of commodity production under socialism. Was the theory of Marx, Engels, and Lenin about socialism wrong, or was their theory on commodity production wrong? Or are we wrong in interpreting what Marx, Engels, and Lenin said about commodity production?[8]

Challenging words indeed! I quote them here because they remind us that Bukharin's blind spots on these issues were typical of socialist thinkers of his time. This helps us to place in

Accumulation of Capital (London, 1951). See J. P. Nettl, *Rosa Luxemburg* (abridged edn., Oxford, 1969), 165–8.

[7] See E. Barone in A. Nove and D. M. Nuti (eds.), *Socialist Economics* (London, 1972).

[8] A. Sergeyev, round table, *Voprosy ekonomiki*, 7 (1988).

context his ideas of the War Communism period, to which we will now turn. I would add that the Bukharin of NEP certainly took a positive view of the role of the market in what he regarded as the 'transition period', but nowhere can we find him speaking of the market–commodity production under *socialism*. I recall a conversation many years ago with the old Soviet economist L. Gatovsky, who said: 'Neither Bukharin nor Preobrazhensky thought that there would be a market under socialism, and both were wrong.' There is a tendency to make of Bukharin a sort of prophet of market socialism. I believe that this is erroneous.

'WAR COMMUNISM'

In his very interesting introduction to a translation of Bukharin's selected writings, Richard B. Day seeks to show that there is a consistent strand in Bukharin's ideas, before and after 'War Communism'.[9] Thus Bukharin took the new Leviathan concept of the capitalist state, as developed in his earlier work *Imperialism* (1915), and applied it to the Soviet Union's dictatorship of the proletariat. To cite *Economics of the Transition Period* (1920): 'Formally this dictatorship will be similar to the epoch of bourgeois dictatorship, meaning that it will be state capitalism *turned inside out*, or state capitalism *dialectically converted into its own opposite* . . . the proletarian state, the collectively organized working class.'[10] It seems to me that the connecting link is a tendency to a sort of youthful theoretical extremism, taking the views common among the Bolsheviks of his time a little too far. If he was inspired by a misinterpretation of the German war economy, which seemed to fit his earlier vision of state capitalism, Lenin also made a similar error, as can be seen in his references to the economy in *State and Revolution* (1917) and other works of the same period. Thus their views of the dominant role supposedly to be played by the central bank are similar. By 1921 experience had taught both Lenin and Bukharin that they had suffered from 'illusions', a word used by both of them looking back at the War Com-

---

[9] R. B. Day, Introduction to N. I. Bukharin, *Selected Writings on the State and the Transition to Socialism* (New York, 1982), p. xxxii.

[10] Bukharin, *Selected Writings*, 56.

munism years. Perhaps one genuine point of difference arose from Bukharin's evident admiration for the ideas of A. A. Bogdanov, whose ideas Lenin had opposed, and whose *Tektologiya*, or the universal theory of organization, was a pioneering approach to systems theory. This could have inclined Bukharin to the view he came to hold on the domination of the 'proletarian state' over everything, including the proletariat.

However, his first disagreement with Lenin was, paradoxically, for quite opposite reasons. In the spring of 1918 Bukharin was to the left, not only over Brest-Litovsk (he was against signing the treaty, for revolutionary war) but also over Lenin's attempt to enforce discipline in factories, to stop further nationalization, to stop local soviets from acting on their own, and even to work with some remaining capitalists and managers. (Lenin called *this* 'state capitalism'). Bukharin was critical, siding with such 'left-Communists' as Osinsky on these issues. Though this policy posture did not last long, it contrasted oddly with Bukharin's views of 1920 vintage. It is another instance of his tendency to swing from one extreme to another. When Lenin, under pressure of circumstances, abandoned the relatively moderate policies of the first months of 1918, Bukharin unreservedly supported him and became a committed supporter of what came to be known as War Communism. His best-known works of this period, *Economics of the Transition Period* and *The ABC of Communism* (1919) (the latter written jointly with his future opponent Preobrazhensky), faithfully reflected the atmosphere of the time. Most of the more extreme views then expressed earned him the applause of the vast bulk of his comrades. In his introduction to a reprint of *Economics of the Transition Period*, Sidney Heitman states that 'it can be viewed only as an inexplicable aberration in Bukharin's thought'.[11] If it is, then the bulk of his comrades at the time suffered from a similar 'aberration'. One hardly needs reminding that Lenin's marginal notes, first published in 1929, approved strongly of the large majority of Bukharin's *economic* propositions.[12]

[11] S. Heitman, Introduction to *Put'. k sotsializmu v Rossii: Izbrannye proizvedeniya N. I. Bukharina* (New York, 1967).

[12] V. I. Lenin, 'Zamechaniya na knigu N. I. Bukharina', in *Leninskiy sbornik*, ed. N. I. Bukharin *et al.*, xi (Moscow, 1929), 362–87.

In fact, he simply generalized from what was happening around him. Thus he developed the concept of 'negative expanded reproduction': the possessing classes resist revolution; sabotage and civil war cause losses; class war and disruption of customary links in and between town and village lead to shrinkage of production. What is more, the proletariat, unlike the bourgeoisie, cannot learn to govern before *its* revolution and will make expensive errors.

In the transition period, asserts Bukharin, value categories such as 'commodity' and 'price' have already ceased to have their former meanings. Under socialism, he believes, political economy as well as the state will wither away.

Indeed as soon as we deal with an organized national economy, all the basic 'problems' of political economy, such as price, value, profit, etc., simply disappear . . . for there the economy is regulated not by the blind forces of the market and competition, but by the consciously implemented *plan* . . . The end of capitalist and commodity society signifies the end of political economy.[13]

By now (1920), commodities have become products and lost their commodity (exchange) character; money also has lost its character; there is 'self-denial' (*samootritsanie*), and wages have ceased to be wages, since there is no longer hired labour. 'Economic theory must move towards thinking in natural units.'[14] As for relations with the peasants, Bukharin speaks of 'the struggle between the state plan of the proletariat, incorporating social labour, and the commodity anarchy and speculative wildness of the peasantry, expressing fragmented property and market forces'.[15] If this seems extreme, and indeed very far from his own views on the peasantry two years on, he bases himself on Lenin, and quotes him: 'The peasant economy remains a small-scale commodity producer. Here we have very wide and deeply rooted bases for capitalism. On this basis capitalism is preserved and resurrects itself in the most tough battle with communism,' and so on.[16] It should not be

---

[13] N. I. Bukharin, *Ekonomika perekhodnogo perioda*, i. *Obshchaya teoriya transformatsionnogo protsessa* (Moscow, 1920), 3. Part ii never appeared.
[14] Ibid.
[15] Ibid.
[16] Ibid.

forgotten what Lenin's views were at this period, and Soviet readers have had a reminder in *Novyy mir*.[17] Lenin did have some criticisms of Bukharin's formulations, which I cite in detail in another work,[18] but most of their ideas were rather similar.

Interestingly, Bukharin quotes approvingly the words 'primitive socialist accumulation', with acknowledgment to V. M. Smirnov (Lenin underlined it and remarked 'ugh'!), but for him it meant not what it later meant to Preobrazhensky, but rather the need to conscript labour for socialist reconstruction, including non-proletarian elements, 'in the first place the peasants'. This links with his extreme position on militarization of labour, an issue on which, in 1920, he was at one with Trotsky. In *Economics of the Transition Period* he advocates 'new types of forms of compulsion . . . the abolition of so-called freedom of labour'.[19] There are among the workers all kinds of defects, such as

individualism, lack of solidarity, sectional interests . . . lack of under-standing of the all-proletarian tasks which find their concentrated expression in the tasks and requirements of the Soviet dictatorship, the workers' state. As these tasks must be fulfilled at any price, it is clear that from the standpoint of the proletariat, in the name of real and not fictional freedom of the working class, *it is necessary to abolish so-called freedom of labour*, since this (such freedom) *cannot be reconciled with a properly organized planned economy and with a planned allocation of labour power*.[20]

Here, too, Lenin in that year made many statements favourable to labour militarization, though he did distance himself from Trotsky's notions about the statization of trade unions at the end of 1920. He also criticized Bukharin for trying to incorporate trade unions into the economic administration.

In *The ABC of Communism* the picture of a future Communist economy is presented in a simple and rather naïve way, but, apart from the shared illusions of the period, it is necessary to

[17] V. Selyunin, 'Is oki', *Novyy mir*, 5 (1988), 162–89.
[18] A. Nove, 'Some Observations on Bukharin and his Ideas', in C. Abramsky (ed.) *Essays in Honour of E. H. Carr* (London, 1974), 186–7.
[19] Bukharin, *Ekonomika perekhodnogo perioda*.
[20] Ibid.

recall that this was a sort of pamphlet intended to inspire the semi-literate, and not a high level statement of theory. It is worth noting, however, that it was very popular, and not only in the Soviet Union.[21]

I will not analyse *The Theory of Historical Materialism* (1920) in detail here, but two brief remarks are necessary. One concerns Bukharin's frequent use, both in this and in earlier works, of the concept of 'equilibrium'. The other, linked with it, and reflecting Bogdanov's influence, concerns thinking in terms of systems theory. Both must be seen in relation to Lenin's criticism of Bukharin's 'not understanding dialectics'. However, it may be worth making the point that in Marxism there is both determinism and voluntarism, and also a necessary coexistence between analysis of systems at rest, in equilibrium (e.g. capitalism in its pure form), *and* of the contradictions which tend to destroy both equilibrium and system. To say, as some critics do, that Bukharin failed to see within-system contradictions is surely unfair. To call him a 'mechanist' is equally so. After all, he had been an active participant in a most 'unmechanist' revolution! Nor do I believe, as do such critics as Day, that Bukharin's policies during NEP can be explained by reference to his philosophical position.[22] One can believe in several different philosophical doctrines and still come to the conclusion that a 'workers'-and-peasants' state' in which the peasants form 80 per cent of the population should not deliberately set out to attack the peasants!

Bukharin swiftly became a supporter of NEP. Writing in 1924, under the title of 'O likvidatorstve nashikh dney', he frankly declared:

The adoption of NEP was the collapse of our illusions . . . This does not mean that the War Communism system was wrong for its time . . . War and blockade compelled us to act thus. But we thought then that our peacetime policy would be a *continuation* of the centralized planning system of that period . . . The illusions of War Communism were

---

[21] The numerous translations of N. I. Bukharin and E. A. Preobrazhensky, *Azbuka kommunizma* (Moscow, 1919), include that by E. and C. Paul, *The ABC of Communism* (London, 1922; repr. London, 1969, with an Introduction by E. H. Carr; also Ann Arbor, Mich., 1966).

[22] Day, Introduction to Bukharin, *Selected Writings*, p. liv.

exploded at the very hour when the proletarian army stormed Perekop [i.e. when the civil war ended].[23]

He wrote so much in and about NEP that in the interests of necessary brevity I will concentrate on two topics only: his conflict with Preobrazhensky (and Trotsky), and the much-discussed question of a 'Bukharinist' alternative to Stalin's 'left turn' of 1928–9. (I agree entirely with a contemporary Soviet historian who expressed doubts as to whether there ever was a Right Deviation;[24] Bukharin stood where Stalin himself had stood before the latter swung in an ultra-left direction.)

Before tackling the controversy over 'primitive socialist accumulation' and Preobrazhensky's *The New Economics* (1926)[25] it is essential to stress that they—Bukharin, Preobrazhensky, Trotsky—had much in common. This is a point well made by the Hungarian scholar, János Mátyás Kovács, who referred to 'the forgotten consensus'.[26] Let me give some examples: Bukharin in 1925 produced the slogan, addressed to the peasants, 'get rich' (*obogashchaytes'*). Trotsky, in 1923, speaking to the Party Congress, recommended that the peasant 'became richer' (*stal bogache*). Both had the same idea in view: given the acceptance of the framework of NEP, given the urgent need for more marketed foodstuffs, clearly the peasant must be given incentives and confidence that success would not land him in the ranks of 'class enemies'. Trotsky in 1923 criticized bureaucratization, and so did Bukharin. For example: 'even proletarian origins and the most calloused hands provided no safeguard against transformation into a new class . . . It is vital not to allow the cadres to become a monopoly caste',[27] and then again he spoke of *'the danger of the degeneration of the proletarian state and the proletarian party'*.[28] Bukharin at no time was opposed to industrialization, and did not deny that the transfer of value into the accumulation fund at the expense of

---

[23] N. I. Bukharin, 'O likvidatorstve nashikh dney', *Bol'shevik*, 2 (1924), 3–9.

[24] A. P. Lanschikov, *Voprosy istorii*, 6 (1988), 30–2.

[25] E. A. Preobrazhensky, *Novaya ekonomika* (2nd edn., Moscow, 1926); trans. B. Pearce, *The New Economics* (Oxford, 1965).

[26] J. M. Kovács, 'The Real Preobrazhensky', paper presented to the 3rd World Congress of Soviet and East European Studies (Washington, 1985).

[27] N. I. Bukharin, *Proletarskaya revolyutsiya i kul'tura* (Petrograd, 1923), 45.

[28] N. I. Bukharin, 'Burzhuaznaya revolyutsiya i revolyutsiya proletarskaya', *Pod znamenem marksizma*, 7–8 (1922).

the petty producers must occur. Nor did Preobrazhensky in 1925 envisage going beyond the confines of NEP; his 'exploitation' of the peasants through the price mechanism, through 'unequal exchange', was based on voluntary exchange between town and country reinforced by taxation, not on coercion and compulsory delivery quotas. There *were* political conflicts, of course. Bukharin did assail Trotsky and Preobrazhensky, and the evidence supports the view that he thought, already in 1923–5, that their line would prove inconsistent with the maintenance of the precarious political–economic equilibrium represented by the market-based 'worker–peasant alliance' (*smychka*) with the peasants. (Trotsky, too, at that time, insisted on the importance of the *smychka*).

Where, then, were the differences in *economic* analysis and policy? There was a difference of emphasis, certainly. Also of language. Preobrazhensky had used such terms as 'exploitation', 'internal colonialism', making parallels with 'primitive capitalist accumulation' of Marx. This was tactless, threatened the *smychka*. State industry should compete effectively with the private sector. If 'the state economy can meet peasant needs better than the private trader, then the *smychka* is safe'. In 1923 there was the 'scissors crisis'; prices were too unfavourable for the peasant. Was this the time to raise the question of unequal exchange, rather than taking steps to lower the costs of, and prices charged by, state industry? In Bukharin's view, such a policy could only impoverish the peasantry and deprive industry of markets.

Bukharin's view of the peasants, of their 'growing into socialism' through co-operation, was, he insisted, consistent with and inspired by Lenin's views expressed in 'On Co-operation' (1923) and in personal discussion. Bukharin combined his belief in NEP and in the *smychka* with the view that, in the absence of revolution in the West, Russia could 'build' socialism, even if very slowly— 'at a tortoise pace' (*cherepash'imi shagami*). To cite his words to the Leningrad Provincial Conference in 1926, where his direct opponents were Zinoviev and Kamenev, who had formed an alliance with Trotsky:

If we do not have confidence in the sufficiency of our internal forces for building socialism, then there was no reason for us to go to the barricades in October; then the Mensheviks were right, that in such a backward country as Russia it was pointless to attempt a socialist revolution; then comrade Trotsky was right in asserting that without the help of a victorious West European proletariat we shall face a conflict with the peasants which we must lose.[29]

By then both sides in the factional struggle had taken up what looked like irreconcilable polemical positions. The Left Opposition mounted a critique of economic policy: it was too favourable to the kulaks, investments were insufficient; Trotsky advocated a wider participation in the international division of labour and a more effective revolutionary policy by the Comintern (1927 saw the Communist disaster in China); Zinoviev denounced 'socialism in one country'; Preobrazhensky published the article in which he argued that the contradictions in which the Soviet Union found itself could not be resolved without revolution in the West.[30] In 1921–5 the economic debate was carried out within a broad consensus; everyone accepted NEP, though some doubtless did so with more conviction than others. But from 1926 both the political struggle and the very real policy dilemmas led to a sharpening of differences.

Economic strains began in 1926–7. On the one hand, growth was very rapid. On the other, there were growing disequilibria, the beginnings of goods' shortages, inflationary pressures, and even then a turn in policy towards restrictions on the kulak and on the private trader.[31] At this period Bukharin was alongside Stalin, and presumably approved these measures, as he must also have approved the reduction in grain-procurement prices also decreed in that year, and the cut in industrial selling prices which contributed to goods' shortages. Was this a consistent position for one who professed to believe in market-based relations with the peasants and in the continuance of NEP? In retreating from 'enrich yourselves', in adopting a policy of 'limiting the kulak', he could be said to be defending

---

[29] Bukharin, *Put' k sotsializmu v Rossii*, ed. Heitman, 340.

[30] E. A. Preobrazhensky, 'Economic Equilibrium in the System of the USSR', *Vestnik Kommunisticheskoy akademii*, 22 (1927); trans. D. A. Filtzer, in E. A. Preobrazhensky, *The Crisis of Soviet Industrialization* (London, 1980), 160–235.

[31] I make a long list of such measures in A. Nove, *An Economic History of the USSR* (London, 1989), 138–42.

an indefensible line: a so-called kulak is a successful middle peasant (*serednyak*), and one cannot build a healthy agriculture on those who turn into class enemies when they prosper, though, of course, Bukharin never advocated their 'liquidation as a class'. Neither, needless to say, did Trotsky or Preobrazhensky (actually this needs to be said, since several contemporary authors in the Soviet Union, including Belov and Mozhaev,[32] blame Trotsky for the collectivization tragedy).

Richard B. Day is also hostile and even stated that 'Bukharin bears an enormous historical responsibility for the onset of forced collectivization'.[33] But then Day also believed that 'the only policy that might have avoided the "grain strike" [the grain-procurements crisis of 1927–8] was that put forward by Trotsky', who 'consistently appealed for accelerated investments in consumer goods industries'.[34] With this proposition I strongly disagree. Trotsky's policies of greater pressure on the kulak plus accelerated investments (which included heavy-industry investment) would surely have made the goods famine more acute, not less, as investments take several years to yield a flow of consumable goods. Furthermore, he opposed price increases. The dilemmas were real. Workers pressed for higher wages, there was still serious urban unemployment, the budget was severely strained. Bukharin was gradually pushed into a position which was in some respects contradictory, and the adoption of an ambitious five-year plan (which he supported) would inevitably lead to further strains, shortages, a widening gap between official and free (or black) market prices, and so to pressure to take action against the private sector. At this point Stalin felt free to ignore his former ally and radically change the policy positions which he had previously held, and which, together with Bukharin, he had defended from criticisms from the Left Opposition. He then went very much further left than the Left Opposition ever dreamed of, as Klyamkin correctly pointed out in *Novyy mir*.[35] And even Stephen Cohen, much more sympathetic to Bukharin than either Carr or Day, wrote

---

[32] See, e.g., B. Mozhaev, 'Muzhiki i baby', *Don*, 3 (1987).
[33] Day, Introduction to Bukharin, *Selected Writings*, p. 1v.
[34] Ibid.
[35] I. Klyamkin, 'Kakaya ulitsa vedet k khramu?', *Novyy mir*, 11 (1987), 150–88.

in his biography 'So it was in December 1927 . . . the Politburo Right found their policies beset with crises and their political position threatened. Bukharin bore a large part of the responsibility for what became their desperate situation,'[36] and this not only because o his part in destroying the Left Opposition, but because of policy inconsistencies.

This implies no sort of defence for, or justification of, Stalin's 'revolution from above' with all its brutalities and excesses. It does lead me to wonder if in 1927–8 Bukharin had a coherent policy alternative, other than to warn (e.g. in his 'Notes of an Economist' (1928)) against unbalanced plans—one cannot build today's factories with tomorrow's bricks. M. Reiman has argued that Bukharin was not a *political* heavyweight; he was a fine writer and a theoretician of quality, but as a political organizer and leader he was far inferior to his ally Rykov.[37] But what concerns us here are coherent policy alternatives. It may be that we are tempted to ascribe to Bukharin *our* concepts of the alternative to Stalinism, which no doubt did exist, but which the real Bukharin neither advocated nor formulated in 1927–8.

I accept that virtually *any* more moderate alternative would have been preferable to what actually occurred. However, the objective difficulties and contradictions rooted in the Revolution itself, even in Leninism, are sometimes overlooked. Yuri Afanas'ev argues that Lenin did not have time to elaborate a conception of socialism, or of how NEP would lead to socialism. There was an NEP, but it was still an open question whether Russia had become nepist.[38] Some Soviet searchers after alternative roads put forward the original version, the more modest one, of the first five-year plan as such a road, with its gradualist approach to collectivization. But since even the relatively small rise in investments which occurred in 1926–7 had already caused serious disequilibria to emerge, would this have been consistent with the maintenance of NEP, in both its economic and its political aspects?

---

[36] Cohen, *Bukharin and the Bolshevik Revolution*, 266.

[37] M. Reiman, *The Birth of Stalinism: The USSR on the Eve of the Second Revolution*, trans. G Saunders (London, 1987).

[38] Y. Afanas'ev, *Literaturnaya Rossiya*, 17 June 1988.

Finally, to return to the question of Bukharin as an economist. About thirty years ago I read Peter Knirsch's book on Bukharin's economic thinking.[39] Knirsch examined in detail Bukharin's ideas before 1921 and virtually ignored his subsequent thought. I asked him why. He replied that after 1921, in his view, Bukharin was a political manœuverer, not a theoretician. At about the same time I spoke with my late colleague Rudolf Schlesinger, who had been Bukharin's secretary in the Comintern. He expressed the view that Bukharin's heart was in War Communism, that, when this collapsed and he shed his 'illusions', his heart was broken. This contrasts with Day's view that he adopted NEP 'with the passion of a convert'.[40] Day also (surely incorrectly) speaks of Bukharin 'eliminating dialectics entirely from the theory of NEP', giving as an example his attitude to the peasant problem, his alleged failure to realize that the smallholder peasantry's interests were not compatible in the long run with the aims of the Bolshevik Revolution. The problem as Bukharin saw it was how to overcome this *evident* contradiction without violence. He (like Lenin in 1923) hoped that gradually the peasantry would incorporate itself through co-operation (first for marketing, then for production too) into a society politically dominated by the Party, which he saw as a vanguard of the working class. Of course he saw the contradiction. Thus in 1926, at the Leningrad Conference, he specifically rejected the notion that a peasant party be legalized, because the peasants would vote for it and not for the Bolsheviks, since 'it would be hard to explain to them' that the Party's role would in the long run be in their interests too.

It is true that before 1921 Bukharin was primarily a theorist. But his later picture of an NEP-based transition to socialism is worth a careful and sympathetic study, even though his writings of the period do overly reflect short-term concerns of an intensely political individual. Despite the different scale of present-day economic problems, the Russian leadership may have lessons still to learn from a longer-term, historical, perspective.

---

[39] P. Knirsch, *Die ökonomischen Anschauungen Nikolaj I. Bucharins* (Berlin, 1959).
[40] Day, Introduction to Bukharin, *Selected Writings*, p. xlvii.

3

Bukharin and the New Economic Policy

Peter Ferdinand

ONE common interpretation holds Bukharin to be a proto-typical advocate and principal defender of the New Economic Policy (NEP) and thereby a precursor of market socialists. Economic reformers in Communist regimes, when struggling to reform the Stalinist command economy, have tended to regard him as 'one of them'. They have viewed him as someone who wished to maintain a mixed economy for the Soviet Union into the 1930s with a continuing major role for market relations in the allocation of national resources, who took a more tolerant view of the peasantry than Stalin, and who wanted a more limited role for the state in the transformation of the Soviet Union into a socialist society. His criticism of Stalinist methods even before they became established, thus became a source of inspiration and justification for subsequent revisionism.

An alternative account was offered by E. H. Carr. He suggested that from 1924 to 1929 Bukharin 'adhered consis-tently to the view that the need to conciliate the peasant should take precedence over the rapid development of industry', and that a particular characteristic of Bukharin was 'the combina-tion of rigidity in ideas with malleability of temperament'.[1] In other words, a work such as Bukharin's *Path to Socialism and the Worker–Peasant Alliance* (1925) could be taken as typical of his views throughout NEP. A third view, or a variant of the second, has blamed Bukharin for concentrating too much on accumulation in agriculture, which led to stagnation in industry under NEP. In turn this intensified the shortage of industrial goods for peasants to buy, with the consequence that

---

[1] E. H. Carr, *A History of Soviet Russia: Socialism in One Country, 1924–1926* (3 vols.; London 1976) i. 185, 187.

Bukharin bears an enormous responsibility for the onset of forced collectivization. This is true both in the sense that he was the principal architect of the policies that produced the 'grain strike' of autumn 1927, and in the sense that, as editor of *Pravda* and the party's leading publicist, he played the key role in successive press campaigns that discredited any alternative leadership to Stalin.[2]

This chapter will challenge these accounts. Above all, it will suggest that by 1927 Bukharin's support for the methods of NEP was by no means as unqualified as it had seemed even two years earlier. It will suggest that Bukharin's views underwent significant modification whenever the Party's economic policies ran into difficulties, as in 1923 with the 'scissors crisis', and then after the 'goods famine' of 1925. Subsequently, he was much more ready to contemplate an enhanced role for the state in allocating national economic priorities as the country moved towards industrialization, and he was more prepared to accept a 'transfer' of resources from the peasantry and agriculture to industry and the workers by some means or other, even though this was still to be a temporary and non-exploitative measure. Underlying such considerations were the crucial questions: how was the Soviet Union to be transformed into a modern socialist society, and what role was the state to play in that transformation process? We will trace the development of his ideas on this and other questions through four main periods. The first, from 1916 to May 1918, can be characterized as one of radical anti-statism, when he placed much greater stress upon the role of the working masses in overthrowing the bourgeois state, and indeed all forms of statism. The second period, from June 1918 to 1920, revealed an increasing acceptance of the coercive role of the state in forcing social progress. The third, from 1921 to 1925, was marked by a high enthusiasm for society itself to carry out its own transformation, and for the state's role to be significantly restricted. The fourth, from 1926 to 1928, showed a more positive view of the role of the state in planning the direction of social progress and in laying down many of the policies which were to be

[2] See R. B. Day, Introduction to N. I. Bukharin: *Selected Writings on the State and the Transition to Socialism* (New York, 1982), pp. liv–lv.

adopted in pursuit of them, but this was accompanied by a continuing reluctance to use naked force.

The point of his periodization is twofold: first, to illustrate the fact of wide oscillations in his ideas; and, secondly, to show that these oscillations took place between converging parameters. In other words, as the 1920s progressed, there developed a greater coherence in his thought. Thus to many people he seemed to be saying the same things throughout NEP. It will be argued, however, that this view is a misapprehension, although it is true that there was greater similarity in his ideas during this period than there had been between 1916 and 1920. Bukharin's views of 1924–5, when he was most outspoken as an advocate of market relations, were certainly not his last on the subject of the economic strategy of building socialism. By 1927 he was more prepared to accept regular intervention by the state to achieve rapid industrialization. On the other hand, it cannot be assumed either that his views of 1927–8, even his 'Notes of an Economist', would have been his last thoughts on the subject. There was still room for evolution.

This chapter will draw its primary materials from Bukharin's own writings. It will also rely, where relevant, upon those of his 'school' of young theoreticians and ideologists. Between the years 1924 and 1928 a number were prominent as editors of *Pravda*, *Bol'shevik*, or other journals and took part in the vigorous intellectual debates of the period. Their views were regarded, especially by opponents, as to all intents and purposes synonymous with Bukharin's. Therefore they are integral to an understanding of 'Bukharinism'. Thereafter, most of their fates remained close to Bukharin's, once they too had lost their positions to the founders of Stalinism.

BUKHARIN THE LEFT REVOLUTIONARY, 1916– MAY 1918

By early 1916 Bukharin had completed his essay 'Toward a Theory of the Imperialist State'. In it he emphasized the similarities, as he saw them, between the views of anarchists and Marxists on the need for the revolutionary destruction of the bourgeois state, and of the state in general. He claimed that it was untrue to suggest that Marxists were 'statists' and anarchists were 'anti-statists'. Both wished to destroy the political organization of the state. According to Bukharin, the real difference between them lay in the Marxists' belief in maintaining economic centralization after the Revolution—a theme which, as we shall see, recurs in his later writings about NEP. Lenin's first reactions to this article were hostile, and he accused Bukharin of 'semi-anarchism'. By early 1917, however, he had accepted many of Bukharin's points, and, when *State and Revolution* was written in August 1917, it bore many similarities with Bukharin's earlier views. Later on, after the October Revolution, Bukharin took an even more intransigent stand than Lenin on the issue of world revolution. As leader of the left Communists, he urged the rejection of the Brest-Litovsk peace treaty and the continuation of the armed struggle to ignite revolution in Europe. He also initially opposed the creation of a full-time, professional Red Army to defend the Revolution, preferring instead to retain militia organizations and 'flying detachments of partisans', which could engage in genuinely revolutionary warfare.[3]

In all three arguments Bukharin's position was generally regarded as being to the left of Lenin—more hostile to the use of proletarian state power to carry through the Revolution, and more ready to rely upon the 'spontaneous' action of the working masses.

BUKHARIN THE RADICAL STATIST, 1918–20

The Civil War changed all that. As it developed from mid-1918, and as the regime was fighting for its life, the Bolsheviks became reconciled to the need for the 'dictatorship of the proletariat' to organize the armed struggle and the production of all that was needed to support the war effort. The same applied to Bukharin. Even though, as editor of *Pravda*, he had no executive responsibility for the regime's policies, he nevertheless came to accept the increasing statification of national life. Its basic justification was the need to crush the armed

---

[3] For more details, see S. F. Cohen, *Bukharin and the Bolshevik Revolution: A Political Biography, 1888–1938* (New York, 1973; 2nd edn., Oxford 1980), chs. 1–3.

resistance of the bourgeoisie, as well as their imperialist supporters. For this to be achieved as quickly as possible, Bukharin argued that the Bolsheviks needed 'the regime of the armed dictatorship of the proletariat'. It was to be 'the lever of economic transformation'. But it would not be enough for the proletarian state simply to destroy. It was also needed to restore the economy by establishing national priorities, by extracting grain surpluses, and by taxes in kind. There was even talk of a unified economic plan. Bukharin expected that the mass of the peasantry would accept this role, since they could see that it was in their own interest—a restored industry would be able to supply them with tools to replace worn-out or damaged equipment, and also fertilizers. In addition, Bukharin envisaged the proletarian state re-educating the bourgeoisie and inculcating modern economic attitudes among the peasantry and even, to some extent, among the workers too. It was part of the rationalization of the socio-economic process, the establishment of the 'regulating influence of a crystallized, socially conscious centre'.[4]

In this phase of his thinking, the principle of centralization occupied a prominent place, as it had for Lenin. As Bukharin put it in his *Programme of the Communists (Bolsheviks)* of May 1918, the greater the centralization, the better. Thus he essentially set out a revolutionary utopia of a highly centralized Communist world state, which would serve as the antithesis of the highly centralized, finance-capitalist world which, he had argued, existed before 1917.[5]

Eventually, the role of the state was supposed to decline. Using a botanical image which was to become much more popular with Bukharin under NEP, he declared that 'the dictatorship of the proletariat will ripen into communism in an evolutionary way, withering away together with the state organization of society'.[6] Nevertheless, there was no suggestion that such an outcome was imminent.

[4] N. I. Bukharin, *Put' k sotsializmu v Rossii: Izbrannye proizvedeniya N. I. Bukharina*, ed. S. Heitman, (New York, 1967), 65, 71, 84, 94, 117, 108–9.
[5] A. G. Löwy, *Der Weltgeschichte ist das Weltgericht. Bucharin: Vision des Kommunismus* (Vienna, 1969), 111–12.
[6] Bukharin, *Put' k sotsializmu v Rossii*, ed. Heitman, 98.

BUKHARIN THE MODERATE ANTI-STATIST, 1921 – 5

The introduction of NEP in 1921 brought about a radical change in Bukharin's attitudes, as it did in those of Lenin. Bukharin did not take the lead in the introduction of NEP. It was above all Lenin's decision, and he had to overcome widespread opposition from within the ranks of the Bolshevik party, including Bukharin.

However, once Lenin had got his way, Bukharin emerged as the best-known spokesman for NEP, seeing himself as Lenin's truest disciple, particularly after Lenin had been incapacitated by illness. NEP was regarded by most Bolsheviks as a retreat from the heights of socialism which had been achieved during War Communism and therefore as something to be regretted. At first, Bukharin was no exception to this rule. But from the latter part of 1921 he came to see it as, first, a necessary retreat, and, secondly, from 1922, the preliminary for a renewed advance upon the forces of capital. In this he was following Lenin, who from 1922 began proclaiming that the retreat was over, and that, just as the Japanese had failed to take Port Arthur by direct assault in 1905 only to succeed by a long siege, so the Bolsheviks had failed to establish socialism in the Soviet Union by direct assault but would do so by the 'siege tactics' of NEP.

Bukharin's optimism about the prospects for achieving this are best exemplified by the phrase which he coined to characterize the whole period of NEP and which was so harshly criticized by his opponents: 'growing into socialism' (*vrastanie v sotsializm*). The underlying thought originated, as with so much in Bukharin's ideas, with Lenin, who had proclaimed in 1917 that there would take place a 'growing over' (*pererastanie*) of the different phases of the revolution, so that one would follow another without any break. Zinoviev also claimed that the term 'growing over' was 'one of the most used and profound terms of Leninism':

The *growing-over* of capitalism based on free competition into monopoly capitalism; the *growing-over* of the bourgeois-democratic revolution into the socialist revolution; the *growing-over* of socialism into communism; the *growing-over* of imperialist war into civil war; the *growing-over* of the general strike into an armed uprising; the *growing-*

over of opportunism into social-chauvinism. On the other hand, take 'the slow *growing-over* of serf-landlord farming into Junker-bourgeois farming' . . . one of the possibilities for the 'Prussian' type of development of peasant Russia, which Lenin considered after 1905. Or the 'historic break-through' from bourgeois to proletarian democracy, the *growing-over, crawling-in* [*vpolzanie*] or the *break* of the former, the *birth* of the latter. . . . Each of these formulas is full of the deepest content, each of them is a model of the application of revolutionary dialectics.[7]

Similarly, after the victory in the Civil War, Bukharin implied that the Bolsheviks would be able to arrange for the smooth progress of the country towards socialism. There would be no need for a further, third, revolution. Instead the process of building socialism would be smooth and organic. It was true that this phrase did little more than crystallize Bukharin's optimism that such a process *could* be carried out. It was not specific about the practical steps that would need to be taken if indeed it was to occur. It showed no awareness of the obvious difficulties that lay on the way and the hard choices that would have to be made. Nor did it always show sufficient sensitivity to the continuing strength of property prejudices on the party of the peasantry. One of Bukharin's young followers claimed in 1924, for example, that 'the withering away of private property in the countryside will take place slowly, gradually, and painlessly, following successes in agricultural technique, electrification, etc.'.[8]

Nevertheless, one direct consequence of this change of line was Bukharin's renewed awakening to the opportunities and need for society itself to build its own version of socialism. Relatively speaking, the role of the state came to be diminished in Bukharin's writing for the next few years. Instead of being in the vanguard of the socialist movement, its role was more to hold the ring, to construct a framework of laws within which the people themselves could build socialism, to establish the incentives which would win over sufficient members of the population, especially peasants, to the cause. The new path to socialism was to be laid on the 'planks' of individual incentive

---

[7] G. Zinoviev, 'Leninizm i dialektika', *Bol'shevik*, 16 (1925), 8 (emphasis in original).
[8] V. N. Astrov, 'K voprosu o kulake', *Bol'shevik*, 1 (1924), 32.

and interest, though individuals were not to be free to pursue)
that incentive and interest just as they chose.

A second consequence of the change was Bukharin's enhanced appreciation of the need for balance or equilibrium
between all the parts of society if society was to survive. Earlier
on, in his 1920 work, *The Theory of Historical Materialism*, he had
shown sensitivity in the abstract to this need of all successful
societies for some kind of internal balance. In turn this pre-
disposed him to trying to maintain balance in the transitional
society.[9] Whereas previously the revolutionary state had
deliberately sought to restructure the whole of society and
thereby manufacture and maintain a new 'equilibrium',
Bukharin came to appreciate that there had to be a new natural
equilibrium. The state could not hold society together, unaided,
all of the time. So this period was also marked for Bukharin, as
for the rest of the regime, by a growing awareness of the
complexity of factors which constitute a social equilibrium. The
chief momentum for the new strategy was to come from the
workers and peasants. The political strategy was to preserve
the worker–peasant alliance which had been forged in the
Revolution, and which, for Bukharin, was the most vital feature
of Bolshevik policy. Anything which threatened that alliance
would, he believed, also fatally undermine the whole regime.
So he was always sensitive to any possible threat to the
'worker–peasant alliance' (*smychka*).

The reason for the introduction of NEP was the increasing
alienation of the peasants. They resented the fact that their
crops were perpetually liable to seizure by marauding troops
and reacted by reducing the crops which they sowed. Once the
Civil War was over, the Party had to do something to restore
the peasants' goodwill. Lenin's solution was to tolerate the
reintroduction of the peasants' right to sell food surpluses once
they had delivered a minimum amount to the state. Thus the
peasants would be given the incentive to grow more, since
they would be assured of being able to keep the proceeds. NEP
was based upon this assumption of incentives.

Of course, it was not the intention of either Lenin or Bukharin

---

[9] U. Stehr, *Vom Kapitalismus zum Kommunismus: Bucharins Beitrag zur
Entwicklung einer sozialistischen Theorie und Gesellschaft* (Hamburg, 1973), 78.

that individuals or groups of them should simply be allowed
to pursue their own self-interest wherever it took them. The
available choices were to be structured by the state. So, for
example, the state retained its ownership of the land, which
was supposed to mean that successful peasants would not be
able to buy land and build up large landholdings. Peasants
instead should be encouraged to invest surplus income in
improvements to the land or to their equipment so that both
they and the state would benefit from increased harvests.
Similarly, although the state began to tolerate a limited amount
of private industry in factories leased from the state and run
according to state regulations on wages, safety, etc., there was
no question of private entrepreneurs being allowed to take
control of elements of heavy industry, i.e. the 'commanding
heights' of the economy. As Bukharin put it in a revealing
passage in *The Path to Socialism and the Worker–Peasant Alliance*:

The strength of Soviet power and its stability are so obvious that the
utter hopelessness of any attempt at conducting an active and sharp
political struggle against the new order is obvious to the bourgeois
strata of our society (NEPmen). These strata have willy-nilly to reconcile themselves to the existing order of things. Within certain limits
this bourgeoisie is allowed economic activity. . . . Does this mean that
the class struggle is ended? Not at all. But this struggle has changed
its form in the most vital fashion.[10]

The state would use its legal powers to support trade unions,
to deprive the bourgeoisie of the vote, to tax them more
heavily, and to support co-operatives in their competition with
private entrepreneurs through special terms for credit, etc. In
all these ways, then, the state would use the market to carry on
class struggle.

Thus the role of the state was far from negligible. Nevertheless it was supposed to be much reduced from War Communism times. Under NEP, the elements of socialism were to
grow through the development of co-operatives, especially
among the peasantry. Lenin described this as being, in Soviet
conditions, all that was still needed for socialism, and Bukharin
described it as the 'high road' (*stolbovaya doroga*) to socialism.

---

[10] Bukharin, *Put' k sotsializmu v Rossii*, ed. Heitman, 280.

The prime motive force for the development of co-operatives was intended to be an increasing realization on the part of the peasants that only by forming such co-operatives would they be able to continue to derive increasing income from their land. To start with they would be able to make small improvements to their land and to their equipment with the small amount of extra cash which they could generate from the new right to dispose of part of their produce. This, in turn, would lead to greater profits. In time they would reach a natural limit on the amount they could earn while still working their small individual plots. That would be the point at which they would begin to appreciate the need to work together in order to take advantage of opportunities for increased mechanization. They would, collectively, begin to be able to afford machines such as tractors. Thus the process of socialization of the land, which all Bolsheviks including Bukharin regarded as absolutely essential for socialism, would come about gradually through small-scale decisions taken by individual farmers throughout the country and in their own good time. It was socialism from below. Bukharin was very keen to emphasize that this strategy was a natural one for the peasants. It did not make any exaggerated demands upon their socialist 'consciousness', which was bound not to be too high. Instead it created a context in which the interests of individual peasants and of the regime as a whole coincided.

This then was one way in which society would be expected to transform itself in the direction of socialism. A further method, to which Bukharin attached considerable importance during NEP, was that of 'cultural revolution'. Again, this was a theme on which Lenin had placed great stress:

For us the cultural revolution is now enough to be a fully socialist country. But for us this cultural revolution represents incredible difficulties both of a purely cultural nature (for we are illiterate) and of a material nature (for to be cultured, we need a certain development of material means of production and a certain material base).[11]

To Lenin, the term 'cultural revolution' involved a great deal. It included obviously 'cultural' concerns, such as literature and

---

[11] V. I. Lenin, 'Zadachi soyuzov molodezhi', *Polnoe sobranie sochinenii* (4th edn., Moscow, 1958–65), xli. 299.

art, although, given the conditions in the Soviet Union at the
time, he was very scathing of what he saw as 'premature'
attempts to impose 'revolutionary' styles of art and literature
upon artists and writers. Instead he regarded a more immediate
task of cultural revolution as spreading literacy widely across
the country. So he urged that the position of the village school-
teacher should be given a high priority in the regime's policies.
Indeed he seemed to regard teachers as the main potential
allies of the Party in the countryside, acting as propagandists
and opinion-leaders for the regime. Both indirectly (through
spreading knowledge and culture), and directly (through
encouraging political support), they would help to solidify the
base of legitimacy of the regime. The spreading of culture
would go hand in hand with the spreading of Soviet power
and authority.

In addition, Lenin was preoccupied with the need for the
regime to absorb advanced methods of industrial organization
and economic management which were to be found in the
West. He would have no truck with Bolsheviks who tended to
be superior about the achievements of Western culture and
science, repeatedly castigating them for 'Communist conceit'
(*komchvanstvo*).

Bukharin also recognized the need to transform the mentality
of workers and peasants. As early as 1923 he declared that the
solution to the tasks of building socialism would lie 'primarily'
in solving the problem of culture in 'our' conditions.[12] He
summarized the problem as follows:

The task . . . the unction, the role of the transitional period lies precisely in ensuring that the working class matures as the class producing
all cultural forces . . . so that it becomes capable of administering
society, and then . . . dissolves into a generally Communist society,
when the dictatorship of the proletariat will inevitably be abolished
and when the remnants of old class divisions will disappear.

New cultural principles are not enough . . . we also need the living
bearers of them.

In practical terms he summed it up, as Lenin had done, in the
phrase: 'We need Marxism plus Americanism.'[13]

---

[12] N. I. Bukharin, *Proletarskaya revolyutsiya i kul'tura* (Petrograd, 1923), 9.
[13] Ibid. 35, 49.

The peasantry too would be expected to undergo a 'cultural' transformation, learning to farm and to trade 'in a cultured fashion'. Most of the modernization of agriculture which was expected to take place as a result of the co-operativization movement was described in these terms of learning to behave economically in a more 'cultured' way. Like Lenin, Bukharin placed much stress upon the role of the village teacher in building links between the regime and the peasantry, in serving as a kind of opinion-leader on behalf of the Bolsheviks. As he put it: 'There is a kinship linking the work of a politician and a primary-school teacher.' Teachers would hopefully serve as 'the bridge between town and country'.[14] There were also the innumerable tasks of transforming the cultural level of 'daily life' (*byt*).

Moreover, many defects of the Soviet regime were interpreted in terms of cultural backwardness: for example, bureaucratism. 'The greatest cause [of bureaucratism] is without doubt cultural backwardness, the "immaturity" of the masses, condemned to this backwardness by the capitalist regime.'[15] Indeed, as will be argued further in Chapter 5, this issue of cultural revolution became ever more important to him. So, for example, in January 1928, on the fourth anniversary of Lenin's death, Bukharin chose to give his commemorative speech not on the problems of the economy or agriculture, which were by then beginning to assume crisis proportions, but on 'Lenin and the Problem of the Cultural Revolution'.

At this stage, the approach of Bukharin to the problems of NEP highlighted ways in which society itself would resolve them. The role of the state, while not insignificant, tended to recede into the background. It took on more the character of 'peaceful', 'cultural', and 'organizational' work. The tasks of state-building were conceived of as holding the ring for society to do its work, for instance, by providing a legal system that would regulate human affairs on an impersonal basis, or providing greater opportunities for democratic participation in the Soviets. This was entirely in keeping with spirit of 'growing

---

[14] N. I. Bukharin, *Les Instituteurs et la jeunesse communiste* (Paris, 1925), 4, 8.
[15] N. I. Bukharin, 'Kul'turnye zadachi i bor'ba s byurokratizmom', *Revolyutsiya i kul'tura*, 2 (5 Dec. 1927), 7.

into' socialism naturally. For Bukharin there were no longer any serious internal enemies to be suppressed. On one occasion in 1924 he ever implied that the phase of the dictatorship of the proletariat was in practical terms over. As he put it, once the working class had won power, once there had been the victorious workers' revolution, *after* the dictatorship of the proletariat, there *began* the organic period of development, the growing into socialism.[16]

This view was obviously not accepted by other Bolsheviks, even by apparent supporters of NEP at the time such as Stalin. In mid-1925, roughly at the same time as Bukharin was producing his *Path to Socialism and the Worker–Peasant Alliance*, Stalin wrote about the dictatorship of the proletariat in quite different terms from those associated with Bukharin: 'The dictatorship of the proletariat is: . . . violence, unrestricted by law, *in relation to the capitalists and landlords.*'[17] In January 1926 Stalin presented his three 'characteristic features' of the dictatorship of the proletariat, and in a way which suggested that dictatorship was still the basic element of Soviet power:

1. The utilization of the power of the proletariat for the suppression of exploiters, for the defence of the country, for the consolidation of ties with the proletariat of other lands, and for the development and victory of the revolution in all countries.
2. The utilization of the power of the proletariat in order to detach the toiling and exploited masses once and for all from the bourgeoisie, to consolidate the alliance of the proletariat with these masses, to enlist these masses for the work of socialist construction, and to ensure the state leadership of these masses by the proletariat.
3. The utilization of the power of the proletariat for the organization of socialism, for the abolition of classes, for the transition to a society without classes, to a society without a state.[18]

Particularly striking in this formulation is the heavy emphasis upon the *power* of the proletariat to bring about socialism. It was a far cry from the notion of 'growing into' socialism.

It is not surprising, therefore, that great suspicion should

---

[16] Bukharin, *Put' k sotsializmu v Rossii*, ed. Heitman, 237–8 (emphasis added).
[17] J. V. Stalin, *Sochineniya* (vols. i–xiii, Moscow, 1946–52), vii. 186.
[18] Ibid. viii. 30.

have been aroused by possibly unguarded comments by Bukharin and his followers which seemed to imply that the Soviet state would not intervene even against kulaks. For example, in 1924 one of Bukharin's followers, Astrov, wrote: 'The kulaks do not hold political power, we do not touch them in politics as long as they do not touch us.' There was a certain literal truth about this at that time, although it did put matters more starkly than perhaps other Bolshevik leaders would have liked. But when he went on to claim that protests against socialism were conditioned only by 'inertia, habit, economic and cultural backwardness',[19] it is easy to see why it sounded naive not only to left-wing opponents of NEP but also to more 'orthodox' Bolsheviks who retained their pre-revolutionary distaste for kulaks. Thus, even with NEP at its height, officials placed varying emphases upon different elements of the regime.

Nevertheless, Bolshevik leaders were united in their desire for industrialization. Bukharin was no exception. The main problem was how fast this could be achieved, and where the main sources of funds were to be found. The terms of the debate were established by Preobrazhensky with his theory of 'primitive socialist accumulation'. He argued that the Party would have to transfer resources from agriculture to industry, at least in the short run, so as to ensure that there were adequate funds, even if it meant 'exploiting' the peasantry.

In 1923 an attempt was made by leftist officials, led by Piatakov at the Supreme Council of National Economy (*Vesenkha*), to engineer such a transfer. Soviet industry raised its prices in order to force peasants to pay more for their machinery and equipment. That would have had the effect of driving resources from agriculture into industry. The consequence, however, was what came to be known as the 'scissors crisis'. Peasants either could not or would not pay the new prices, so they stopped buying industrial goods. Industry could not sell its output and so fell into a crisis.

Bukharin's position in this debate was that nothing should be done to jeopardize the worker–peasant alliance. For the next three years this caused him to advocate a relatively

[19] Astrov, 'K voprosu o kulake', 29, 32.

moderate rate of progress towards industrialization. Two factors were crucial.

The first was ethical. He refused to believe that any would-be socialist system should seek to 'exploit' any of its citizens, let alone the majority of them. His attitude towards Preobrazhensky was determined as much as anything by the fact that the latter had quite explicitly called for the exploitation of the peasantry in his initial versions of the law of primitive socialist accumulation. Even though he had later toned down his statements on the subject, this changed nothing as far as Bukharin was concerned.[20] He believed that the earlier version still represented Preobrazhensky's instincts, even if he was no longer so open about them. So for several years Bukharin resolutely opposed any economic policies which smacked of exploitation. The peasants, he believed, had to be treated as fairly as the workers.

The second reason why Bukharin opposed the economic programme of the left wing of the party was his experience of the 'scissors crisis'. For Bukharin the 'lessons of 1923' (and he repeatedly used the phrase in succeeding years) were the impracticality of the proposals of the Left, not just their immorality. The crisis had undermined the business plans of industry and in so doing had brought the economy to the verge of collapse. Fortunately, it was a crisis which was overcome relatively easily, since it only required the re-establishment of greater 'equilibrium' between agricultural and industrial prices for trade to begin again, and for the economy as a whole to continue its revival. But for Bukharin it dominated his thinking about development policy for the next three years.

Bukharin, like Preobrazhensky, had no doubts about the need for resources in some way to flow from the agricultural sector to industry. But at this time he was extremely reticent about the role of the state in that process. In an article first written at the end of 1924, he accepted the need for industry to acquire resources at the expense of 'petty commodity producers', chiefly peasants, but he used the most neutral term possible to describe the way in which that process would take place. He wrote of the 'passage' or 'transition' (*perekhod*) of

<hr />

[20] Carr, *Socialism in One Country*, i. 219–20.

such resources from the one to the other, which made it seem neutral and unforced.[21] To Bukharin during these years, the solution lay in the circulation of goods, in practice in stimulating peasant demand for industrial products. The positive lesson which he drew from the successful resolution of the 'scissors crisis' was that reducing industrial prices stimulated peasant demand. So over the next few years the policy which the Soviet regime imposed upon industry, with Bukharin's approval, was the opposite of the one which had led to the 'scissors crisis'. Instead of trying to extract maximum resources from the peasantry through high prices, the regime tried to generate growth through ever lower industrial prices. As savings came to be made in industry through greater productivity and through reducing bureaucratism, they were to be passed on to the agricultural sector through lower prices. The hope was that, in turn, agricultural producers would order increased quantities of industrial products and machinery. Agriculture, however, was not under the same pressure to make savings. Thus the net result of such policies was, if anything, to generate accumulation in the agricultural rather than the industrial sector. In the short run, it certainly did not make easier the task of large-scale capital investment, which the Left argued was absolutely essential if the Soviet Union was to be transformed into a modern industrialized state. Moreover, it had one other perverse effect. Since Soviet industry was incapable of meeting the full demand for its products as prices were forced down through government decree, middlemen were presented with a golden opportunity to make profits by buying goods in short supply at the low state prices and then reselling them to the highest bidder. In this way state policies actually transferred profits from state industry to private speculators.

Even so, such a policy did bring substantial results. The economy grew at an impressive rate. But this was largely because the regime was able to bring back into production facilities which had been damaged in the Revolution and Civil War. The cost of repairing such factories was obviously less than having to build new ones. So the cost of industrial growth

---

[21] N. I. Bukharin, *K voprosu o trotskizme* (Moscow and Leningrad, 1925), 68.

was correspondingly lower than it would be once all existing spare capacity had been put back into production. Yet until 1926 Bukharin remained almost naïvely optimistic. People on the left wing of the Party were much more far-sighted about this. As Cohen puts it, Bukharin remained 'dazzled' by the stormy economic growth of 1923–6, when industrial output in one year increased by 60 per cent, and in the next by 40 per cent.[22] He continued to insist that the path to socialism in the future would be the same as it had been over the previous few years, namely through expanding demand and the circulation of goods rather than directly through increased investment.

The end of 1925, however, saw a new economic crisis. An unexpected shortage of grain collections led to the curtailment of the foreign trade programme, and in particular the reduction of imports of foreign machinery needed for industry. The reasons for the grain shortage were partly heavy rain at harvest-time and poor organization of the grain-purchasing agencies, but also a reluctance on the part of the more prosperous peasants to sell surplus grain while there were insufficient consumer goods for them to buy with the proceeds. In other words, industry was unable to meet the potential demand of the peasantry. This, in turn, threatened the growth of the whole economy. And, since industry was approaching its pre-war level of output, it was becoming more clear that something would have to be done to expand industrial capacity. Basically this meant increased industrial investment, and fairly rapidly. As Bukharin thought over the implications of this crisis, he began to adjust his ideas to the need for greater state intervention in and direction of investment, as well as greater state planning of the economy.

It was not just a question of Bukharin changing his ideas, though. This was also a time when government agencies responsible for overall planning and management of the economy, Gosplan and *Vesenkha*, began to play a more prominent part in the direction of future policy. Up till that time they had simply been too inexperienced to be able to play such a role. But now their expertise and confidence were growing.

---

[22] S. F. Cohen, Bukharin and Russian Bolshevism, 1888–1927', Ph.D. thesis (Columbia University, 1969), 445.

Policy-making began to depend less upon contributions from individual Party leaders and especially from ideologists such as Bukharin. Conceivably, too, the increasing amount of work on plans for industrialization which was being done by Gosplan meant that the scale of resources which would need to be mobilized became more apparent to the Party leadership. That, at least, is the charitable explanation. Up to this point it had been the Left which presented 'structural' analyses of the problems of the Soviet economy and their figures were automatically seen as suspect. It was at any rate noticeable that before 1926 Bukharin's writings on the economy were remarkably thin on figures of any kind.

BUKHARIN THE MODERATE STATIST, 1926–8

By the end of 1925, the fourteenth Party Congress had already resolved that the Soviet Union should pursue a policy of industrialization and the development of the production of the means of production. A leading article in *Bol'shevik* proclaimed the pre-eminent role of industry: 'The socialist steamer (urban industry) at present with steam up will haul the rural barge after it along the co-operative navigation channel to the open sea.'[23] In the aftermath of the Congress, Gosplan began to talk of disproportions between agriculture and industry.[24] A member of the Central Committee who was associated with Bukharin, Stetsky, admitted this, although he played down the extent of the disproportions by claiming that government miscalculations had been a major factor in the crisis of the previous autumn.[25] When challenged by Preobrazhensky to state the rate of capital investment he wanted, he replied by citing the preliminary control figures for the period 1925/6–1929/30, which had been submitted to Gosplan by the economist Strumilin, who was in charge of the team at Gosplan responsible for producing the first draft figures of a five-year plan. By implication, therefore, he accepted Strumilin's proposals for the rate of capital investment, which amounted to a

---

[23] *Bol'shevik*, 3–4 (1925), 6.
[24] Carr, *Socialism in One Country*, i. 343.
[25] A. I. Stetsky, 'Khozyaystvennye zatrudneniya', *Pravda*, 6 Feb. 1926, 2.

minimum of 16 000 million roubles in the state sector. Roughly two-thirds of this was to come from accumulation within industry and transport but this still left approximately 5,500 million which would have to come from agriculture. This was potentially an enormous sum, but how was the process of 'transfer' to take place?

In spring 1926 Stetsky pinned his faith on credit co-operatives, which would invest in industry because it would be profitable to do so. Unfortunately, at that time deposits in savings banks only amounted to 60 million roubles. At that rate accumulation over five years would only amount to 300 million roubles, i.e. only about 5 per cent of the estimated requirement. Nevertheless Stetsky claimed that accumulation was increasing with every year, and 'soon' these monetary accumulations in peasant savings, co-operatives, etc., would amount to hundreds of millions.[26] At this time, therefore, he at least remained true to the outline of policies which Bukharin had sketched in his *Path to Socialism and the Worker–Peasant Alliance*, even though it was doubtful whether alone it could be enough to meet the requirements.

At roughly the same time, another young Bukharinist, this time one employed by Gosplan of the Russian Republic, Gol'denberg, took up the same theme in a series of occasional articles which appeared in the spring and summer of 1926. In April he declared that there was no doubt about the need for 'pumping across' (*perekachka*) the surpluses of NEPmen and kulaks from agriculture to industry. He even suggested that one could not reject in principle the transfer of the funds of the middle peasants too, although he stressed the need to support co-operatives, including credit co-operatives, as the primary method of facilitating the flow of resources from agriculture to industry.[27] This was a stronger statement than Bukharin's 'transition' to sixteen months earlier. Then in June he asserted that heavy industry would have to take priority over light industry, although at the same time he took care to guard his flank by attacking Preobrazhensky again as a 'super-industrializer'. He declared that industrialization required that

---

[26] A. I. Stetsky, 'Ob industrializatsii', *Pravda*, 29 Apr. 1926, 2.
[27] E. Gol'denberg, 'Zapozdalyy refleks', *Bol'shevik*, 7–8 (1926), 31.

production of the means of production must grow faster than production of the means of consumption, and that therefore it could not begin from the 'calico end'.[28]

In his analysis, Gol'denberg relied upon a recent study by Strumilin which claimed that there were even greater hidden reserves in industry than had been previously suspected. In particular, he pointed to the effect of abolishing private owner- ship of land. He claimed that before the Revolution at least half of industry's profits had been siphoned off by the bourgeoisie for their own private consumption. From this he drew the following conclusion: 'The complete abolition of unproductive consumption by the basic group of the bourgeoisie—that is the fundamental reason explaining the specific opportunities for the rapid rate of growth of our industry.'[29]

Thus even greater pressure was placed upon policy-makers to find sources of accumulation in industry as well as in agri- culture. There began a hunt for possible increases in efficiency which could supplement other sources of accumulation. Of the Bukharinists, the outcome of this search could be seen in a book on Soviet economics written by one of Bukharin's 'pupils', Aykhenval'd. It first appeared in early 1927 and by 1929 had gone through five editions and 100,000 copies in Russian and Ukrainian. Almost immediately it became the standard reading on economics for all candidates for admission to the Institute of Red Professors. It included a warm introduction from Bukharin himself and in 1929 it was described as having energetically propagandized Bukharinist views. At the same time, however, it offered an extended commentary upon the plans for devel- opment as formulated at that time by Gosplan and *Vesenkha*. This is perhaps not surprising as, according to Nicolaevsky, Aykhenval'd was employed by Gosplan.[30] Thus the book can also be read as a synthesis of general principles associated with Bukharin and of policies formulated by government agencies.

Aykhenval'd advanced a number of modernization schemes designed to increase agricultural output. The most striking

[28] E. Gol'denberg, 'Voprosy ekonomicheskogo kursa', *Bol'shevik*, 11, (1926), 7–16.
[29] E. Gol'denberg, 'Otvet t. Preobrazhenskomu', *Bol'shevik*, 15–16 (1926), 84–95.
[30] Cohen, 'Bukharin and Russian Bolshevism', 582, n. 89.

concerned the continued predominance of the three-field system, rather than more modern systems of crop-rotation. As a result, he estimated, 28–30 million desyatinas of land were lying fallow at any given time. More intensive working of the land through improved crop-rotation could reduce that amount by up to two-thirds, and the extra 18–20 million desyatinas thus obtained would represent approximately one-fifth of the total area sown. In itself this would go a long way to alleviating the problem of land hunger. There were many other relatively simple ways of significantly improving agricultural output. He mentioned more rational consolidation of peasant plots, simple land-improvement schemes, greater regional specialization of agricultural production to make better use of local conditions, rather than growing a subsistence amount of grain everywhere, and simple improvements in agricultural equipment. This would supplement the benefits of the gradual introduction of industrial products such as tractors and fertilizers. Most of these improvements could be made by the peasants them-selves. The state would provide facilities that would show peasants how to become more 'cultured' farmers, but it could not coerce them, at least not *en masse*.[31]

Concerning accumulation in industry, Aykhenval'd pointed out that the basic solution to this problem was technical innovation, but that at least in the short term it was also possible to look to greater intensification of labour. He noted that, according to official figures, time off for holidays and sickness in 1923–4 was still three times higher than in 1913, and that simple absenteeism was twice as high. He did, how-ever, suggest that, as pre-war levels of productivity were restored, it would be less and less possible to rely on inten-sification of labour as a significant source of savings.

Nevertheless there were many other sources of potential savings. One was greater standardization of products. Why, for example, was it necessary to produce 150,000 types of knife when 1,000 might be sufficient? A second, and even more important, source was the introduction of more scientific methods of working. This included the attempt to increase the

[31] A. Aykhenval'd, *Sovetskaya ekonomika (ekonomika i ekonomicheskaya politika SSSR)*, (Moscow and Leningrad, 1927; 2nd edn., 1928), 135–56.

rate of circulation of capital—in some trusts the production and trading cycle took place 'at a tortoise pace', with raw materials and fuel often lying unused for months in warehouses. It had been calculated in 1924 that, if circulating capital throughout state industry were speeded up by just one day, it would either save four and a half million roubles, or enable the production at no extra cost of a further nine million roubles' worth of goods. In the United States capital circulated much faster. If the total production cycle for cars at Ford Motor Company was a mere three days, why did it take the ironically named Skorokhod ('Quick walk') factory thirty-one days to produce a pair of shoes?[32]

A further measure to increase scientific organization of labour was the drive to reduce bureaucratism. Aykhenval'd claimed that hundreds of millions of roubles were swallowed by the unwieldy bureaucratic apparatus. He mentioned that in March 1927 *Vesenkha* had taken steps to reduce centralized authority over trusts so that they could more flexibly adapt to the market and cut administrative costs, which he described as a merit of capitalism.[33]

Even given all these possible sources of accumulation within industry itself, Aykhenval'd accepted that they would not in themselves be sufficient for all the needs of industrialization. Some funds would have to come from agriculture. Indeed, apart from encouraging peasants to set up their own food-processing plants, and the state using its foreign-trade mono-poly to take the difference between the price paid to peasants for grain and its selling price on world markets, he indicated that the chief means for transferring funds to industry should be through peasant deposits in savings banks or subscriptions to state loans. He accepted that a heavy progressive income tax should be imposed on kulaks (at that time equivalent to 25 per cent of their income), but he rejected the demand of the Opposition for an extra 200–300 million roubles to be taken from the kulaks, as this would mean the ruin of their farming and in turn the disruption of food and raw material supplies for industry.[34]

[32] Ibid. 85–9, 109–110.
[33] Ibid. 109, 63–5.
[34] Ibid. 113, 240–1.

It is clear from this outline of the views of Bukharin's close followers that from 1926 onwards they were prepared to accept a state-induced transfer of funds from agriculture and the peasantry to industry and the workers, provided it was moderate in scope and as voluntary as possible. The state could increase taxation of kulaks and rich peasants, but only within strict limits.

Bukharin's own pronouncements on the subject were more sparse in 1927, but in his famous 'Notes of an Economist', which was intended to be a definitive statement of his views on industrialization, he stated that the opponents of industrialization were opposed to any kind of transfer of resources, which would slow down the tempo of industrialization, whilst the Trotskyists wanted a transfer that was as high as technically feasible. The truth, Bukharin wrote, lay in the middle.[35] Thus he, too, had come round to the view that the state would have to play a part in the transfer of resources.

The second area of economic policy-making in which Bukharin seemed to accept an enhanced role for the state after 1926 was planning. It is difficult to discern from his writings during the earlier phase of NEP exactly what his position was. It does seem, however, that he never abandoned the idea that industrialization and planning would develop hand in hand. Even though he was enthusiastic about the role of the market in reviving the economy, he never seems to have believed in it as an impartial efficient allocator of resources which worked best when left most alone. He repeatedly stressed that in the conditions of NEP the market represented a kind of class struggle. So the role of the state even then was in some way to 'rig' the market so that it favoured the rise of co-operative forms of farming and collectivist principles in general. For example, Bukharin made much of the fact that the state would continue to own the land, which would, he claimed, prevent the rise of a capitalist class of landowners who would buy up the land of weaker peasants. Also, the state would offer cheap credit, loans, and other financial concessions to peasants to enable them to form co-operatives and compete with richer peasants. Thus one of the functions of the state, according to

[35] Bukharin, *Put' k sotsializmu v Rossii*, ed. Heitman, 387.

Bukharin, was to ensure that peasants would come to see that only co-operatives held out the prospect of prosperity. Thus increased taxation of kulaks and rich peasants was entirely in keeping with this goal. Likewise, the state would use its fiscal powers to prevent bourgeois entrepreneurs from building up great wealth in the cities. And the state would use its powers over the pricing of industrial products (at least in theory) to ensure that industrial enterprises which were leased to capitalists would not be able to charge extortionate prices.

Thus even in *The Path to Socialism and the Worker–Peasant Alliance*, which is one of the most enthusiastic defences of market relations and NEP, he wrote:

Ultimately the development of market relations will destroy itself because, as state industry and co-operatives crush all other economic forms and drive them out of the market precisely on the basis of these market relations with their buying and selling, money, credit, stock-exchange, etc., so the market itself will sooner or later wither away, for all will be replaced by the distribution of products through the state and co-operatives.[36]

He is clearly here reluctant to associate the market with either state or co-operative enterprises. There seems to be no scope for a market to play a part in allocating resources between such enterprises. Indeed in Bukharin's mind there continued to linger a vague identification of industrialization with centralization and planning of decision-making, just as there had been in 1916. In the same work he looked forward to 'a unified, organized economy' and to progress in industry towards 'an order of things when the whole of industry is united by a general plan, under which nothing is wasted, when there are no unnecessary expenses, and under which the cost of products becomes ever less'. In the short run he regarded such a situation as impossible, most of all because of the existence of a multitude of small peasant farms. But in the long run:

The advantages of *large-scale* production in general will reveal themselves; ever greater savings and profit will be obtained in the state economy as it becomes more planned, i.e. from the planned and most rational use of all material and labour resources; ever greater sums will

[36] Ibid. 289.

be at the disposal of state power, which will be capable of helping ever more widely with the organization of the peasantry through the formation of co-operatives.[37]

The attraction of planning for Bukharin and other Bolsheviks was that it was part of the more general process of introducing science into life It had been part of their ideas from before the Revolution. To some extent this could be seen as a natural social process which would not need the intervention of the state to bring about. On the other hand, the establishment of state planning institutions and the gradual expansion of their work in the 1920s meant that the Soviet state was taking an increasingly prominent role in the process. And, whether or not in theory Bukharin's talk of the increasing centralization of decision-making in industry necessarily implied that the state would take the lead, it was certainly compatible with it. There is no evidence that Bukharin rejected this and quite a lot to suggest that he approved.

Thus, in both the recognition of the need for the state to play a more prominent role in redistributing resources between agriculture and industry, and also in the expanding role of overall planning by the state, it is clear that in the period 1926–8 Bukharin was no longer the defender of the market and of the interests of the peasantry at all costs that he had appeared in 1925.

This is not to say that he had clear answers to all the problems confronting the Soviet Union at that time. For example, although he was now prepared to contemplate some state-induced transfers of resources to industry from agriculture, he still wanted to rely to a large extent on the voluntary savings of peasants. However, there was still an enormous gap between the size of peasant deposits in savings institutions in 1927 and what Soviet planners believed was needed for industrialization to take place. It is not clear that Bukharin would have been prepared to countenance the pressure which the state might have felt necessary even if there had not been the grain crisis at the end of 1927 and if the planned industrialization had not been upped even further in 1928. Nor were the peasants being rapidly persuaded of the advantages of co-operative farming, as he had optimistically believed in 1925. A tiny proportion of land was under collective cultivation by 1928.

Equally importantly, neither Bukharin nor his group of followers devoted much attention to trying to ascertain the real extent of differentiation among the peasantry as NEP developed, and this despite repeated accusations by Oppositionists that it was indeed growing rapidly. Instead such information as the regime did possess on the subject had been collected by the Commissariat of Agriculture, and in the eyes of many Old Bolsheviks this was suspect because of the number of former Socialist Revolutionaries or their supporters whom it employed. At the very least this lack of concern on the part of Bukharin suggested to some complacency, or even indifference. In that sense Day's accusation that Bukharin was undialectical in his thinking because he failed to appreciate the importance of private property for the peasant is justified.[38]

Nevertheless it is also clear that he had modified his views on NEP since 1925, as the policies, the regime, and the situation in the country at large had changed. He had come to accept the need to give primacy to industrialization over agricultural development, provided it did not lead to any kind of 'exploitation' of the peasantry. He had come to accept that the state would have to maintain a prominent leading role in the building of socialism—and he had begun to write as if he believed it as well.

CONCLUSION

This chapter has demonstrated that it is wrong to see Bukharin as an unreconstructed advocate of market socialism. His views evolved in the course of NEP, and did so in the direction of a greater role for planning and the state. Like many other Bolsheviks, he became increasingly attracted to planning as the practical possibilities for achieving it became greater. Bukharin was a particularly clear example of this, chiefly because he had been so strongly associated with the methods of NEP in the period up to 1925, but he was not unique. In any case, from

---

[38] Day, Introduction to Bukharin, *Selected Writings*, pp. liii–lv.

1926 onwards his role in economic policy-making declined, particularly as he became more preoccupied with international affairs and the Comintern. Government economic agencies such as Gosplan acquired greater stature and prominence. Although their perspectives were similar to Bukharin's,[39] and although some of his protégés occupied leading positions within them, policies were modified.

So, on the one hand it seems unfair to pin on Bukharin 'enormous historical responsibility for the onset of forced collectivization',[40] because he was the 'principal architect' of the policies that produced the 'grain strike' at the end of 1927, and because he played a key role in successive press campaigns that discredited any alternative leadership to Stalin. In fact, Bukharin, despite all his pre-eminence in the field of ideology under NEP, never seems to have won over many people employed as ideologists in the party. A good deal of the assault on the Right Deviation after 1928 was led by ideological workers and officials, such as Bauman, who briefly became Molotov's deputy in Moscow in 1929. But, on the other hand, it seems mistaken to view Bukharin as the precursor of modern market socialists, since his view of the market remained that it would decline and ultimately disappear as Communism approached.[41] One obvious difference between Bukharin and the advocates of economic perestroika today is that in the meantime directive planning and the command economy have been tried in the Soviet Union and they appear ultimately to have failed. Maybe Bukharin would have come to the same conclusion if he had lived long enough to see the same results. But at the time the instinct for planning and all that it implied in terms of the greater rationalization and human control of the economy were far too strong.

Does this mean, then, that Bukharin's ideas should be

[39] See, e.g., Bazarov's use of the term 'dynamic equilibrium', which was particularly associated with Bukharin's *Theory of Historical Materialism*, mentioned in P. A Diaconoff, 'Gosplan and the Politics of Soviet Planning', Ph.D. thesis (Indiana University, 1973), 81.

[40] Day, Introduction to Bukharin, *Selected Writings*, p. lv.

[41] See also Nove's view that 'socialism [for Bukharin] . . . would *not* be any species of market economy' (A. Nove, 'Some Observations on Bukharin and his Ideas', in C. Abramsky (ed.), *Essays in Honour of E. H. Carr* (London, 1974), 199.

viewed simply as a product of their time, with little relevance to the problems of building socialism today in the Soviet Union? In fact it can be argued that the political reforms which Bukharin advocated in the 1920s, rather than economic reforms, are precursors of perestroika (Bukharin even used the same term). For example, the call for a revival of the Soviets, for a more impartial legal system, for greater professionalization of administration all appeared in Bukharin's *Path to Socialism and the Worker–Peasant Alliance* in 1925. Then, too, there is Bukharin's sensitivity to moral scruples, his unwillingness to sacrifice them for a higher cause, which resonates with the preoccupation with social justice which can be observed in some Soviet reformers now. And in autumn 1928, although it was then too late, Bukharin wondered aloud whether in fact there was not too much centralization in the Soviet Union and whether it might not be time to make a move in the direction of Marx's commune state[42]—though how this was to be reconciled with the developments in the direction of a planned economy and his earlier comments about increasing centralization in the industrial sector of the economy was not elucidated. Despite this, decentralization might have become for Bukharin as important as it appears to be becoming for Soviet reformers now.

However, one conclusion is clear: in 1928 Bukharin was still looking for new additional ways of building socialism. From the point of view of theory, this sounds attractive. Bukharin was always innovative and original. Cohen characterized him as 'the seeking Marxist'.[43] In a professor this would be stimulating. For a would-be leader in a regime based upon orthodox dogma, it was not such a strength. As this chapter has emphasized, there had been major oscillations in his ideas on building socialism since 1916. Although the gap between the parameters of these oscillations had narrowed in the 1920s, it certainly had not disappeared. It was not clear how predictable or acceptable his policy suggestions would be in the future. Would be suddenly fly off at a tangent and expect everyone to follow him? Still worse, would he do so in a crisis? In a novel

---

[42] Bukhanin, *Put' k sotsializmu v Rossii*, ed. Heitman 396.
[43] Cohen, *Bukharin and the Bolshevik Revolution*, 15.

written in the 1960s by Astrov, the one survivor of Bukharin's small 'school' of ideologists, Lenin's sister Mariya Ul'yanova is made to say of Bukharin: 'He's always full of impulsive ideas. . . . If it's not one thing, it's another.'[44] The problem with Bukharin was that he was indeed impulsive. His political career was littered with incautious lapses of the tongue, such as his encouragement for peasants to 'enrich themselves'. It would always be difficult to predict how he would react in a crisis. It seems reasonable to assume, for instance, that in 1928 he behaved quite differently from the way in which Stalin expected. If this unpredictability is put alongside his well-known weakness for political organization—he once described himself as the worst organizer in the world—and therefore his failure to organize a group of loyal Old Bolshevik supporters properly, this helps to explain why most other Bolshevik leaders turned to support the man they thought more predictable, more reliable in a crisis: Stalin.

[44] V. N. Astrov, *Krucha*, (Moscow and Leningrad, 1966), 285.

4

Bukharin and the Countryside

V. P. Danilov

THE ideas of N. I. Bukharin have given rise to intense interest amongst Soviet scholars and amongst the public at large. He is widely regarded as the leading spokesman for a non-Stalinist approach to social development and as the last Bolshevik theorist to argue openly against the establishment of the Stalinist bureaucratic despotism. Moreover, Bukharin and his supporters put forward numerous ideological and practical solutions to problems which still beset the Soviet economy and society. While the scope of this chapter is restricted to rural aspects of 'Bukharin's alternative'—which, given the peasant character of the Soviet Union, had decisive importance—it will also touch on more general features of Bukharin's views before and during the New Economic Policy (NEP). After all, it was in defence of NEP that he articulated his 'alternative' to Stalinism.

As we know, Bukharin stood on the far left of the Party during the immediate post-revolutionary years. His *Economics of the Transition Period* (1920) is rightly seen as an apologia for the policy of War Communism. Although he soon abandoned this viewpoint, the lessons of those years did not disappear without trace. Subsequently, no one provides more penetrating exposés of leftist mistakes. He was clearly speaking at first hand in diagnosing 'leftism' as an 'infantile disease'. Personal experience of this illness stood him in good stead later for the difficult task of refuting the call for economic compulsion and administrative-command management as the motive forces of social development. And this critical post-mortem of War Communism in turn assisted his further analysis: an original and fruitful attempt to understand and develop the Leninist ideas of NEP.

At the heart of this new analysis, most clearly set out in *The Path to Socialism and the Worker–Peasant Alliance* (1925), lay the notion of co-operation. Years later Bukharin revealed to Boris Nicolaevsky,

When I wrote it I included my [last] conversations with Lenin about the articles he had already published [such as 'Better Less but Better', 'On Co-operation'] and those not yet published. I tried in that pamphlet to keep to only what Lenin thought, what he told me. . . . The main poin of his testament was that it is possible to reach socialism without applying more force against the peasantry.[1]

The elaboration of this Leninist idea was probably Bukharin's single most important contribution to the formation of Party policy in the years 1925–8. For instance, he and his followers were the key authors of the Fourteenth Party Congress resolution (1925) on the pace of industrialization and the need to accelerate economic and cultural development of the Soviet Union. Similarly, the speeding up of the economic reconstruction process, especially in agriculture, approved by the Fifteenth Party Congress (1927), also fully corresponded to his analysis of the prevailing situation and his priorities for the Party and state. Thus, the Party in these years accepted and approved ideas for the transition to socialism that had been formulated— on the basis of Lenin's last testament—by Bukharin.

THEORETICAL ORIGINS

We should note that the central focus of Bukharin's policy towards the countryside—one fully endorsed by Lenin's co-operative plan—was first worked out by the great specialist and theoretician of co-operation, A. V. Chayanov. Indeed, Chayanov's theory is sufficiently fundamental to Bukharin's thinking to warrant a somewhat fuller analysis. Detailed examination of Chayanov's theory will provide a useful commentary on the position Bukharin subsequently adopted.

Scholarly study of the notion of 'co-operative collectivization' originated in response to questions raised by the Russian Revolution. We recall that collectivization was made an absolute priority of Soviet agrarian policy in autumn 1918, when the

---

[1] B. Nicolaevsky, *Power and the Soviet Elite: 'The Letter of a "Old Bolshevik"' and Other Essays* (New York, 1965), 13.

first attempt to unite peasant and collective agriculture was launched. Necessarily, this could not bring results on a large scale, though the birth of a kolkhoz movement was a significant event. It led, however, to a critical examination of the potentialities for and obstacles to collectivization. Thus, Chayanov's book *Basic Ideas and Forms of Organization of Peasant Co-operation* (1919) emphasized 'the limits of co-operative collectivization of farming' and rejected 'co-operative socialization of peasant agriculture as a whole'. It pointed out many difficulties, such as 'stimulation of work', the 'organization of labour' and 'the will for form'—i.e. management.[2] We know from much subsequent experience how intractable such problems can be.

Chayanov's critique of the idea of collective (*artel'*) farming, has two main aspects. First, the idea is not rejected out of hand, but forms a constituent part of his overall conception of co-operative development of the countryside. Secondly, and more importantly, the idea of 'co-operative collectivization' was worked out on the same basis on which the idea of collective farming arose and flourished, as its continuation and extension. To do so requires a detailed understanding of the organization and production structure of peasant agriculture, identifying and matching the capacities of previously disparate and isolated individual units. Chayanov showed, as early as 1919, that such a distinction would avert 'the ruin of those sections of the economy in which small-scale family production was technically more suitable than large scale', also making it possible 'to identify and re-organize into large-scale co-operative entreprises . . . where such amalgamation would have significant positive effect'. Ultimately, it would be possible so to re-organize all teams, functions, work, etc., 'on the scale and on the social basis which was most appropriate'. Thus 'large-scale collective enterprises of the co-operative type' would develop alongside the peasant economy and gradually replace it.[3]

According to Chayanov, 'co-operative collectivization' is the best or even 'the only possible' way to introduce 'elements of

---

[2] A. V. Chayanov, *Osnovnye idei i formi organizatsii krest'yanskoy kooperatsii* (Moscow, 1919) 301, 303–5.
[3] Ibid. 15–16.

large-scale economy, industrialization, and state planning' into the peasant economy. It comes about on a purely voluntary basis, relying upon 'self-collectivization'.[4]

Few people recognized the originality and profundity of his theory, especially in the conditions of 1919 and 1920. But I have no doubt that it received positive endorsement in Lenin's article 'On Co-operation' (1923), notably in its conclusion that, for peasant Russia, the growth of co-operation was identical to the growth of socialism. The experience of co-operative development during the 1920s, and Lenin's ideas, gave Chayanov material for elaborating his concept of 'co-operative collectivization'. In a second edition of his book, completed on 1 December 1926, he stated that the outcome of 'vertical concentration' of production, achieved through co-operation, would be that

the whole system evolves qualitatively from a system of peasant economy which co-operates in certain branches of its activity, into a system of social co-operative rural economy, constructed on the basis of the socialization of capital, while leaving the technical performance of some processes in the private economies of members, a principle of technical assignment.[5]

By this stage, Chayanov did not rule out the possible combination of 'vertical' and 'horizontal' concentration of production in agriculture as a whole, under which 'the whole peasant economy without exception is finally amalgamated into a single commune and organized on an optimal area of 300–800 hectares'. But he did not consider this the best outcome and stressed rather that it must in 'no way affect our basic system of purchase-credit-market and production co-operative, which will still be organized as before. The difference is that, instead of small-scale peasant economy, members of the primary co-operative will belong to the commune'.[6]

This process of 'co-operative collectivization' did express a basic tendency and, in the last analysis, the essence of the growth of rural co-operatives in the 1920s. Such a trans-

[4] Ibid. 24.
[5] A. V. Chayanov, *Osnovnye idei i formi organizatsii sel'skokhozyaystvennoy kooperatsii* (rev. and enlarged 2nd edn., Moscow, 1927), 13.
[6] Ibid. 341–2.

formation was an organic process, capable of spontaneous development, but by no means uncontrolled. On the contrary, it became more possible in conditions created by the socialist Revolution, above all those that were conscious, purposefully assisted, regular and governed (*rukovodimych*). 'Co-operative collectivization' was a socio-economic process actually taking place in the countryside during the 1920s. It was the objective basis for a genuine alternative to the Stalinist methods of collectivization.

BUKHARIN'S THEORY

Bukharin viewed the question of the peasants' path to socialism primarily from the theoretical aspect. Taking up the new idea of 'co-operative collectivization', he wrote that

the small peasant economy suffers from its 'smallness'. . . it will compensate for this defect by co-operative organization, supported by the proletarian state power, and will therefore in precisely the same way conquer for itself the advantages of all large-scale unification, and utilize the advantages and profits received from co-operation, in its struggle against the private kulak farming.[7]

He envisaged this in two stages. First, under NEP, co-operation via the market would bring wider rural strata into a system of economic links with general sections of the national economy (state-owned industry, the banks, etc.). Secondly, the process of increased co-operation would bring peasants 'from the organization of trade . . . into the joint organization of production'. The transition 'to increasingly collective forms of economy' would be very protracted. It would depend on technical re-equipment of agricultural labour 'reaching its maximum extent' with the electrification of agriculture.[8] Consequently, agricultural co-operation was an organic process, not purely voluntary and gradualist, but taking place as the result of requirements internal to the peasant economy itself.

At all stages of the transformation, multiple forms of co-operation must be used, extended and interacting: pro-

---

[7] N. I. Bukharin, *Put' k sotsializmu i raboche-krest'yanskiy soyuz* (Moscow and Leningrad, 1925; 4th edn., 1927), 65.

[8] Ibid. 33, 36–8.

duction, trade, and credit. The importance of the 'co-operative-collectivization' principle is clearly shown by the practical experience of Soviet kolkhoz development. Only now, more than half a century later, have we begun to restore the essential conditions for bringing about all forms of co-operation, including market relations.

However, the Bukharinite construction of a 'co-operative ladder' is very questionable. It tried to link forms of co-operation with the social structure of the countryside: kolkhozes for poor peasants, co-operatives for middle peasants, credit co-operatives for the kulaks. Hence arose the suggestions that 'kulak co-operative nests' could arise which would be drawn into the overall economic system of socialism, subordinated to it, and gradually reconstituted by it.[9] Bukharin's presentation was purely theoretical. This might seem to be the last tribute to that scholasticism, reflecting the abstract and logical formulations, often characteristic of his writings. But we should add that there was no basis for the accusation that he defended kulak interests or denied the existence of class struggle.

In refuting that charge, it is sufficient to review Bukharin's works of the period. These set out the main forms of struggle against kulaks, seen as rural exploiters. The chief method, in his view, was economic displacement, principally through co-operatives. 'To these rural hucksters we must oppose not the organs of direct coercion but our own good co-operative shops. Against the village usurer we must employ, in the first place, a battery of our credit associations.'[10] This was the struggle against exploitative relationships carried out by 'NEPist' means, in conditions of overall economic development.

The accusation that Bukharin was opposed to collectivization in principle, and indeed rejected the very idea of collective agriculture, is equally unfounded. The Bukharin plan for a socialist transformation of agriculture did rule out mass collectivization as a starting-point. It retained that for the future as a final consummation. Bukharin dealt with the question of relations between co-operative and collective processes at an all-union meeting of kolkhozes in March 1925:

[9] Ibid. 47–50.
[10] Ibid. 56–7.

We must not launch socialist construction in the countryside with the mass organization of collective production enterprises. On the contrary, the highway [*stolbovaya doroga*] lies in a co-operative line . . . collective economy is not the main road, it is one of the contributory roads, but none the less essential to the main. When peasant co-operatives are boosted by advanced technology, electrification, when we have more tractors, then the transition to collective agriculture will be greatly enhanced. One side of the process will help the other, one hand will join the other in a gigantic flood, leading us to socialism.[11]

The distinction between co-operation and collectivization came under severe criticism in 1928–9. This reflected the continuing predominance of kolkhoz formation and the weakness in organization of the co-operative movement. In ideological terms, much depended on presenting the transition to collective agriculture as the ultimate goal of socialist transformation. It could be argued, though, that the concept of 'co-operative collectivization' *had* received further treatment in Bukharin's works as the ultimate socialist goal.

In a theoretical account of the co-operative process in agriculture, the question of a completion date for the transition to socialism does not arise. The time-scale comes into question only in practice, when the peasantry must carry it out. However, it is wrong to state that Bukharin entirely ignored the time-factor. It was referred to in the 1927 Party Congress resolutions on co-operative peasant agriculture and the offensive against the kulaks. Likewise, the need to preserve and strengthen the NEP system by economic measures is emphasized elsewhere. No deadline nor tempo, nor any other detailed implementation of this transition, was established by the Congress. What is more, the Congress emphasized the importance of all forms of co-operative and envisaged their widest expansion.[12] Bukharin himself had publicly outlined a new course for Party agrarian policy shortly before the Congress.[13] It is hardly surprising that, when the Congress

[11] N. I. Bukharin, 'Doklad. Vsesoyuznoe soveshchanie s-kh. kollektivov', *Pravda*, 6 Mar. 1925, 3.
[12] *KPSS v rezolyutsiyakh*, iv (Moscow, 1970), 57–60.
[13] N. I. Bukharin, 'Ob itogakh ob"yedinennogo plenuma TsK i TsKK VKP(b)', *Pravda*, 4 Nov. 1927, and *Ocheredniye zadachi partii. Doklad na XVI Moskovskoy gubernskoy partkonferentsii 20 noyabrya 1927 g.* (Moscow and Leningrad, 1928), 28–33.

announced its offensive against the kulaks, this was associated with 'the question as posed by Bukharin'.[14]

The argument between Bukharin, Rykov, and their supporters on the one hand, and the Stalinist leadership on the other, came later. It was not concerned with such questions as: whether or not to accelerate industrialization, whether or not to co-operate with peasant agriculture, whether or not to attack the kulak. It concerned the ways in which to do so: should the Party confine itself to economic measures and extend the NEP system or should it turn to arbitrary, administrative-political measures, not shrinking from the use of sheer force?

The grain-collections crisis of the winter 1927–8 certainly posed a threat to the plans for industrialization and complicated the economic position. The initiation of widespread and more systematic use of 'extreme measures'—that is, non-economic, administrative–coercive methods of grain collection—broke up NEP. It ruptured the vital economic link between town and countryside. The potential growth of small-scale peasant farming was abruptly curtailed and the 1927 Congress resolution was reinterpreted as the call for a crash programme of collectivization, to be achieved decisively and at high speed.

In this increasingly complex situation, the Bukharin group proposed a way out based on NEP: preserve the policy of improving the peasant economy and developing trade-credit forms of co-operation; raise the price of bread; maintain a voluntary kolkhoz movement through voluntary renunciation of extreme measures. This was rejected on the grounds that the implied pace of industrialization was too slow and the 'concessions' to the peasantry were excessive. The Stalinist leadership denounced their policies as Right Opportunist, and—worse still—'pro-kulak' and seeking 'capitalist restoration'.

'BUKHARIN'S ALTERNATIVE'

Thus arose the 'Bukharin alternative'—a non-Stalinist approach to industrialization of the country and the socialist transformation of peasant agriculture. None the less, the clash between the Bukharinite and Stalinist positions does not

---

[14] *Pyatnadtsatyy s"yezd VKP(b): sten. otchet* (Moscow, 1962), ii. 1229–1231.

exhaust the number of ways of resolving the problems facing the Soviet Union at the end of the 1920s. There were various possibilities, according to differing concepts of the new society, its essential features, and means of development. There were profound differences between them as regards ends and means, those in power and the masses, and their own leadership function. In the contest between these views, all sight of common ground was lost. I think Kamenev was right in his ill-fated note of his conversation on 11 June 1928, when he quoted Bukharin: 'Differences between us and Stalin are incomparably more serious than all our former differences with you.' To demonstrate this it is only necessary to contrast Stalin's behaviour, already evident in 1928, with Trotsky's views expressed in *Towards Capitalism or Socialism?* or with the platform of the New Opposition at the 1927 Congress.

A fundamental divergence of views between Bukharin and Stalin first came into the open during their assessment of the difficult winter of 1927–8. We can see this in *Pravda*'s account of the April 1928 Plenum. Stalin explained the grain-procurements crisis as the result of NEP's strengthening the kulaks against Soviet power. The so-called 'Shakhty affair' (the first rigged trial of 'wreckers') was allegedly evidence of a plot by the technical intelligentsia against Soviet power, as agents of world capitalism. All difficulties were attributed to enemies: 'We have enemies within. We have external enemies. We must not forget this for a single moment.' Such was Stalin's general explanation. It followed that solutions to difficulties must involve the merciless annihilation of 'class enemies', above all the kulaks.

By contrast, Bukharin's explanation stressed the mistakes of those in power: 'We know that the chief instruments of economic pressure lie in our hands, and possession of them makes us invincible in domestic policy, unless we make major blunders. The kulak represents a serious danger only if he can use our mistakes.' Bukharin concluded that the shortcomings of the previous winter stemmed from the way in which society had been administered 'by ourselves'. Consequently, the alternatives were clear: *either* the Stalinist line of centring future policy upon enhanced struggle with enemies (if they did not exist they could be created through extreme measures and further Shakhty affairs) and by administrative-command methods, *or* the Bukharin line of improving Party and government work, carrying out industrialization and co-operative agriculture with due regard to actual conditions, preserving and perfecting the economic mechanisms of NEP.

The conflict between these two conceptions was most fully expressed over economic planning. Bukharin's long article 'Notes of an Economist' of 30 September 1928 demonstrated the unsoundness of voluntarist planning, singling out for special criticism the 'lack of co-ordination' in capital construction because it planned' the construction of factories 'today' with building materials (bricks and so on) to be produced 'tomorrow'. Bukharin's attack was directed not only at very high tempos of industrialization—as his critics maintained— but at voluntarist absurdities, disregard for objective conditions, and potential 'bottlenecks', inevitably reducing real growth and ultimately rendering the extra efforts of society worthless. Bukharin's last article published as a member of the Party leadership was his lecture 'Lenin's Political Testament' (January 1929). The title itself was a challenge to Stalin—it recalled Lenin's last letters. It opposed throughout the Stalinist course of replacing NEP with widespread use of administrative-repressive measures towards the peasantry, and defended the idea of bringing about a socialist transformation in the interests of the whole working population, through their conscious efforts.

Even this superficial glance at his published articles shows the conditional nature of 'Bukharin's alternative'. The question clearly arises: would NEP suffice to carry out the transition to socialism? In responding, we must first of all emphasize that NEP of the late 1920s was not reducible to one or another set of specific policies, as sometimes alleged. The question was not whether to extend some part or other of its specific mechanisms (which shows, incidentally, how underdeveloped NEP was). Even so, it became fashionable to speak of the contradictions of NEP, of its exhaustion, by referring to problems much more in evidence in 1922–4 than in 1926–7. By contrast, the statements of Bukharin and his supporters between April 1928 and April 1929—the period of their struggle against the

Stalinists—all indicate that the debate concerned matters of principle, not of detail. For instance, Bukharin's speech on the programme of the Comintern included a very important definition: 'In what does the essence of NEP consist? On what is it based? At the Central Committee Plenum of the Party the question gave rise to great argument. In my view, the decisive feature of NEP is its maintenance—by one means or other—of market relations. That is the initial criterion which defines the essence of NEP.'[15]

In this speech, Bukharin advances and defends the thesis of the 'universality' of NEP as opposed to the thesis of the necessity for direct forms of transition to socialist organization. He spoke of the 'NEP method', that is of an economic policy that preserves the right balance between socialized industry and small-scale enterprise, thus allowing for co-operation on the basis of mutual economic interest. According to Bukharin, real alternatives take into account the essence and direction of policy as a whole, rather than seeking pragmatic solutions to specific problems, although even in such instances the existence of his alternative is not in doubt.

Moreover, as a well-versed economist and politician, Bukharin linked such overall policies with resolving particular problems and tasks. In this connection, he did deal with questions of tempos, economic growth, and, above all, industrialization. A contradiction is sometimes seen between the insistence that extreme measures be forbidden, and hopes for a high speed of economic growth. But there is no such contradiction in Bukharin's thought. He regarded accelerated economic growth as the product of a whole series of measures designed over a long period, and not for immediate short-run effect. During his previously unpublished speech to the Central Committee Plenum of April 1929, Bukharin made the interesting and significant statement that

further tempos of the kind we have adopted may be even greater. We may develop them but only in carefully prepared circumstances and conditions, where agriculture has been developed as a base for

---

[15] *Pravda*, 17 Aug. 1928.

industrialization and there is a rapid economic turnover between town and countryside. Moreover, thanks to a number of mistakes on our part (such as an inflexible price system; over-assessment of agricultural taxes; erratic shifts in policy forcing earlier extraordinary measures in the first round as the product of previous mistakes; a system of closed commodity exchange), agriculture—grain sector—is not increased but reduced.

And further:

The problem is not that the tempo of construction is beyond our powers; it causes increasing and exceptional difficulties because we do not have a correct relationship to the basic masses of the peasantry. If we made certain changes in this respect, we should make a five-year plan of great construction work completely realistic not only as feasible, but guaranteed.

These changes would guarantee the solution of the problem, 'combining kolkhoz and sovkhoz construction with raising the level of individual poor-middle peasants'.

The attention of many commentators on the Bukharinite programme of 1928–9 has been attracted only to the question of 'extreme measures'. In fact, they often mention his acceptance of the 'first round' of extreme measures. Leaving aside the fact that for Bukharin they were the result of 'previous mistakes', the main point was in emphasizing their 'extraordinariness' as a system of extracting tribute from the countryside for industrialization and in the denial of extra-economic coercion in relations between the town and countryside. He counterposes 'extraordinariness' with his programme of 'expansion of commodity-exchange' on the basis of improved levels of agricultural output and resolving its problem of accumulation 'through market relations'.

The final removal of Bukharin from participation in the political leadership of the Party and country in autumn 1929 marked the end of the struggle for this variant of socialist development and of defence of the 'Bukharin alternative'. It meant that the question of the feasibility of his programme was never investigated. In my opinion, such an assessment can be carried out objectively. Ultimately, the criterion of truth is practice. Stalinist policy practised in the 1930s gives the final verdict in favour of the 'Bukharin alternative'.

AFTERMATH

The political defeat of Bukharin and his followers was not the defeat of their ideas or theories. On the contrary, all subsequent experience of the development of our society proves the correctness of the basic ideas and principles of the 'Bukharin alternative', and their accordance with Lenin's views on the path to building socialism in the Soviet Union. Nothing is more false than the Stalinist myth about the 'right opportunism' of Bukharin, Rykov, Tomsky, and their followers, alleging that they came out against industrialization and socialist transformation of agriculture, that they defended the kulak interest, and so on. The thoughtless and mindless acceleration of industrialization and collectivization, forced on the country by the Stalinist leadership, led to the disruption of the first and second five-year plans, the failure to fulfil the tasks set by them for industry and agriculture, the disorganization of economic linkages, and futile waste of material and human resources. Finally, it resulted in the catastrophic famine of 1932–3, in rural areas of the Ukraine, North Caucasus, the Lower and Middle Volga, the South Urals, and Kazakhstan, which cost millions of lives. This was perhaps the most terrible consequence of that 'choice of paths' that took place in 1928–9, which truly was a 'revolution from above' carried out by the Stalinist leadership. One of the most active and determined opponents of the installation of the command-administrative system and Stalinist despotism as a whole was N. I. Bukharin.

PART II

POLITICS AND INTERNATIONAL RELATIONS

5

Bukharin and the State

Neil Harding

THE very fact that Bukharin's rehabilitation was so long coming indicates that the political costs of this exercise were carefully weighed. For the Party to admit that it had been responsible for the judicial murder of the man Lenin referred to as the favourite son of the Party and its most outstanding theorist was brave and dangerous. Dangerous because it obviously impugned its past judgement on crucial issues, its procedures, and its moral integrity: it was obliged to admit to fratricide. There must also have been an equally careful consideration of the potential benefits. Bukharin's rehabilitation would oblige the Stalinists to come out of the woodwork and declare themselves. Those who still believed in the enduring importance of a command economy and the tight monopoly of Party control over every level of state and society must have seen the threat that rehabilitation posed. The threat was there as all parties knew because Bukharinism carried with it an alternative to the Stalinist party–state. It promised looser control by the state, a more densely-textured society, a variety of forms of property holding, and a degree of autonomy to social groups. In this notation, of course, Bukharinism was emblematic of perestroika and its enemies could plausibly be identified as enemies of Gorbachev.

Since pressing matters of power and policy are intimately connected with the campaign for Bukharin's rehabilitation, it is small wonder that his own ambiguous and highly volatile ideas on the state are conveniently ignored. Current orthodoxy— now as unimpeachable as its Stalinist predecessor—forces Bukharin into its mould. He has been appropriated as the authentic Bolshevik source for present policies, the true disciple of Lenin's mature reflections, and the Russian who established the intellectual *bona fides* of a humane and moderate socialism. The Party is consciously rewriting its own history and, as a necessary part of that process, is obliged to present a highly selective account of Bukharin's thought. Hence the economic, political, social, and cultural policies of Stalin are now portrayed as a disastrous usurpation of the true Bolshevik tradition. Yet the line of continuity with the founding fathers of the movement must be re-established as a precondition for restoring the legitimacy of the Party itself. This requires, in its turn, an open admission of the heavy responsibility and the guilt the Party bears for the enormities of Stalin's rule and a cleansing from its ranks of those who are unrepentant. Bukharin is the Party's prophylactic.

With such issues at stake it is small wonder that Bukharin has been converted, almost overnight, from a non-person into an icon. It is easy to forget that Bukharin's reflections on the proper relationship between state, economy, and society, in the period from 1921 to his death in 1938, were radically at odds with his earlier theories. Moreover, we are apt to overlook the fact that among these earlier theories was the fullest and most thorough rescript for the Stalinist state formation that was to claim Bukharin himself as its most illustrious victim. Within the space of five years, from 1916 to 1921, Bukharin ran the gamut of possible Marxist perspectives on the nature of the socialist state. As ever, he took them to their extreme conclusions. More than any other prominent Bolshevik, he was temperamentally and intellectually disposed to construct broad-ranging and absolutized theoretical systems from contingent circumstances. His life was an adventure in the dialectic. For too long, perhaps, he failed to acknowledge the catastrophic impact abstracted ideas could have upon the lives of a whole people when they became joined to irresponsible and unaccountable state power.

Like all the leading Bolsheviks, Bukharin considered political structures and modes of management to be neutral. They were in themselves neither good nor bad, but good or bad according to the class purposes to which they were put. This is not to say that he professed the same reductionist relativism that then characterized all Marxist writing on politics. But even when there were glimmerings of a more subtle approach, in, for instance, his reflection on the centrality of ideology as the cement of the state, there was always the fateful 'ultimately' that reduced ideas, institutions, and practices to class economic interest. In this myopic scenario ideas, institutions, conventions, and practices are not permitted to breathe a life of their own; they have no real being and no autonomy. This is the general plaint that can be brought against all Marxist theory of the state—it exists in a sort of limbo, a world of shadows precisely because it is set in a landscape without politics. The fatal flaw of Bukharin's analysis of the imperialist state is precisely his methodological commitment to explaining all political phenomena in class-economic terms. In his prescriptions for the young socialist republic it is, once again, the view that electoral practices, rules of accountability, and procedural propriety are at best neutral in the class sense and therefore of marginal importance, and at worst are veils and deceptions to disguise class purpose and economic interest. His theory of the state is flawed by the impossibility of his being able to acknowledge an autonomy for politics. Ultimately this derives from the Marxist metaphysic in which he so fervently believed and that was the bedrock of all his intellectual and practical activities.

According to this catechism, the world in all its natural, physical, social, and psychical appearances *is* knowable and to know it is to know the laws that inform it. In the social realm, where the struggle of classes is the motor of change, the task in hand is to demarcate the class interests and historical objectives of the principal and subsidiary classes involved. The integrity of the whole structure of this social analysis rests upon the related axiomatic propositions that there *is* a single and unitary interest binding all those sharing a common relationship to the ownership (or non-ownership) of the means of production and, secondly, that this class interest is discernible and knowable. It may, of course, not be immediately manifest. All sorts of false awareness bred of utopian projects, antiquated conceptions, or intellectual and physical oppression may intrude to blur the picture and stymie, for some time at least, effective action to promote class interests. History is the solvent of these illusions; practical experience is the avenue towards effective organization. Both will combine to make real and, therefore, to make manifest the unity and homogeneity of class interest and objectives. In all of this, politics does have its transient and limited role to play. It distils and articulates the rival interests, it moulds them into self-conscious groupings organized on a national and international plane. It purges illusions and increasingly shows the contending parties in their true lights. It is the theatre in which the decisive battles are prepared, battlelines drawn up, and the adversaries prepared for the fray. But it is not and cannot be the locus for the resolution of the dialectical clash of interests and objectives. At the crucial point, the battle is transferred from parliament to the street, from the war of words of newspapers and pamphlets to the physical confrontation of armed groups. The prize to be fought for is possession of the state and therewith of mastery over society.

The state is, throughout, conceived of instrumentally. First one class uses t to bludgeon the opposition and to secure the triumph of its exploitative processes, then the next class uses it until, eventually, the proletariat takes hold of it to usher in the final era of non-exploitative relations. In this era, politics is rendered redundant or even harmful. What could its practice reveal apart from the lingering remnants of outmoded class positions, that is, the reassertion of exploitative economic interests? In the era of the transitional dictatorship of the proletariat the state casts off the spurious pretensions of universality with which it has in all previous epochs dressed itself, and unabashedly proclaims itself a *class* state committed to implementing the interests and objectives of the working class. But these interests are, axiomatically, homogeneous and unitary. There can be no objective basis for genuine, legitimate, and basic disputation as to what they might be. The working class must, therefore, have an authoritative agency through which its common class interests are distilled, elaborated, and applied. In the transitional period this agency can only be the Party.

The state is a body that embraces the whole of the class, indeed all of the working people in town and country. It will, therefore, unless properly guided, reflect the degrees of backwardness of culture, consciousness, and organizational ability of those that comprise it. The Party, by contrast, does not express the variety of craft, local, ethnic, or occupational

interests within the working class; its business is not to ag-
gregate a great variety of differing interests and to articulate
the lowest common denominator of consent. Its role is to
express the generalized essence of the proletarian cause
specifically with regard to the most generalized source of
authority within society, that is, the state. Whenever, therefore,
Bukharin talks of the proletarian state being the highest and
most authoritative organization of socialist society, we need to
recall that it is so by dint of its inclusiveness and its coercive
economic, legal, and administrative means of obliging every
individual to do its bidding. But in and of itself, simply as a
set of administrative apparatuses, the state, as we have seen,
expressed no purposes and had no ends of its own to pursue.
Those ends, those purposes, had to be brought to it from without and the only agency that could therefore give it direction
and meaning was the proletarian party. It was this conception
of the state the led Bukharin, like all of the Bolsheviks, to
disparage the importance of procedural safeguards, balance of
powers, judicial review, and even democratic accountability as
means to restrain and restrict political power, or at least to
make it responsible. All of these devices and practices were
important only in terms of a wholly different liberal metaphysic
that denied the possibility of 'objective truth' in social matters
and that made the individual rather than the corporate group,
the epistemological and historical subject. The awful and im-
placcable logic of Bukharin's position was poignantly revealed
at his own trial—he who had before all others popularized
militant materialism and class identity could not now resort to
the language of liberalism and individual rights. He was caught
in a web of his own making.

THE STATE IN GENERAL

Bukharin never wholly escaped the reductionism of the Marxist
account of the state, but there are, none the less, important
innovative aspects of his analysis that have only recently
featured as major questions in Marxist thinking on the state.
Bukharin was not only prepared to acknowledge the 'relative'
autonomy of the bourgeois state but became the first to suggest
that, in its final and perfected form, it was the decisive mech-

anism for restructuring both the forces and the relations of
production. In this formulation, the state emerges not as the
passive reflection of the economic substructure of society; not
as the determined expression of the productive forces, *but
rather as their determining agency*. He was the first to arrive at
the startlingly novel (and apparently heretical) notion that the
superstructural state could, and in fact did, determine the
economic base of society and all other social relations. This
is Bukharin's most daring and singular contribution to the
Marxist theory of the state. It is also a notion fraught with the
most momentous potential. For, if the bourgeoisie, in its epoch
of instability and peril, could use the state in this way, did it
not follow that the proletariat could do likewise? Moreover,
that it not only *could* but *had to* in order to survive. As ever,
Bukharin became captivated by his own theoretical conjectures
and elaborated a theory of the proletarian state that was, in all
but its objectives and class control, the mirror image of his
analysis of the imperialist state formation.

One of the more interesting and provocative of Bukharin's
thoughts on the state is his insistence that it must be grasped
as a relation not a thing. Proportionate to the stage of development, it does, of course, dispose of all sorts of physical
assets—ministries, offices, prisons, courts, rifles, and battle-
ships. It has differentiated hierarchies of functionaries to staff
these institutions—politicians, civil servants and bureaucrats,
police and judges, gaolers and soldiers and sailors.[1] But all
these, taken simply *in abstracto*, do not cumulatively express
the essence of the state. That essence is to be discerned in a
relationship of those dominating to those dominated: 'Society,
except in its initial stage, was always *class* society; its production relations were those of domination and submission; its
political system was a reflection and an expression of this
condition.'[2] As patterns of exploitation changed from those of
serf to lord, journeyman to master, proletarian to entrepreneur,
the relations of domination within the economic substructure

---

[1] N. I. Bukharin, *Teoriya istoricheskogo materializma: Populyarnyy uchebnik
marksistskoy sotsiologii* (Moscow, 1921); trans. as *Historical Materialism: A System
of Sociology* (London, 1926), 152.
[2] Ibid. 177.

of society also had to change and along with them the form of the state. The distinctiveness of Bukharin's approach is his quite sophisticated historical sociology. The real story to be told, the real substance of history, is to be excavated from the debris in men's minds that mistakes things for men. It is a disposition that crudely sees, in a technological determinist sort of way, progress embodied in the wheel, the plough, the windmill, steam engine, or electric motor. In and of themselves, Bukharin says, these things disclose no meanings any more than do the physical attributes of state power. Their true meanings are to be discovered beneath these phenomenal and tangible things. They are but instruments and tools of varying sorts by means of which one group exerts its power and control over others. They express a power relation; a class relation that is, as we shall see, embedded not only in things but in a ramified and increasingly coherent system of institutions, rites, popular ideas, and psychology; riveted together by ideology as much as by coercive institutions and economic subjugation:

it is obvious that the 'essence' of the state is not in the *thing* but in the *social* relation; not in the centralised administration as such, but in the *class envelope* of the centralised administration. As capital is not a thing (as is, for instance, a machine), but a social relation between workers and employers, so centralisation *per se* by no means necessarily signifies a state organisation; it does not become a state organisation until it expresses a class relation.[3]

Class relations are, of course, intimately bound to the division of labour within society which, in its turn, is reflected in the nexus of bodies that comprise the state. We have already observed that Bukharin had noticed the differentiated functions of politicians, judges, policemen, gaolers, and soldiers. To these must be added the crucially important roles that are performed by those that serve its ideological apparatuses:

The bourgeoisie is well aware that it cannot control the working masses by the use of force alone. It is necessary that the workers' brains should be completely enmeshed as if in a spider's web . . . the capitalist state maintains specialists to stupefy and subdue the pro-

[3] Ibid. 303.

letariat. It maintains bourgeois teachers and professors, the clergy, bourgeois authors and journalists.[4]

The work of 'ideological labour as such'[5] assumes increasing importance as the process of the concentration of capital increases and as, consequently, the social and political insecurity of the bourgeoisie becomes more pronounced. Its role is to promote and foster a range of expectations and popular dispositions that will be unquestioningly accepted—a social psychology that sets limits to discourse and sets the agenda for politics: 'The social psychology is a sort of supply-chamber for ideology; or, it may be compared with a salt solution out of which the ideology is crystallized . . . The ideology systematizes that which hitherto has been not systematized, *i.e.* the social psychology. *The ideologies are a coagulated social psychology.*'[6] These ideologies, which, as we have seen, are not abstractly conjured out of thin air but are themselves systematizations of a broadly held political culture assiduously cultivated by the state, are of very considerable importance in binding the people to the state. They 'are not playthings, but in many ways serve as girders to maintain the equilibrium of the entire social body', they 'serve as rivets to hold together the existing order'.[7]

Bukharin has, quite clearly, moved from the somewhat simplistic formulations of Marx and Engels that gave warrant to those who were disposed to view the state simply as a set of coercive and punitive agencies—separate bodies of armed men in one guise or another. This state, so it was argued, stood separate from and above society, obliging it by threats of force. Bukharin's analysis is much more complex and sophisticated. As the bourgeois state develops and matures, he argues, the distinction between society and state is increasingly undermined. Organizations and institutions that had, hitherto, prided themselves or their autonomy, were increasingly suborned and subsumed within the general apparatus of power. The

---

[4] N. I. Bukharin and E. Preobrazhensky, *Azbuka kommunizma* (Moscow, 1919); trans. E. and C. Paul as *The ABC of Communism* (London, 1922; repr. London, 1969, with an Introduction by E. H. Carr; also Ann Arbor, Mich., 1966), 44.

[5] *Historical Materialism*, 218.

[6] Ibid. 215.

[7] Ibid. 255.

distinction between economic and political life was, in the epoch of monopoly capitalism, finally eroded. The banking and political élites became fused, the state exercised increasing control not only over general fiscal policy but also over the whole organization of industry and commerce, appropriating to itself the commanding heights of the economy. Simultaneously the churches, universities, school system, newspapers and the publishing world, trade unions, and voluntary associations were annexed as so many subordinate departments. They became quasi-governmental agencies. Vital powers of society were sucked up by the state, and its diverse and plural groupings were amalgamated in a single omnipotent and omnipresent power.

This analysis, as we shall see, was to have a very considerable impact not only upon Bukharin's analysis of the imperialist state formation but also upon his theorization of the dictatorship of the proletariat. For the moment let us notice two highly original and inter-related propositions:

1. Modern state forms cannot be reduced to coercive agencies that become more and more divorced from society as class contradictions become increasingly acute. The state, on the contrary, enmeshes society (the proletariat included) in a fine web of ideological, organizational, fiscal, and economic structures, making it difficult to target it as a purely negative and alien phenomenon.

2. At the most basic theoretical level the state, at the apogee of its development, far from passively reflecting and being determined by the economic base of society, emerges as the active subject organizing and directing this economic base. Superstructure determines base.

THE BOURGEOIS STATE

I have, elsewhere, attempted to reconstruct in some detail the continuum of argument that led Bukharin from his analysis of finance or monopoly capital to his brilliant and neglected theory of the imperialist state.[8] I will here do no more than

---

[8] N. Harding, 'Authority, Power and the State, 1916–20', in T. H. Rigby, A. H. Brown, and P. Reddaway (eds.), *Authority, Power and Policy in the USSR:*

summarize these points of Bukharin's analysis that are important for an understanding of the rest of this chapter.

Despite Lenin's valedictory (and thoroughly opaque) comment in his 'Testament' that Bukharin had never fully understood the dialectic,[9] it must be said that Bukharin's conception
of the bourgeois state was eminently dialectical. More than
any other Marxist of his generation he was concerned to
understand it not as a fixed and reified thing but as a set of
relationships in constant flux. The basic change that Bukharin
observed was the transition from the limited, liberal, pluralist,
night-watchman state that accorded with the phase of genuinely
competitive industrial capitalism to the omnipotent, illiberal,
totalitarian theory (and practice) of the imperialist state that
coincided with the rise of monopoly or finance capitalism at the
turn of the century. In social terms this transition reflected
the progressive shrinking of the social base of bourgeois
dominance which followed from the accelerated concentration
of capital. The multiform, relatively autonomous, and often
conflicting forms of capital—entrepreneurial, manufacturing,
industrial, landed, banking—were rapidly swallowed up by
finance capital based on the all-conquering national banks. This
meant the effective displacement and destruction of the social
groups that had affirmed themselves through these forms of
capital. In proportion, therefore, as finance capital succeeded
in its object of concentrating the entire capital resources in
the hands of a clique of the magnates of finance capital, it
simultaneously eroded the social basis of the bourgeois order.
This was bound to have political implications. Politics could
not be left to the competitive interplay of plural political forces,
which could no longer be assumed to have a spontaneous

Essays Dedicated to Leonard Schapiro (London, 1980), 32–56. I have explored the
impact of Bukharin's analysis of the imperialist state upon Lenin in Harding,
Lenin's Political Thought, ii (London and New York, 1981), 92–8, 100–9.

[9] Lenin's 'Testament' took the form of a letter to the Thirteenth Party
Congress. It contained cryptic assessments of leading personnel, including the
famous indictment of Stalin as being 'too rude' and the recommendation that
he be removed from his post as General-Secretary of the Party. Of Bukharin he
wrote: 'Bukharin is not only a most valuable and major theorist of the Party; he
is also rightly classified as fully Marxist only with great reserve, for there is
something scholastic about him (he has never made a study of dialectics, and,
I think, never fully understood it)' (V. I. Lenin, *Collected Works* (45 vols.;
Moscow, 1960–70), xxxvi. 595).

interest in the preservation of monopoly capital. The state itself would have to become an active agency in the management of the political life of society. It would have to use its considerable power to suborn the labour movement through the bribery of its upper strata, through ubiquitous propaganda and ideological habituation. Through its control of the media of communication and its direction of foreign policy, it was now able to foment antagonisms with competitor states and to portray the world as a place of hostile predators—one that imperatively demanded internal unity as a condition for the national mission to be played out. Resistance or opposition to the 'national' ideology became tantamount to treason. In wartime it actually did become treason and so could be dealt with judicially by the abstract impartiality of the law.

In the age of imperialism, therefore, the bourgeois state was, *in abstracto* at least, able to create the economic and political conditions for its own reproduction. The fusion of economic and political power that Bukharin described in his *Imperialism and World Economy* (1920) created an *organized* capitalism, a planned capitalism that therefore had the capacity, at least notionally, to avoid the destabilizing effects of the anarchy of production. This anarchic planlessness, that Marx had diagnosed as the Achilles heel of capitalism and the mark of its irrationality, had largely been overcome. Trusts, cartels, combines, and, above all, the big banks had begun this process of rationalizing production and bringing it into synchrony with demand. The wartime state completed the process. The state capitalist trust now commanded the heights of the economy, bringing much of it under nationalization. It decided upon the allocation of capital resources through its control over the major banks. It set prices through cartels, monopoly pricing mechanisms, and its fiscal policies. It controlled competition internally through trustification and externally via tariffs. It set the rewards of labour through its systems of rationing, welfare, and its legal interventions into the conditions and restraints governing collective bargaining, strikes, and so forth. The state capitalist trust, in short, did not neglect any aspect of the conditions for the reproducibility of its own mode of economic and political domination.

One senses in Bukharin's account an esteem bordering on

admiration for the integral logic of the structure of ideas and
institutions of the imperialist state. Here was an enemy to
be reckoned with. He was audacious, subtle, yet ruthless in
pursuit of its self-interest. He was admirably organized and co-
ordinated in both the economic as well as the political planes.
He was ideologically astute and breathed a courage and
audacity born of his fragile situation. Above all he had learnt to
use the state quite purposefully as the last bastion available to
guarantee the maintenance of his own powers and privileges.
Here was an enemy from whom much might be learned.
Bukharin barely attempted to disguise his captivation with the
efficiency and omnipotence of this state formation and early on
began to apply its organizational model to remedy the shortcomings of the infant socialist republic.

We might, at this stage, wonder whether Bukharin had not
rather overplayed his hand in stretching Marx's admiration for
the resilience and class consciousness of the bourgeoisie to
its extreme limits. He seemed, at times, almost in danger of
treading the same path as the Struves and Tugan Baranovskys
who heaped so much 'Marxist' praise on capitalism as a
modernizing force that they had ended up embracing it
as liberals. But this comparison would be quite mistaken.
Bukharin's objective and inspiration was quite otherwise: it
was to revive the lost heroic of the Marxian schema. The
greatest impediment to that was the vulgar historical optimism
of the revisionists, and the mishmash of Lib–Labism. Like
Lenin, his targets were that host of Western Marxists basking
in the pathetic and mechanistic belief that history necessarily
demonstrated the unfolding of the immanent socialist ideal.
Do what they liked, struggle as they might, the bourgeoisie
was fated to implement socializing policies. To such myopic
optimists, every nationalization, every intrusion of the state
into the management of industry, welfare, and education, was
proof of the inevitability of socialism. Their happy conclusion
from this analysis was that *economically* organized capitalism
must issue in socialism and that *politically* the growing consciousness and organization of the labouring majority would
ensure the growing-over of democracy into social democracy.
For Bukharin, such optimism bred quietism, responsibility,
incorporation, and was an apostasy to the militant heroism of
the proletariat's historic mission.

The first condition for reconstituting militant heroism was to replace this heady optimism with a refreshing dose of historical pessimism. Like Lenin he did not believe that the proletariat would spontaneously and necessarily acquire sufficient self-organization, consciousness, and resolve to realize its historic mission. Still less did he believe that the bourgeois state would spontaneously self-destruct or benignly legislate itself away. On the contrary, he painted a picture of an all-conquering magisterial power, splendidly armed and organized for its own defence, mobilizing all resources physical, coercive, psychological and ideological, economic and military for its own preservation. Its co-ordinated and differentiated agencies reached right down into every aspect of the lives of its subjects, controlling and directing everything and everyone. Here was Bukharin's deliberately nightmarish vision of the new Leviathan: 'Thus there arises the finished form of the contemporary robber state, an iron organization, which envelopes the living body of society with its tenacious, grasping claws. It is—the new Leviathan, beside which the fantasy of Thomas Hobbes seems but a child's plaything.'[10] This was not the benign and doddering power of social democratic mythology, able to survive only by emasculating itself in perpetual concessions, but an awesome enemy that threatened to absorb the whole economy, and society, even the working class. Nothing short of titanic struggle could overcome it. Armed to the teeth, contemptuous of democratic formalities, this formidable opponent would go down fighting. It followed that the battle against it would be one with no quarter given, in which victory would go to the best organized, best armed, and, above all, to the most inspired and resolutely committed. As with the bourgeoisie, so too with the proletariat, politics would yield place to war—the decisive battles for the prevalence of one mode of production over another would be fought not in debating chambers but on barricades.

Bukharin believed that the fatal flaw in the integrated structure of the state capitalist trust was that its ideology, its economic structure and social mobilization, could only justify themselves by the perceived threat of imminent war. This

---

[10] N. I. Bukharin, 'K teorii imperialisticheskogo gosudarstva' (1915), in *Revolyutsiya prava*, i (Moscow, 1925), 30.

threat could only be sustained if, periodically, the state was actually engaged in war with its competitors. Militarism and the militarization of everyday life were therefore necessary, intrinsic features of state monopoly capitalism. But this meant that taxes would have to be raised, living standards reduced, and, above all that millions would have to be mobilized to fight and die for their country. There would come the point when those confronted with the imminent threat of death would ponder the reasons for their own self-sacrifice. Pain, mutilation and death on a mass scale would inevitably pose the existential problem—'What is it all for?' At this point socialist propaganda could begin to dissolve the imperialist state formation. When this existential 'and primal question' was widely posed, the socialist answer to it would receive wide currency. Thus war and its disastrous consequences would finally unyoke the working classes from the chariot of the imperialist state.

THE 'COMMUNIST' STATE

By 1916 Bukharin concluded that it was high time to smash the state and to consign it to the rubbish dump of history. The imperialist robber state had raised the state formation to its ultimate barbaric expression as an engine of war within and without. All productive endeavour had been turned to generating destruction and escalating fratricide: This frenzied monster, swollen with blood, would have to be dispatched or the world would irrevocably be plunged into barbarism. This did not mean however, that Bukharin had succumbed, as Lenin alleged, to a petty bourgeois anarchist utopia. The difference between anarchism and Marxism, Bukharin insisted, lay in their attitudes towards the organization of production and distribution rather than in their attitudes towards the state. The elimination of the state did not at all portend the end of centralized control and direction of industry. On the contrary, by comparison with capitalism, socialism would have a thoroughly centralized economic structure. It would be an *organized society based on labour*; it must, therefore, be a *planned* society.

In such a social order, production will be organized. No longer will one enterprise compete with another; the factories, workshops, mines, and other productive institutions will all be subdivisions, as it were, of one vast people's workshop, which will embrace the entire national economy of production. It is obvious that so comprehensive an organization presupposes a general plan of production.[11]

Everything must be precisely calculated—the need for labour, capital, and consumer goods—and this task will be the domain of statistical bureaux or book-keeping offices, 'and when the social order is like a well-oiled machine, all will work in accordance with the indications of these statistical bureaux'.[12] When classes have been done away with, when there are no more permanent managers, when people develop a variety of skills and administrative experience, 'There will be no need for special ministers of State, for police and prisons, for laws and decrees . . .'[13] The function of the state will, in this situation, 'be reduced to that of a central accountant's office',[14] discharging its benign tasks of overseeing the administration of things.

Here the old Marxist dish reappears on the menu, spiced with a little demotic Saint-Simonianism. We should notice (as do all commentators examining the Marxian original) how sparse and vague are Bukharin's comments on the future order of things. Particularly lamentable are Bukharin's conspicuous silences on the transformation of those relations of domination and subordination that had ever characterized class society and, in his own account, had ever constituted the very essence of the state. He did, temporarily, flirt with the idea of workers' control, though it never became an articulated or central feature of his theoretical system. Yet it is difficult to import any coherence to the development of Bukharin's thought without some such pivotal idea. If, after all, his main sociological plaint against class-based societies was the frozen patterns of domination and subordination arising fundamentally from within the social relations of production, we ought to expect some well-elaborated reflections on how Bukharin proposed trans-

[11] Bukharin and Preobrazhensky, *The ABC of Communism*, 69–70.
[12] Ibid. 74.
[13] Ibid. 71–4.
[14] Ibid. 329, 338.

forming and eliminating them under socialism. This is no
minor point. Inferentially at least, it is the sum and substance
of Bukharin's project for socialism. But here, once again,
Bukharin's silences speak eloquently of the ambiguities within
the Marxist tradition as a whole. The romantic dream of free
unalienated men, disposing of a variety of skills and themselves participating in every aspect of the new administration,
fits ill with the more rationalist, progressivist, and positivist
strains that, on the whole, dominated Russian Bolshevism. The
quandary is obvious—how to reconcile the dream of self-acting
non-dominated individuals with the countervailing vision of
the planned and organized society.

The only way of overcoming this unarticulated tension was
to presume that all (or at least the great majority of) free men of
right reason would voluntarily assent to the organizational
structures and planning directives and accept the restraints and
discipline they necessarily entailed. The unspoken assumption
that binds the Communist state is that right reason and the
class interest of the immense majority happily coincide. Right
reason, is, in this context, the application of scientific materialism to the problems of economic and social organization.
Neither Bukharin nor Lenin doubts that this exercise will yield
only *one* optimal plan and a social order given by objective,
indisputable evidence. This optimal economic plan, and its
appropriate social order, will also conform to the long-term
interests of the working class. Communism, in this Bukharinist–
Leninist guise, is clearly premissed on a materialist metaphysic
in which evidence replaces conjecture, statistics speculation,
and positive knowledge utopian aspiration.

It is evident that, in this positivist universe, there can be
no space for politics in the sense of the canvassing of rival
formulations of public policy, alternative specifications of
economic and social priorities, or the aggregation and articu-
lation of differing interests within society. As in the Saint-
Simonian original, disputatious and discursive politics is part
of mankind's pre-history. In the era of positive or scientific
knowledge it has at best no purposes to serve and at worst
becomes a theatre of the absurd where people not yet come to
adequate reason or class awareness fall prey to the vagaries of
mere opinion and utopian schemes.

Democracy, then, could only display itself as universal participation in a common *productive* enterprise that promised, in the future, to allow all to participate in the managerial process[15] of allocating resources and distributing the product. Just as, at root, the bourgeois state is an economic structure whose *raison d'être* is to protect those who extract surplus value and to guarantee the conditions for the reproduction of the cycle of capitalist production and realization, so too the socialist–Communist administrative structure is *wholly* an economic organization. 'Taking it as a whole, the proletarian state mechanism becomes transformed into a huge organization for the management of economic life.'[16] The bourgeoisie needed the cloak of democratic politics and the charade of parliamentary talking shops[17] only as a veil to disguise where real power lay. The frothy externalities of bourgeois politics were but legitimating devices through which the state power of the monopolistic barons of finance capital could posture as the representative of a *general,* cross-class, and *national* interest. The proof of this hypothesis, for Lenin as for Bukharin, was revealed in those moments of crisis of the bourgeois order when class conflict became acute or when war between the armed state capitalist trusts broke out. At such times, quite unceremoniously and with barely a debate, the vaunted political and civil rights, parliamentary control of the executive, and so forth were swept aside. 'Bourgeois dictatorship attains its climax in state capitalism.'[18] The conclusion was clear. So long as the bourgeois state was able, through propaganda and ideological saturation, to retain the loyalties of the majority to its political system, it was happy to bask in legitimate power. If threatened, however, it would not hesitate to enforce its will through simple force.

The proletarian state, by contrast, had no pressing need for such institutional contrivances of political legitimacy. It had no need to create the veils and disguises necessary to those who attempted to sell their particular interest as the general interest.

---

[15] Ibid. 190–1.
[16] Ibid. 338.
[17] Ibid. 181.
[18] Ibid. 119.

Given that the proletarian state reflected and articulated the interests of the immense majority, and given that the policies it pursued could be justified by appealing to indisputable and objective evidence, it had no need of elaborate legitimating procedures. The coincidence of individual interests with class interests and the general interest would, of course, take some time to reveal itself. It would, probably, be the task of two or perhaps three generations.[19] Through education, propaganda, and proper work practices, people would become habituated to merge their conception of self with the goals of the social whole and come to will as their own will those patterns of behaviour best adapted to realizing those social goals. The ideal Bukharin now specified was a society without groups or mediating associations[20] where 'The individual human being does not belong to himself, but to society, to the human race. The individual can only live and thrive owing to the existence of society.' For such individuals education is a schooling in labour and education of this sort was far too serious a matter to be left to the overwhelming incompetence of 99 per cent of mothers.[21] The state, through all its agencies, becomes a propaganda state, forming the minds and directing the energies of all its individual members.

THE PROLETARIAN DICTATORSHIP

Throughout 1917 both Bukharin and Lenin believed that the socialist Revolution signified the leap out of the stultifying and bloody dictatorship of the imperialist bourgeoisie directly into the realm of freedom. In the immediate aftermath of October there was little talk of transitional or intermediary forms. Bukharin in particular was passionately committed to the international spread of the Revolution, and the logic of this attachment required emphasis upon the inspirational appeal of Communism as a radically new and free society. He had to demonstrate that there *was* an alternative to the prison and charnel house of the contemporary capitalist state. The op-

---

[19] Ibid. 74.
[20] Ibid. 74.
[21] Ibid. 233–6.

pressed peoples of the world would not be won over by the prospect of exchanging one dictatorship for another, but could potentially be inspired by the promise of popular power. Bukharin clung to the integrity of his conception of popular power and international revolution longer than Lenin, but by 1919 he too, under the dual pressure of internal opposition and external isolation, was compelled to alter his prescriptions for the proletarian state. The sum of this revision, already outlined in *The ABC of Communism* (1919) and consummated in *Economics of the Transition Period* (1920), was that the contemporary world offered only two possible alternatives: either the dictatorship of the imperialist bourgeoisie or the dictatorship of the proletariat.

There was a certain robust toughness to this formulation that matched the desperate times in which the infant socialist republic found itself. The carnage of the First World War had given way to the savagery of the Civil War. Simply in order to survive the Bolsheviks had had to centralize their slender resources. Soldiers and workers alike had been mobilized and subjected to military discipline. The diffuse power structure of the Soviets had been rapidly usurped by the concentrated centralism of Sovnarkom, Cheka, and Red Army. Desperate times demand desperate remedies. Bukharin was to find the theoretical remedy in his own analysis of the imperialist state. As *it* had responded to its situation of internal and external isolation, so, in like fashion, would the state power of the proletariat. Their contexts were almost wholly comparable. Each found itself increasingly isolated internally, with a relatively tiny social base upon which to rely. Each had to face the armed might of hostile and predatory states. Each had to strive, against mounting odds, to guarantee the reproduction of its mode of production. In this last respect, the Soviet government suffered from far greater impediments than its capitalist rivals. The industry it had inherited had been almost wholly devastated, or lay idle for want of raw materials, transport, fuel, and skilled workers. In the extremity of its crisis the Soviet regime could, Bukharin now argued, do no other than mimic and replicate precisely the structures of power and control that had so successfully served the imperialist bourgeoisie. Bukharin's was the most cogent and far-reaching of all the Bolsheviks' attempts at theorizing the dictatorship of the proletariat. It is a paradox of Marxist theory in the twentieth century that one of its dominant notions—the dictatorship of the proletariat—was articulated at a time when its authors all acknowledged that the proletariat had been declassed, and was, in all its essential features, derived from their model of he imperialist state. In Bukharin's case, these apparent paradoxes received their most extreme formulation. For him, the two rival state forms were both antipodes and twins. They were twins in that they had the same physiognomy and were dressed in the same clothes. They were only antipodes in what he chose to call their class essences. By this he meant that in the one case the finance aristocracy ran the state to subserve *its* interests, and in the other the proletariat did likewise. The only difference between them 'lies in this, that in the one case industry is organised by the bourgeois state, and that in the other case it is organised by the proletarian state'.[22] The *forms* of organization adopted, were, as we shall see, the same.

The imperial st state had swallowed up society, absorbing into itself all the hitherto autonomous partial and particular trade, denominational, youth, cultural, and political organizations: 'Under State capitalism all these separate organisations fuse with the bourgeois State; they become, as it were, State departments, and they work in accordance with a general plan, subject to the "high command . . . in this manner the whole of life is militarised . . ."'[23] The state was crucial not only in harnessing the economy to serve the interests of a particular class but in mobilizing and absorbing the energy of all of society. Far from killing Leviathan, the proletariat have to tame him and make him do their bidding. Bukharin had come to this conclusion in 1919 and was already overtly linking the two 'rival' state forms.

Let us recall what the bourgeoisie did in order to secure its greatest successes. It built up the system of state capitalism, associating all its other organisations more closely with the State power, this applying in especial measure to its economic organisations (syndicates, trusts, and employers' associations). The proletariat, which has to carry to

---

[22] Ibid. 161.
[23] Ibid. 118.

a successful issue its struggle against capital, must in like manner centralise its organisations. It has its soviets of workers' delegates, which constitute its instruments of State authority, it has trade unions; it has cooperatives. Manifestly if their work is to be effective they must be mutually interconnected. The question now arises, with which organisation must the others be linked up. The answer is simple. We must select the greatest and most powerful of all. Such an organism is constituted by the State organisation of the working class, by the Soviet power. It follows, therefore, that THE TRADE UNIONS AND THE COOPERATIVES MUST DEVELOP IN SUCH A WAY THAT THEY WILL BE TRANS-FORMED INTO ECONOMIC DEPARTMENTS AND INSTRUMENTS OF THE STATE AUTHORITY; THEY MUST BE 'STATIFIED'.[24]

In *Economics of the Transition Period* Bukharin carried this analysis to its fateful conclusion. He now represented the administrative structures extemporized in the Civil War not as accidental or adventitious, nor as temporary derelictions from the goals of socialism, but as historically necessary and inevitable. It had been an illusion, he now acknowledged, to imagine that the revolution could smash the *political* structures of coercion, whilst simultaneously appropriating and redirecting the *economic* structures of capitalism.[25]

The more thoroughgoing and radical the revolution, the more frankly destructive its impact upon the economy. It had not only resulted in the wholesale destruction of productive forces, means of communication, raw materials, and scarce skilled labour; it had also, and more fundamentally, broken the crucial linkage between the technical intelligentsia and the working class. Bukharin lists in some detail the economic costs of revolution, concluding that 'the result is a diminution, a deficit, a stagnation and meanwhile also a laming of the *process of reproduction*'.[26] In a more abstruse (and self-contradictory) Marxist formulation Bukharin laments the Soviet Union's entry into a critical epoch of *'expanded negative reproduction'*.[27] The Revolution, in short, had not ushered in a realm of milk and honey. It had wreaked devastation and absolute want. Its

[24] Ibid. 278–9 (bold capitals in original).
[25] N. I. Bukharin, *Ekonomika perekhodnogo perioda*, i. *Obshchaya teoriya trans-formatsionnogo protsessa* (Moscow, 1920); trans. as *Economics of the Transformation Period* (New York, 1971), 56–7.
[26] Ibid. 106–10.
[27] Ibid. 45.

economic results had been entirely negative. Not merely had capitalism been destroyed but along with it the whole economic substructure—everything had fallen into dissolution. 'A "temporary anarchy" is, therefore, objectively considered, an absolutely inevitable stage of the revolutionary process which finds its expression in the collapse of the old "apparatus".'[28] Positive restructuring of the economic base was imperative to make good the destructive impact of this critical revolutionary epoch, where the whole possibility of repeating the cycle of production was gravely questioned.[29]

This task defined the substance of the proletarian dictatorship. It had urgently to restore discipline and cohesion within the social relations of production—this meant that the dislocated system of collegial administration would have to be replaced by one-man management[30] and the strictest exactitude and accountability of all involved in the productive process. Specialists and the technical intelligentsia would have to return to positions of authority and made answerable not to their direct work-mates but solely to the proletarian state.[31] The necessary 'model of proletarian–militarised production' demanded 'the greatest exactitude, the unconditional and undisputed discipline, speed in decision-making, unity of will and therefore minimal consultation and discussion, a minimal number of councils, maximal unanimity'.[32] In order to achieve this unanimity, this cohesion, it was obvious to Bukharin that the proletariat itselt would have to be purged of its virulent antipathy to the 'bourgeois specialists' (*spetsy*), and abandon its commitments to egalitarianism and collegial styles of administration. State coercion would, therefore, have to be used against the ruling class itself, against the proletariat. It would have to be turned '*inward*, by constituting a factor of the *self organisation and the compulsory self-discipline of the working people*'.[33] The hollow sophistry of this formulation thuds through its italicized presentation. Bukharin's whole theoretical focus

---

[28] Ibid. 56.
[29] Ibid. 43.
[30] Ibid. 126.
[31] Ibid. 74–7.
[32] Ibid. 127–8.
[33] Ibid. 151.

has altered profoundly. Revolution has not remedied the planlessness and privations of capitalist production and exchange, but exacerbated them. Revolution has not restructured social and economic relations, in order to ensure harmonious reciprocity between all those engaged in the productive process, but, rather, has intensified animosities and prejudices and split the social and professional groups one from another.

Only the state can remedy these deficiencies, dragging the Soviet Union out of an epoch of dissolution and crisis into a period of positive restructuring. Only it can authoritatively direct labour, making labour mobilization compulsory for all. Only the state can reintroduce comprehensive discipline and accountability and set in train a period of 'primitive socialist accumulation' as a condition for regenerating industry and the re-creation of a proletarian base.[34] In short, the state must imperatively intervene in every aspect of the management of the economy, of trade, and of the disposal of labour power and its rewards, so as to generate the preconditions for the repeatability of its cycle of production and hence its own survival. The striking similarity of the objectives and *modus operandi* of the proletarian state to the imperialist state is evident and explicit: 'In the system of state capitalism the economically-active subject is the *capitalist state*, the collective total *capitalist*. In the dictatorship of the proletariat, the economically active subject is the *proletarian* state, the collectively organised working class.'[35]

It is the superstructural state that, in times of crisis, is obliged to intervene and restructure the economy and, along with it, all social relations: 'revolutionary state power is the mightiest lever of economic revolution'.[36] To do so, and to counter the opposition even of some sections of the ruling class itself (for such is its isolation), the state must concentrate within itself all the dislocated coercive and administrative energies of society. As with the imperialist state, so too with the dictatorship of the proletariat, what counts is the class essence of its policies and

[34] Ibid. 110–11.
[35] Ibid. 117.
[36] Ibid. 151.

orientation. The rival structures of dictatorial state capitalism and the dictatorship of the proletariat are distinguishable in this respect only. Otherwise the dictatorship of the proletariat is to mirror the dictatorship of the imperialist bourgeoisie:

> Now we must raise the question as to the general principle of the system of organisation of the proletarian apparatus . . . It is clear that the same method is formally necessary for the working class as for the bourgeoisie at the time of state capitalism. This organisational method exists in the coordination of all proletarian organisations with one all-encompassing organisation, i.e. with the state organisation of the working class, with the *soviet state of the proletariat*. The 'étatisation' [*ogosudarstvlenie*] of the trade unions and the effectual étatisation of all mass organisations of the proletariat result from the internal logic of the process of transformation itself. The minutest cells of the labour apparatus must transform themselves into agents of the general process of organisation, which is systematically directed and led by the collective reason of the working class, which finds its material embodiment in the highest and most all-encompassing organisation, in its state apparatus. Thus the system of state capitalism dialectically transforms itself into its own inversion, into the state form of workers' socialism.[37]

Bukharin has retreated to the formulation of his own 1915 account of the imperialist state.[38] *Economics of the Transition Period* remains the fullest and most sophisticated account of the dictatorship of the proletariat. It was a vindication of total power that rejoiced in the unchallengeable monism of its structure[39]—a hierarchy of centralized authority patterns that was to mark all of its economic, social, judicial, political, and coercive institutions. It is the state that is reified as the sole authentic exponent of the *real* will of the proletariat, one of whose essential tasks will be to reform the *felt* will of the extensively corrupted proletarian masses.[40] Above all, it fell to the state to restructure and revivify industry and in the process to recreate the proletariat. To do this, however, the state would have to direct the labour power of everyone within society and

---

[37] Ibid. 79. (The English translation has 'nationalisation' for *ogosudarstvlenie* (see *Ekonomika perekhodnogo perioda*, 71–2). I have rendered this as 'étatisation'.)

[38] Bukharin, 'K teorii imperialisticheskogo gosudarstva'.

[39] Bukharin, *Economics of the Transformation Period*, 50.

[40] Ibid. 156.

it would, moreover, have to initiate a more-or-less prolonged period of primitive socialist accumulation through which this process of rebuilding could be accomplished. Necessarily, therefore, the state would not merely have to confront the recalcitrants within the proletariat but would also have to exercise widespread coercion against the peasantry. For all these reasons the proletarian state could be nothing other than the 'concentrated application of force'.[41]

In 1920 Bukharin dreamed his last heroic dream of the cohorts of the conscious and determined, militantly imposing their stamp on a recalcitrant social order and a hostile world. It was a call to arms for the last great battle, in which order would be imposed upon anarchy, and productive efficiency on a devastated economy. This would-be triumph of the will retained only the most tenuous links with the Marxism from which it sprang. Although he was to renounce the programme of his own *Economics of the Transition Period* within a year, Bukharin had lent the weight of his own very considerable theoretical authority to a lasting Bolshevik belief in the power and untrammelled authority of the state to remake human psychology, social relations, and economic structures. His formulation of the role and functions of the dictatorship of the proletariat were to embarrass and stymie him in his later controversies with the Left and were to leave him defenceless when Stalin appropriated this programme as his own eight years later. One of the more bitter ironies of Soviet history is that Bukharin himself most comprehensively established the theoretical basis for omnipotent state authority.

THE MIXED STATE

Economics of the Transition Period was Bukharin's last major theoretical study on the subject of the state; his later reflections were briefer, more sporadic, and less self-consciously theorized. They were none the worse for that. From 1921 onwards, prompted largely by Lenin's sober and often pessimistic assessments of the future of socialism in the Soviet Union, his

[41] Ibid. 160.

thought undergoes a final and conclusive volte-face. No doubt domestic events inspired this sudden and abrupt change of direction. By then, the evidence of internal isolation of the regime became inescapable. Peasant insurrection on a wide scale was, perhaps, predictable and ultimately manageable. But when this coincided with increasing unrest from the few remaining centres of proletarian strength, trade-union opposition, and the anti-Bolshevik revolt of the stronghold of Kronstadt, it became apparent that the regime would have fundamentally to alter its policies and immediate objectives in order to survive. The great danger, Bukharin now agreed with Lenin, was to upset the all-important 'alliance' (*smychka*) between the proletariat and the peasantry. In the last months of 1920 and of spring 1921 Bukharin became painfully aware that the regime's hold upon power was now so very very fragile, and its human and material resources so pitifully weak, that only the most cautious and gradual policies would serve. The aggressive, barn-storming theorizing of the *Economics of the Transition Period* was abruptly replaced by the moderate accommodation of his leading articles in *Pravda*. In place of militant class war he now consistently preached the urgency of programmes of social conciliation, pouring scorn on the Preobrazhenskys and Trotskys, the 'third-revolution' apostles, who remained wedded to the chimerical heroism of War Communism.

But it was not solely the precarious balance of class forces within the Soviet Union that led Bukharin to these conclusions. He came to share with Lenin a profound unease about the competence and utility of the state apparatus itself. Indeed (as ever) he goes further than Lenin and underscores the real dangers of the state absorbing society. And he does so not simply because, like Lenin, he has become aware of the incompetence and high-handedness of the majority of the bureaucrats (*chinovniki*) of the Soviet state. Unlike Lenin, he has suddenly come to appreciate the importance of the web of relatively autonomous voluntary associations. These are now portrayed, not as obstacles and impediments to centralized power, nor as nests of particular interests that needed to be sublimated in the all-encompassing state, but as positive and complementary agencies with which, imperatively, the state had to secure a lasting partnership. He called for the creation of *'hundreds and thousands of small and large rapidly expanding voluntary societies, circles and associations'.*[42]

The state was to become a listening state, working in close collaboration with a multitude of voluntary associations, hearing and acting upon their aspirations and their grievances. Far from being 'the sole economically active subject' portrayed in the *Economics of the Transition Period*, the state was to enter into partnership with the network of co-operatives and with the trade unions. Its task was that of gradually and organically restructuring production relations and drawing the scattered productive units into a planned and integrated economy. Above all, he insisted, 'Our economy exists for the consumer, not the consumer for the economy. This is a point which must never be forgotten. The "New Economy" differs from the old in taking as its standards the needs of the masses ...'[43] Bukharin belatedly became aware of the dangers of degeneration into a 'dictatorship over needs'. Primitive socialist accumulation spelt precisely that. It necessarily implied direction of labour, administrative control over its remuneration, centralized control of investment resources, concentrated upon production of the means of production rather than means of consumption. He now acknowledged that all of this could not be accomplished without the rupture of the *smychka*, a wholesale war of the state against society, the extinction of the independence of voluntary associations and the end of politics.

Only in his final years of power does Bukharin, somewhat hesitantly, search for a space for a genuine politics. He does concede that the system of Soviet power need not, indeed ought not, to be informed by a 'monism of its structure'. He admits the desirability of a multiplicity of relatively autonomous voluntary organizations of the most diverse sorts. In acknowledging and fostering this incipient social and economic pluralism he goes considerably further than any other prominent Bolshevik. The fateful gap in his uncompleted analysis is an unpreparedness to grant such social diversity any legal guarantee or any institutionalized form of expression. Central

---

[42] N. I. Bukharin, 'Zadachi vypusknika-Sverdlovtsa', *Zapiski Kommunisticheskogo universiteta imeni Ya. M. Sverdlova*, ii (Moscow, 1924), 255–9.

[43] *Pravda*, 30 Sept. 1928, 2.

to this neglect was surely the naive relativism deep within the Marxist tradition in regard to political institutions and procedures. At the outset of this chapter I examined the sources of this ingrained relativism in Bukharin's thought. It never left him and, consequently, his advocacy of a pre-political pluralism in his later writings has a somewhat unreal air. It is outlined in a political vacuum and is bereft of the institutional and procedural guarantees that alone could give it space in which to develop and to create its own identity.

Such precisely were the problems confronting Gorbachev and his reforms. To step outside the limitations Bukharin set, to proceed from an ambiguous social pluralism to negotiate a genuine institutionalized political pluralism was imperatively necessary if the reforms were to attain popular credibility and mobilizing power. The price to be paid was, however, the emergence of autonomous political groups that rapidly challenged the authority of the Party and proceeded to expose the hollow metaphysic upon which it was based. The rehabilitation of Bukharin highlighted the persistent ambiguity of the relationship be ween state and society in the Marxist tradition without in any way resolving it. In retrospect indeed it seems that far from arresting the decline of Soviet Marxism it accelerated it.

6

Bukharin's International Alternative

Anna di Biagio

THE questions I want to raise are, first, whether it is possible to speak of Bukharin's thought as an original and autonomous construction in the area of international politics; and, secondly, whether it is correct to say that Bukharin lacked full awareness of the interaction existing between the Soviet Union's domestic and foreign policy and whether this was one of the causes of his downfall. I do not pretend to be able to give a full answer to questions that would require more detailed and exhaustive examination than I can offer here. However, I would like to mention that many of the observations that follow have sprung from a forthcoming work of mine on relations between the Soviet Union and Europe in the years of the New Economic Policy (NEP).

BUKHARIN'S RETHINKING OF BOLSHEVISM

Many historians share the view that Bukharin developed the theses and political programmes of NEP by building upon Lenin's testamentary legacy. The key idea of this legacy can be summed up in the call to pursue more modest, realistic, and less ambitious aims, which he addressed to his colleagues and successors at the head of the Party, particularly in his last article, 'Better less, but better'.[1]

Signs of a rethinking of the precepts recommended to the Party in the foreign-policy area are recognizable in Lenin from early 1921. At the Tenth Party Congress he had made a bravely

---

[1] For a detailed study of Lenin's 'Testament', see M. Lewin, *Le Dernier Combat de Lénine* (Paris, 1967) trans. as *Lenin's Last Struggle* (London, 1975).

self-critical pronouncement about the decision to continue the
Warsaw offensive in the course of the Russo–Polish war. He
admitted that the source of this 'mistake' lay in a serious over-
evaluation of the Soviet Union's military strength. A few
months later, on the occasion of the Third Comintern Congress,
Lenin had recognized the possibility of a 'certain temporary
equilibrium' being established between the two camps. He
declared the need for the Soviet Union to connect itself with
the capitalist world as a prerequisite for its survival and domestic
economic development. In the course of 1922 there is no lack of
signs of a progressive crumbling of the confidence Lenin had
previously placed in the revolutionary outcome of a new world
war. Now he was in doubt about the precept he had laid down
for Soviet diplomacy in 1918: to make use of interimperialist
contradictions as the most efficient means to establish guarantees of security

However, Lenin did no more than point out the new international dangers. He was not able, or lacked the time, to work
out a foreign-policy programme endowed with a coherent
doctrine on war and the proper means of avoiding it, based
constructively on a new comprehensive vision of the domestic
problems of the Soviet Union of NEP.[2] Bukharin was evidently
pushing things a bit far when in 1929, he proposed an interpretation of Lenin's 'Testament' as 'part of a great forward-
looking plan embracing the whole of our work as communists'.[3]
This emphasis, though, does not lessen the Aesopian value of
his interpretation, which offers a clear understanding not so
much of the scope of Lenin's doctrinal revision as of Bukharin's
own programmatic proposals and his vision of the future of
socialism in the Soviet Union.

Stephen Cohen has maintained that Bukharin's ideas on
foreign policy were, from 1925 on, in 'uneasy conflict' with his
evolutionary approaches to domestic policy. In analysing the
international situation, he argues, Bukharin had limited himself to reviving his 1915–16 concepts of state capitalism, which
had led him to postulate a European capitalism vulnerable only

---

[2] For a more extended discussion of this subject, see A. di Biagio, 'I
bolscevichi e il sistema di Versailles (1919–1923)', *Studi storici* 2 (1986), 479–82.
[3] N. I. Bukharin, 'Politicheskoe zaveshchanie Lenina', *Pravda*, 24 Jan. 1929.

during a new world war.[4] In its first phase, Bukharin's rethinking of Bolshevism in the new perspectives opened up by
NEP was limited to the area of the Soviet Union's domestic
problems. In early 1924, when he observed that a 'peaceful'
change of the 'face of class struggle' would have made a
'definitive victory' for socialism in the Soviet Union possible,
he still pointed out: 'We are here setting aside problems of an
external nature.' The latter were not, however, immune for
long from attempts at revision; even if these were at first
limited to Bukharin's hope, expressed from the podium at the
Thirteenth Party Congress (May 1924), for the validity of the
old analytical tools for interpreting a much-changed international situation to be reconsidered. Bukharin spoke about 'new
and original facts', namely a certain 'stabilization' in Central
Europe, particularly in Germany, and the formation of the first
British Labour government. But he made an even more significant point: the pivot of the international constellation was
moving westwards.

For the time being Bukharin refrained from drawing political
conclusions from his analysis. But Krasin, at the same Party
meeting, was much more explicit. The People's Commissar of
Foreign Trade made himself spokesman for other leaders, such
as Litvinov, who had never fully shared Lenin's choice at
Genoa to align with 'defeated Germany' against the imperialist
Entente. Krasin called for a revision of the 'political considerations' that had brought the Soviet government to set up pre-
ferential relations with Germany, relations often prejudicial to
its own economic interests.[5] A common political denominator
might have been established between Krasin's appeal to re-
consider the Rapallo policy and Bukharin's invitation to face up
to the westward shift of the focal point of world events: the
need to reduce the value of the German issue in predictions of
revolutionary perspectives in Europe, and thus to shake off a
kind of hypnosis that had taken hold of the Bolshevik leadership following the Second Comintern Congress (July 1920): that
is the idea that in the Versailles system the German problem

[4] S. F. Cohen, *Bukharin and the Bolshevik Revolution: A Political Biography,
1888–1938* (New York, 1973, 2nd edn. Oxford, 1980), 44, 255–6.
[5] *Trinadtsatyy s"yezd VKP(b). Mai 1924 g.: sten. otchet* (Moscow, 1924; repr.
1963), 308–9, 311 (Bukharin), 139, 144 (Krasin).

was insoluble, which would automatically bring advantages both for the revolutionary cause and for the interests of the Soviet state.

The theory of the inevitability (*neizbezhnost'*) of imperialist wars, put forward by Lenin in 1916 in opposition to Kautsky's 'new ultra-imperialist policy', had rooted in Bolshevik thinking a peculiar vision of international relations in the capitalist world as a succession of conflicts between economic and military interests and of disastrous wars. This was an essentially catastrophist view of the capitalist world, but a reassuring one for Soviet security. The insurmountable antagonisms existing in the hostile camp should make the new regime safe from the danger of the setting-up of an anti-Soviet bloc. This conviction gathered strength during the Brest-Litovsk peace negotiations and was not *diminished* by the hard trials of the Western powers' intervention in the Civil War. The Bolshevik leadership continued to believe in the efficacy of that 'protective shield'.

It was the German government's acceptance of the Dawes Plan that raised, for the Soviet leaders, the spectre of a temporary solution to the main bones of contention among the Western powers, and at the same time that of the formation of a 'united anti-Soviet front'. The Plan's potential success would in fact have meant the overcoming of one of the main interimperialist contradictions that had hitherto been the basis for the Soviet government's belief in its own immunity from foreign threat. The collapse of this illusion laid bare the inconsistencies in the precepts elaborated by Lenin himself for maintaining the country's security.

In the wake of the discussion which arose inside the Soviet Party concerning relationships between the Soviet Union and the capitalist world, in particular of the discovery that a process of stabilization was taking place in Central Europe, ever more insistent voices began to be heard calling for a revision of Lenin's theory of the inevitability of imperialist wars as a necessary first step towards updating the parameters of both Narkomindel and Comintern. Even before Bukharin, Varga, Radek, and Rakovsky had arrived at a different view of the possible factors governing the security of the state, through the alarming recognition that the chief capitalist powers were coming to a temporary agreement on co-operation in order to pacify the Europe created by Versailles. It was, therefore, necessary to be involved in the reordering of the European system in order to prevent the 'Anglo-Saxon bloc' from reaching a stable settlement of international relations without Soviet Union participation and in its disfavour. Rakovsky made himself the spokesman of this approach, which he called 'proletarian pacifism', when in July 1924 he announced the Soviet Union's readiness to provide security guarantees to France, against the threat of war arising from the 'growing nationalist movement in Germany'.[6] Both Varga and Radek tried to stimulate new interpretive analyses of the international situation among Communists asking them not to rule out *a priori* the ultraimperialist hypothesis proposed anew by Hilferding at the beginning of 1924, in evaluating all the changes produced by the world war.

Bukharin did not draw back from this discussion. For some time he had admitted the possibility that contemporary capitalism, with its osmosis of politics and economics, might resolve its gravest internal contradictions and achieve a certain stability; within national limits only, however, and at the cost of simultaneously provoking the multiplying of these contradictions at international level. The virtual exclusion of an imminent revolutionary crisis arising domestically in one of the capitalist countries, and its transference to international level, laid Bukharin's thesis open to accusation of making revolutionary potential dependent solely on the perspective of a new world war. But this criticism assumed that a new world war would promote new revolutions. Bukharin himself, early in 1924, had responded, 'assuming the inevitability of war does not mean hoping for it'. Even before denouncing Preobrazhensky's law, in a 'burst of moral indignation' (December 1924), he had argued with even more passionate 'ethical rhetoric' at the fifth Comintern Congress, against the 'theory of the prosperity of war', expounded by the dissident German Communist, B. Roninger, in order to contest Bukharin's theory of 'expanded negative production'.[7]

---

[6] *Izvestiya*, 2 Aug. 1924.
[7] *Protokoll. Fünfter Kongreß der kommunistischen Internationale* (Hamburg, 1924), 517.

Bukharin did not answer Hilferding by denying the desirability of a time when war might be actually avoidable. He tried to counter the social democratic leader's fatalistic optimism in foreseeing an era in which the danger of war would be eliminated by the logic of the very evolution of world capitalism. For Bukharin, this fatalistic optimism would feed and justify a passive inert attitude towards the big international issues and *de facto* obstruct the 'struggle against the danger of war'. But very soon Bukharin had to recognize that, even in his own Party, passivity and indifference held sway on international issues and that there were many 'silly optimists who, over-estimating the situation, bury their heads in the sand and feed on dreams'.[8]

SOCIALISM IN ONE COUNTRY

As is well known, the theory of socialism in one country began to take hold in parallel with the recognition of capitalist stabilization. But the Soviet Party leadership did not adopt a unanimous position, nor draw the same conclusions from the acknowledgement of a stabilization process and its implications for Soviet foreign policy. Differences in Party line and interpretation were looming from the outset, not only between the Central Committee majority and the Left of the party, but also among members of the majority itself, particularly between Stalin and Bukharin.[9]

Stalin's version of socialism in one country was aimed at overcoming the country's backwardness at the fastest possible tempo. It involved great underestimation of outside threats, a substantial disengagement from international issues, and reversion to the kind of propagandistic approach to the outside world that had been a feature of Soviet foreign policy in the new regime's first years. Acknowledgement of capitalist stabilization went side by side in Stalin's view with revival of

---

[8] N. I. Bukharin, 'Obshchie itogi nashego razvitiya i ego perspektivy', *Pravda*, 24 Oct. 1924, 5.

[9] No light was shed on these differences between Stalin and Bukharin, even in the otherwise fundamental reconstruction of the mid-1920s' debate by E. H. Carr, *A History of Soviet Russia: Socialism in One Country, 1924–1926* (3 vols.; London, 1958–64), iii.

Lenin's 'waiting' tactics at the time of Brest which prescribed 'not accepting battle with the imperialist giants' and waiting for a new internecine war in the enemy camp further to weaken it. This was a tactic that relegated Soviet foreign policy to a passive role of acceptance of the country's isolation in order to avoid the risks of being involved in international troubles, thereby allowing the government to devote itself to the priority task of building up the Soviet state's 'power'.

All Stalin's speeches on the international situation from his first entry into the foreign-policy field in 1924 had one end in view: the reaffirmation of the theory of the inevitability of imperialist wars, presented as an indisputable 'principle of Leninism'. And his fidelity to this principle was unshakeable. The outline on foreign policy he presented to the Fourteenth Party Congress (December 1925) was reiterated, without substantial changes, in his last publication: 'The struggle between capitalist countries' would always prove 'stronger' than the contradiction between the two camps. This would permanently act as an objective factor for the Soviet Union's security.[10]

In 1925 the authority enjoyed by Stalin within the Soviet Party leadership was not yet such as to ensure that his opinions would become the general line. The Fourteenth Congress for the first time accepted the idea that the new threat to Soviet security brought about by the capitalist stabilization necessitated a search for 'peaceful co-existence' among states and among political forces in the capitalist world, in order to consolidate 'economic ties' abroad and to create new *atouts* for the Soviet Union's defence, through the adopting of a new slogan: 'struggle for peace, struggle against new imperialist wars and armed aggression against the Soviet Union'.[11]

The Fourteenth Congress resolution, in part dealing with international policy, substantially reflected the political pro-

---

[10] J. V. Stalin, *Economic Problems of Socialism in the USSR* (Moscow, 1952), Ch. 6. For a further discussion of the inevitability of imperialist wars, see A. di Biagio, 'La teoria dell'inevitabilità della guerra', paper submitted at the International Conference 'The Twentieth Congress of the CPSU' (Florence, 2–5 October, 1986), published in F. Gori (ed.), *Il XX Congresso del PCUS* (Milan, 1988), 59–73.

[11] *KPSS v rezolyutsiyakh*, iii (Moscow, 1970), 245.

posals supported at this time by Bukharin. These were founded on the idea that a situation of 'equilibrium' between the two camps might benefit the Soviet Union, provided that the Party leadership took steps domestically to accept the 'national face' of Russian socialism without 'being ashamed that the socialism we are building will inevitably be a backward kind of socialist construction', and while maintaining the 'worker–peasant alliance (*smychka*). This domestic doctrine had a foreign-policy corollary Bukharin saw the *smychka* as the 'root' of the Bolsheviks' success both in October and in the course of the Civil War and foreign intervention. The Soviet regime's successes would continue in future to depend on the ability to keep the allies who had brought about this victory: the Russian peasants at home and the 'Western toiling masses' internationally [12]

But the idea of building a 'backward socialism' was considered unacceptable by broad, and influential, sectors of the Soviet Party; and not by Stalin alone. The Fourteenth Congress accepted the prospectives of domestic economic development as outlined by Stalin in his report: the determination to transform the Soviet Union into an industrially developed 'independent economic unit'. Thus, after the Fourteenth Congress, certain principles were firmly installed into Party doctrine: the imbalance in the Soviet economy between industry and agriculture had to be overcome through the former's expansion; industrialization had to be brought about by developing the production of capital goods and financed from domestic resources. Even if the supporters of industrialization did not put these principles into practice at once, they nevertheless could no longer be openly contested. A first decisive step had been taken towards the affirmation of the Stalinist socialism in one country Bukharin seemed unaware of this and did not understand that acceptance of these principles in domestic policy would soon necessitate adoption of Stalin's line in foreign policy too.

[12] N. I. Bukharin, *Put' k sotsializmu i raboche-krest'yanskiy soyuz* (Moscow and Leningrad, 1925; 4th edn., 1927); repr. *Put' k sotsializmu v Rossii: Izbrannye proizvedeniya N I. Bukharina*, ed. S. Heitman (New York, 1967), 312–13.

BUKHARIN'S ALTERNATIVE IN INTERNATIONAL POLITICS

At the end of 1926 Bukharin asked for a new look at the international policy positions of both the Soviet Party and foreign Communist parties.[13] It is at this time that sizeable differences within the majority coalition of the Central Committee first became public.

At the Fifteenth Party Conference (October 1926) Bukharin raised some 'major questions of principle', centring round the finding of symptoms in Germany of a process of 'rationalization in foreign policy', of an extension to international level of the trends to unification and the formation of cartels, which until then he had recognized only at domestic level. The importance of this admission was clarified by Bukharin himself in the course of his speech when he asked whether the social democratic thesis of 'super-imperialism' was not acquiring a semblance of reality in the light of the new events taking place in Germany. He raised strong doubts as to the universal validity of the conclusions drawn by Lenin in his *Imperialism* (1917), and confessed that, in his view, it would not have been 'altogether correct' to apply Lenin's analyses 'mechanically and point by point' to the post-war situation. They should be checked against the 'particular features' of the actual historical period.[14]

Polemical reaction was aroused at the meeting by Bukharin's call for re-examination of Soviet and Communist attitudes of supporting Germany as a 'subjected nation-State'. Manuil'sky in fact denied the existence in Germany of the *Machtmittel* which, according to Bukharin, would allow it to conduct an 'imperialist policy', and he predicted a future world war, setting ascendant US imperialism against its declining British counterpart.[15] This forecast, an *idée fixe* of Trotsky since 1921, served to reassure listeners as to the dangers to Soviet security that Bukharin's analysis on the new features of the German

---

[13] For a more extended discussion of Bukharin's ideas about international politics in 1926–8, see A. di Biagio, 'Il Pervonachal'ny proekt tezisov di Bucharin al VI Congresso del Komintern', *Quaderni della Fondazione G. Feltrinelli*, 17 (1981).

[14] *Pyatnadtsataya konferentsiya VKP(b)* (Moscow and Leningrad, 1927), 16–17, 29–30, 91–1.

[15] Ibid. 50–2.

situation suggested, and to contest the need to change the
Rapallo policy. On the assumption of a new, inevitable internecine war in the capitalist world, the Soviet Union's isolation
would work in favour of its national security and guarantee
its own non-involvement in that war. But, as Bukharin himself would later point out, the prediction of a future Anglo-
American war prevented the Soviet leadership from facing
up to the immediate and probable picture: a war among the
European powers, provoked by the 'contradictions of the
Versailles system', that could not fail to involve the Soviet
Union too.[16]

   To a meeting on 13 November 1926 at the Institute of World
Economics and Politics, Radek made a strong plea for abandonment of a 'mystical conception' of the theory of the inevitability of war, and for an end to the 'superficial attitude'
Soviet leaders customarily took towards the perils of isolation.[17]
This fell on deaf ears. Raising the problem of the absence of
international security guarantees also meant questioning the
determination to industrialize the country at the 'frenetic
tempo' (Bukharin) necessary to 'catch and overtake' the capitalist countries. At the end of 1926 this determination was
shared by a large part of the Politburo majority, and not just by
representatives of the Left Opposition.

   The Fifteenth Party Conference adopted no resolutions on
the international situation. Bukharin managed, nevertheless,
to secure formal approval for a turning-point (*perelom*) in
the Comintern's political line, at the Seventh Plenum of the
Comintern (December 1926). During the meeting of the Executive, Bukharin pointedly stressed the new elements in his
thinking, so as to bring up again for discussion a large number
of the axioms that Communists had derived from Lenin's
Imperialism. He now acknowledged a 'certain real ground' in
the analyses proposed by Hilferding in his early 1924 article:
pacific unification of Europe was 'probable'. Nevertheless—in
Bukharin's opinion—a policy of *entente* by the capitalist states
would not, as Hilferding suggested, bring about an era of
'realistic pacifism', but rather a 'reproduction at a higher

[16] *Protokoll. Erweiterte Exekutive der kommunistischen Internationale. Moskau, 22
November-16 Dezember 1926* (Hamburg and Berlin, 1927).
[17] K. Radek, *Mirovoye khozyaystvo i mirovaya politika*, 10–11, (1926), 11–16.

level' of the danger of war in general which, theoretically, could not be separated from the danger of 'intervention' against the Soviet Union. The polemic against Hilferding thus served to provide Bukharin with a further argument in support of his call for a reconsideration of the catastrophic consequences and destructive effect that a 'new war between the imperialist powers in Europe' would mean for the whole world, for the Soviet Union, and for the scope of the international revolutionary movement.

The new political 'strategy' Bukharin proposed to the Comintern was summarized in his request to shift the 'centre of gravity' of its actions from Central Europe to Britain. Working in the new conditions of capitalist stabilization, it would in fact have been possible to follow with greater coherence and commitment the road opened by the experience of Anglo-Soviet trade-union co-operation (the Anglo-Russian Committee), with 'correct revolutionary application' of the united-front policy. There was another reason why Bukharin denied the existence of a 'real revolutionary situation' in Germany. That country had suffered more than others from the outcome of the world war. The fact that it was a 'defeated and oppressed' country gave rise to a process of stabilization which, by contrast with other countries such as Britain, presaged a 'clear move to the right' by the ruling classes, in both domestic and foreign policy. Germany was manifestly the European power most inclined towards policies that would sharpen international tensions and provoke another world war. Therefore, the Soviet government should stop nourishing illusions of the insolubility of the German problem and abandon its support for the countries defeated in the world war laid down by Lenin in 1920, and reiterated by him in the Rapallo Treaty. It was necessary to adopt a foreign-policy programme that offered security guarantees by preventing a new world war, one that would deal a 'destructive blow to the whole social and economic order, incomparably greater than that dealt by the 1914–18 war'. The Comintern, in its role of 'world party of the revolution', should turn itself into the 'most solid guarantee of real world-wide peace'.[18]

[18] N. I. Bukharin, *Die kapitalistische Stabilisierung und die proletarische Revolution* (Moscow, 1926).

THE DOWNFALL

Early in 1927 Bukharin also tried to get approval from the
Soviet party for a *perelom*, reminding a meeting in Moscow that
'the great struggle between us and the capitalist world will
ultimately by resolved not so much by technical and military
strength as by the hearts of the broad working masses'.[19] But
Bukharin was not able to propose openly a revision of the
Leninist 'law' of inter-imperialist contradiction as a permanent
factor for the Soviet Union's security (reaffirmed by Stalin at
the Seventh Plenum of the Comintern). He was forced, therefore, to paint an alarmingly exaggerated picture of his country's
position in the international field. It may be assumed that he
himself did not foresee the panic effect produced by his urgent
plea to take account of the lack of 'guarantees against foreign
attack'. A 'silly war psychosis' (as Litvinov defined it) spread
suddenly through both the country and the Party.

The 'super-industrializers' saw the possibility of making
instrumental use, on the domestic scene, of these alarmist
analyses of the Soviet Union's international position. In fact,
the war psychosis, paradoxically provoked by Bukharin,
allowed the Stalinists to wage a battle on two fronts: one,
against the Left opposition and against 'factionalism'; the
other, against resistance within its own majority to accepting
the line of accelerated industrial development. The battle
against the moderate front was not limited to following its own
ends in the sphere of domestic politics alone. It was in the field
of international policy that the first consistent results of that
battle emerged.

The outcome of the proceedings of the Eighth Plenum of the
Comintern (May 1927) represents a decisive step in the defeat
of the line on international politics supported by Bukharin. His
view was rendered meaningless, and further discussion was
prevented by the introduction of a distinction between the
danger of a new imperialist war and the danger of anti-Soviet
intervention. This distinction would have made adoption of
Bukharin's proposal to fight for 'general peace' into a useless
'concession to pacifism', particularly to the left wing of the

[19] *Pravda* 13 Jan. 1927.

social democrats, who now came to represent for Communists a 'greater danger than the open and cynical treachery' perpetrated by the right-wing leaders of the Second International, because it was dosing the masses with the 'opium of a sentimental and sterile pacifism'.[20]

Bukharin's proposal to make the struggle for peace the pivot of the Comintern's political action in Europe would have helped to create new, more effective forms of support for the Soviet state's defence, provided the latter undertook to build 'bridges' to the European proletariat, which remained affiliated in great majority to the social democrat parties, and to seek a 'compromise between reformism and communism', with an eye to 'keeping at least neutral and formally tied those who might openly pass to the imperialist camp'.[21]

The conclusions reached by the Eighth Plenum of the Comintern testify that an increasingly influential section of the Soviet party's leadership did not think it necessary to turn to the Comintern to defend the country's security. This is partly confirmed by the fact that at this sitting foreign Communist parties were peremptorily forbidden to take up the proposals being made by the Soviet government to other European governments on the disarmament issue. And on this basis a 'distinction of principle' was drawn for the first time between the Soviet state's foreign policy and Comintern policies, in the opposite direction from the political co-ordination implicit in the *perelom* that Bukharin had previously advocated.[22]

In August 1927 the Soviet party formally accepted the idea that it would be the 'dynamics of development' itself, that is, an objective law of history, that would automatically act to 'postpone' the clash between capitalism and socialism.[23]

This axiom, reaffirmed by Stalin at the Fifteenth Congress (December 1927), for a time dispelled the doubts raised by Bukharin as to the unconditional neutrality of the Rapallo partner, and seemed to render any active intervention of the Soviet state towards the outside for guaranteeing its security

---

[20] See resolutions in *Kommunisticheskiy Internatsional v dokumentakh* (Moscow, 1933), 711–16.
[21] N. I. Bukharin, 'Itogi plenuma IKKI', *Pravda*, 28 June 1927.
[22] See resolution in *Kommunisticheskiy Internatsional v dokumentakh*, 708.
[23] *KPSS v rezolyutsiakh*, iii, 463–71.

unnecessary. But this lasted only until those 'surprise factors' that Togliatti had warned of from the rostrum at the Sixth Comintern Congress in August 1928 appeared on the European scene.

The first draft of the thesis 'On the International Situation and the Tasks of the Communist International' to be discussed at the Sixth Congress of the Communist International in July–August 1928 is kept in the Trotsky Archives at the Houghton Library in Harvard University. This text has been neglected by Western scholars, who apparently have never made use of it in their analyses of Bukharin's political ideas on international politics. Stalin's speech of April 1929 is almost the only source relied on by them when dealing with the problem of the contents of the first draft. As a consequence of the new light thrown on the subject by this document, Bukharin's analysis on international politics appears more consistent than is usually thought.

I attempt a detailed examination of the document, elsewhere,[24] stressing the change which the original draft suffered during the Sixth Congress. I conclude that the final resolution approved by the Congress still reflected some of the original points which Bukharin proposed. However, the overall political meaning of the first draft was substantially altered. In the essay introducing Bukharin's text, I show the crucial points characterizing Bukharin's position, starting from the Seventh Plenum of the Comintern to the Sixth Congress. A dramatic change in the Comintern line intervened in May 1927, when the Eighth Plenum of the Comintern issued a resolution on 'The War and the War Danger', rejecting at the same time Bukharin's and Togliatti's amendment in favour of the 'struggle for peace'. By contrast, when building up his 'socialism in one country', Stalin had worked out a scheme based on the Leninist theory of the inevitability of imperialistic wars, in order to give a realistic look to the hypothesis according to which the Soviet government could delay a war between the two hostile fields. Stalin proposed this scheme again, after the end of the Second World War, without modifications,

---

[24] For a further discussion of the importance of Togliatti's speech at the Sixth Congress of the Comintern, see A. di Biagio, 'Il Pervonachal'ny proekt', 24–5.

notwithstanding the criticism of some Soviet leaders, who judged his schema inadequate to meet the new reality of the post-war world.

At the Twentieth Party Congress Khrushchev declared that war between the two competing camps was no longer unavoidable, thanks to the power that the socialist system had achieved. In this way he carried out only a partial revision of Stalin's dogma, and barred all attempts to perform an ideological adaptation to the demands of politics and propaganda roused by the relaunch of peaceful coexistence as a strategic plan.

Bukharin's foreign-policy programme defeated at the end of the 1920s differed substantially not only from Stalin's model,[25] but also from the positions prevalent in the Soviet government during the time of Lenin's leadership. In foreign policy there was much more continuity between Lenin and Stalin than between Lenin and Bukharin. Perhaps this was one of the reasons underlying Bukharin's defeat. His programme could not be ratified by the Party because it considered unacceptable in principle any attempt to rethink not just Stalin's 'Leninism' but still more Lenin's 'Leninism'.

[25] See di Biagio, 'La teoria dell'inevitabilità della guerra'.

Part III

CULTURE AND SCIENCE

7

Bukharin's Theory of Cultural Revolution

John Biggart

THE apparent hiatus between the developmental theory contained in Lenin's last writings and the practice of Stalin's 'cultural revolution' has puzzled historians, for the 'cultural revolution' was clearly an abandonment of the policies outlined by Lenin after the Civil War. In search of theoretical continuities between these two phases of Soviet development, historians have tended to explain Stalinism as a regression to the utopianism of War Communism or as a confiscation of the ideas of the Left Opposition.[1] In this chapter I shall argue that, whereas Bukharin is generally considered to have been the custodian of 'Leninism' and a supporter of gradual change during the New Economic Policy (NEP), in fact his theory of cultural revolution differed significantly from that of Lenin. Bukharin advocated a radical break with the NEP system and his ideas represent a link in official thinking between late Leninism and Stalinism.[2]

This chapter will also argue that through Bukharin a number of the ideas of Alexander Malinovsky-Bogdanov found their way, in modified form, into official ideology. The extent of Bogdanov's influence upon Soviet intellectual life during the 1920s is only now being realized, but as early as 1928 Bukharin

[1] Sheila Fitzpatrick, to whose works on the 'cultural revolution' we are all indebted, is as preplexed as anyone as to the intellectual origins of Stalin's programme and as to Bukharin's role. See her introduction and contribution to S. Fitzpatrick (ed.), *The Cultural Revolution in Russia, 1928–1931* (Bloomington, Ind., 1978) and her *Education and Social Mobility in the Soviet Union, 1921–1934* (Cambridge, 1979).

[2] Of course, as Laszlo Szamuely has pointed out, Lenin himself for a period endorsed the policy of War Communism. The convention of applying the term 'Leninism' only to his later, NEP, strategy is, therefore, misleading. See L. Szamuely, *First Models of the Socialist Economic Systems* (Budapest, 1974).

had admitted that Bogdanov had 'played a major role in the development of the Party and of social thought in Russia. Many of us were brought up on his *Short Course in Economic Science* and were captivated by his writings. For quite some time he was one of the greatest theoreticians of Marxism.'[3]

BOURGEOIS CULTURE AND PROLETARIAN CULTURE

Following a decision of the Politburo on 31 August 1922 to launch a public debate on the question of cultural revolution, Bukharin expounded his own theory in a series of lectures, articles, and debates which were published during the years 1922–3.[4] His first contribution was an article for *Pod znamenem marksizma*, which appeared over the summer. On 9 October 1922 Bukharin addressed the Moscow Party organization, and his lecture was published in *Pravda* two days later. On 16 December 1922 he once again presented his ideas to the Moscow Party organization, this time in debate with Yakovlev, whose articles had appeared in *Pravda* on 24 and 25 October. Both sides of this debate were published by the Moscow Committee of the Russian Communist Party in its journal *Sputnik kommunista*. Finally, Bukharin delivered a lecture to a Party forum in Petrograd on 5 February 1923.[4]

In his classification of cultural systems Bukharin distin-

---

[3] N. I. Bukharin, 'A. A. Bogdanov' (obituary), *Pravda*, 8 Apr. 1928. The influence of Bogdanov upon Bukharin is discussed in: I. Susiluoto, *The Origins and Development of Systems Thinking in the Soviet Union: Political and Philosophical Controversies from Bogdanov to Present-Day Re-Evaluations* (Helsinki, 1982). For recent Soviet appraisals of the importance of Bogdanov, see the introduction to the re-edition of his *Tektologiya*: *Vseobshchaya organizatsionnaya nauka* (2nd edn., 2 vols., Moscow, 1989), and the discussion of a lecture of N. S. Shukhov (1989), in 'Voprosy sotsializma v ekonomicheskoy literature 20-ykh godov', *Voprosy ekonomiki*, 4 (1990) The contributions of Bogdanov and Bukharin to equilibrium theory are examined in G. D. Gloveli, 'A. A. Bogdanov and N. I. Bukharin: sblizheniya i razmezhevaniya', in I. D. Semenov and G. D. Gloveli, *N. I. Bukharin: Issledovanie nauchnogo naslediya (politiko-ekonomicheskiy aspekt)*, (Institut Ekonomiki, Akademiya Nauk SSSR, Sovet Molodykh Uchenykh; Moscow, 1988); and A. A. Belykh, 'The Theory of Equilibrium of A. A. Bogdanov and Soviet Economic Discussions of the 1920s', *Soviet Studies* (July 1990), 571–87.

[4] N. I. Bukharin, 'Burzhuaznaya revolyutsiya i revolyutsiya proletarskaya', *Pod znamenem marksizma*, 7–8 (1922), 61–82; 'Problema kul'tury v epokhu rabochei revolyutsii', *Pravda*, 11 Oct. 1922; 'Diskussiya po voprosu o postanovke kul'turnoy problemy', *Sputnik kommunista*, 19 (1923).

guished between what he called: first, the methods and principles (*metody i printsipy*) of a particular culture; secondly, its complexity or intensity (*intensivnost'*); and, thirdly, the extent of its dissemination (*ekstensivnost'*). Thus, as regards 'methods and principles', it was the special achievement of the bourgeoisie to have replaced an immobile and hierarchical society with one which liberated the individual. It had replaced a static with a dynamic world view, the dogmatism amd otherworldliness of feudal, priestly, ideology with science and the critical outlook of the 'thinking individual'. It had placed a higher value on practicality and had achieved a greater degree of control over nature.

As regards 'complexity', though the world-view of feudal society had attained a high level of sophistication (as in the works of Thomas Aquinas), the bourgeoisie, in the Encyclopaedia of the French materialists, had produced a 'cultural codex' which was superior by far. Finally, whereas feudal culture had displayed a pronounced caste character (learning had been concentrated mainly in the monasteries and even kings had sometimes been illiterate), the bourgeoisie, even before it attained political power, had embarked on the democratization of education.[5]

During the 1920s Bukharin frequently disparaged the general theory of development of Alexander Bogdanov, but in his description of the cultural values of the proletariat under capitalism he borrowed freely, if selectively, from Bogdanov's work.[6] In its structure, methods, and principles, Bukharin argued, proletarian culture was superior to bourgeois culture. Rejecting the 'fetishes' (absolute values and categorical imperatives) of the bourgeoisie, the proletariat had acquired its

---

[5] Bukharin, 'Burzhuaznaya revolyutsiya', 69–70; *Proletarskaya revolyutsiya i kul'tura*, 27–8.

[6] Bogdanov assembled what he considered to be his most significant writings on the subject in his anthology *O proletarskoy kul'ture, 1904–1924* (Moscow and Leningrad, 1925). On the theory and practice of 'Bogdanovism', see G. Gorzka, *A. Bogdanov und der russische Proletkult* (Frankfurt and New York, 1980); K. Mänicke-Gyöngyösi, *'Proletarische Wissenschaft' und 'sozialistische Menscheitsreligion' als Modelle proletarischer Kultur* (Berlin, 1982); Z. Sochor, *Revolution and Culture: The Bogdanov–Lenin Controversy* (Ithaca, NY, and London, 1988); and L. Mally, *Culture of the Future: The Proletkult Movement in Revolutionary Russia* (Berkeley, Calif., and Oxford, 1990).

own system of ethics grounded in principles of expediency
(*tselesoobraznost'*. At a time when the bourgeoisie was preoccupied with mysticism, theosophy, and the occult, and
displayed overt symptoms of decay, the proletariat sought out
the practical applications of knowledge. Although the capitalist
division of labour made for a fragmentation of individual
branches of knowledge (an 'anarchy of cultural-intellectual
production'), the proletariat, unified by its experience of
production and of social struggle, looked for the interconnectedness of things, the unifying principles in every sphere
of human knowledge.

However, it was only in the social sciences (in the teachings
of Marx) that the proletariat had attained the 'intensity' of
cultural development of the bourgeoisie. The proletariat had
been unable to produce its own cohort of scientists, engineers,
technicians, agronomists, artists, architects, geologists, its own
organizers of the economy. In its 'extensive' development the
proletariat was also backward: the great mass of workers remained technically and politically uneducated, captive to the
prejudices inculcated by the bourgeois educational system and
the church; hence, for example, their adhesion to social democratic parties; hence, also, the 'Catholic-worker' phenomenon.[7]

MATURATION OF PROLETARIAN CULTURE

In contradistinction to 'social democratic theorists', Bukharin
rejected the idea that an extended period of capitalist development and bourgeois democracy was necessary as a precondition of the cultural development of the working class. On the
contrary, although bourgeois culture had developed fully
'within the womb' of feudal society, the development of
proletarian culture under capitalism was not analogous.[8]

---

[7] Bukharin, 'Burzhuaznaya revolyutsiya', 74–5; *Proletarskaya revolyutsiya i kul'tura*, 28–31.

[8] In criticizing 'social democratic theorists' Bukharin may have had in mind Potresov, who in *Nasha zarya* in 1913 had argued that 'the culture of any class-divided society was produced by the ruling class of that society' and had described the culture of the working class as a dominated culture. For a summary of the debate on this question before 1917, see J. Biggart, 'Cultural Revolution', in H. Shukman (ed.), *The Blackwell Encyclopedia of the Russian Revolution* (Oxford, 1988).

Capitalism, Bukharin argued, had been associated with the spread of towns within the feudal countryside. Its development had been comprehensive and had involved economic growth, the creation of a new hierarchy of social relations, and, above all, the formation of 'an administrative-command staff of great proprietors'.[9] Even if, in the early stages of capitalist accumulation, the feudal authorities, by virtue of their control over the state, had been able to appropriate part of the surplus product created by the bourgeoisie, the relationship of the feudal powers to the nascent bourgeoisie had not been one of exploitation or domination. As the bourgeoisie increasingly gained control over the surplus product, so also it had acquired control over education. Over time, even within the confines of the feudal system, the bourgeoisie had been able to acquire a cultural ascendancy over the feudal classes.[10]

Has there ever in any feudal regime been a landlord who was the real master of the school or who exercised a monopoly control over education? Far from it. Even under the feudal regime the technician, the student, the researcher in the laboratory were under the direction, control, and tutelage of the new class, the bourgeoisie which had not yet attained political power but which was the preponderant cultural force and at a higher cultural level than the class which it was destined to overthrow.[11]

By contrast, neither the proletariat nor socialist production relations had developed, nor could they develop, on anything like the same scale within capitalist society. Whereas the bourgeoisie had acquired its own economic base, the proletariat, besieged within towns controlled by the bourgeoisie, had been unable even in the most advanced capitalist countries to create a fully fledged alternative economy or society.[12] The relationship of the bourgeoisie to the proletariat was one of exploitation. The budget of the manual worker was that which was sufficient for the reproduction of his labour power and contained hardly any surplus. The ruling class exercised monopoly control of education and ensured that its offspring

[9] Bukharin, 'Burzhuaznaya revolyutsiya', 63–4.
[10] Ibid. 68; see also Bukharin, *Proletarskaya revolyutsiya i kul'tura*, 18.
[11] Bukharin, *Proletarskaya revolyutsiya i kul'tura*, 22.
[12] Bukharin, 'Burzhuaznaya revolyutsiya', 65–6.

were trained in schools appropriate to their destined place in society.[13] To the extent that production became more concentrated and centralized, the proletariat acquired some experience of the social nature of work (*sotrudnichestvo*), and in workers recruited into the technical intelligentsia and in activists of the labour movement it acquired the skeleton of a future 'administrative industrial command-staff' (*administrativnaya proizvodstvennaya verkhushka*); but in general the proletariat was able to acquire only the most limited experience of self-government. 'It is obtuse to think that in any capitalist society, even the finest and most developed, the working class can attain a level of culture superior to that of the bourgeoisie which it is destined to overthrow'.[14] The implication of Bukharin's argument was that for the bourgeoisie the cultural revolution preceded the political revolution, whereas for the proletariat the reverse was the case: the seizure of political power was a necessary precondition of cultural development. According to Bukharin, it was only during the 'transition period' which followed upon the seizure of power that the proletariat could effectively 'grow into' socialism.[15] Its dilemma during the transition period, as during the period of bourgeois hegemony, was how to exercise control over the process of its own 'cultural accumulation'. This led Bukharin to contemplate the role of the intelligentsia in relation to the proletariat both before and after the seizure of power.

'ORGANIC DEGENERATION' AND 'BUREAUCRATIC SOCIALISM'

Whereas the bourgeoisie had experienced scarcely any need to recruit leaders from classes hostile to it, the backwardness of the proletariat under capitalism had made for a dependence upon déclassé elements (*vykhodtsy, perebezhentsy*), notably from the intelligentsia. It was no accident, Bukharin argued, that Marxism, 'the most complete, correct proletarian ideology', had been worked out by Marx, Engels, and their pupils;[16] and

---

[13] Ibid. 70.
[14] Bukharin, *Proletarskaya revolyutsiya i kul'tura*, 22.
[15] Bukharin, 'Diskussiya po voprosu o postanovke kul'turnoy problemy', 97.
[16] Bukharin, 'Burzhuaznaya revolyutsiya', 78.

even within the labour movement the working class was 'to a significant degree ruled by a cadre of leaders who came from a different milieu',[17] as witness the role of the Fabians in the British trade movement and the influence of the editorial board of the revisionist *Sozialistische Monatshefte* over the German Social Democratic Party. Within Russian social democracy, too, leadership had been provided by professional revolutionaries from the intelligentsia.[18]

The problem with this relationship was that, whereas the cultural distance separating a bourgeois political leader from the average member of his class had not been great, the cultural and psychological distance separating the leader of a proletarian party from the proletariat was considerable. The bourgeois leader shared his educational and social background and experience with those on whose behalf he acted; but a leader of the proletariat, if he came from another class, would often lack the instinctive collectivist responses of the industrial worker.[19] Once the proletariat had come to power, this problem became more acute. Lacking the qualified specialists, organizers, and cadres needed to carry out the huge range of tasks which it had undertaken, the proletariat was obliged to recruit from within a hostile stratum: 'even in the most revolutionary parties like our own Communist Party (and there is no point in concealing this) there is a definite élite [*verkhushka*] of leaders who are to a significant degree migrants [*vykhodtsy*] from another class'.[20] Whilst it was 'utopian' to think that the proletariat could dispense with the assistance of the intelligentsia, at the same time 'it cannot be denied that this state of affairs brings with it a great danger ... this is the danger of a degeneration (*organicheskoe pererozhdenie*) of the proletarian state and of the proletarian party'.[21]

It was at this point that Bukharin drew out certain implications for the Soviet system of the theories of Bogdanov. In 1917, in a new edition of his 'Universal Organizational Science' (*Tektologiya*), Bogdanov had gone as far as he ever would in

---

[17] Ibid. 77.
[18] Bukharin, 'Burzhuaznaya revolyutsiya', 78.
[19] Ibid.
[20] Bukharin, *Proletarskaya revolyutsiya i kul'tura*, 24.
[21] Ibid. 79; 'Diskussiya', 97.

providing a social and political profile of the intelligentsia in
the period after the First World War. In a chapter entitled
'Contemporary ideals', which had not appeared in previous
editions and in which he described the ideologies of the two
major social classes, bourgeoisie and industrial proletariat,
Bogdanov noted that, at a time when the differentiation of
these two classes was still incomplete, one could identify a
number of intermediary strata (*promezhutochnye gruppirovki*),
one of which comprised the 'greater part of the scientific–
technical intelligentsia, though not its upper elements, who
had thrown in their lot with the bourgeoisie, or the lower, who
were siding with the toiling proletariat'. This stratum had
acquired an ideology of its own which envisaged:

the planned organization of production and distribution under the
management [*rukovodstvo*] of economists, engineers, doctors, and
lawyers, in short of the intelligentsia itself. This would entail, of
course, the creation of privileged conditions for the intelligentsia itself,
but also of materially satisfactory conditions for the working class. In
this way the conditions making for class struggle would be abolished
and a harmony o interests achieved.[22]

The political form required for the realization of this ideal
would be in most cases a 'centralized republic' and the pro-
ponents of this system, for example, the majority of the French
radical socialists, described their ideal as 'state socialism'.
However, for Bogdanov, other meanings were contained
within this slogan:

There are many features of the old estate society [*soslovnyy stroy*]
which still exercise a powerful influence. In Europe the most typical
are the Catholic priesthood and the backward stratum of the landlord
class. These elements either cling to the old estate ideals or update
them. In countries where a significant proportion of the bureaucratic
intelligentsia (*chinovnich'ei intelligentsii*) is linked with the landowning
estate, or identifies with it, one form which this modernised ideology
adopts is that of 'state socialism'. Indeed, it would be more correct to
speak of 'bureaucratic socialism', for a system in which production
and distribution are organised by an hierarchy of officials (*chinovnikov*)
headed by a moral-patriarchal monarchical power lies somewhere

---

[22] A. A. Bogdanov, *Vseobshchaya organizatsionnaya nauka (Tektologiya)* (2 vols.;
Moscow, 1917), ii. 140.

between the ideal of the technical intelligentsia and the feudal-estate ideal.[23]

Bogdanov's preface to this edition of *Tektologiya* was signed on 26 September 1916 and his readers were doubtless intended to see in the above paragraph an Aesopian reference to bureaucratic–socialist tendencies within the Tsarist regime. In his writings produced during the Revolution and Civil War Bogdanov had identified functional similarities between pre-Soviet state capitalism and Soviet War Communism. In these works, however, while refusing to acknowledge the Soviet regime as 'a dictatorship of the proletariat', he had refrained from any attempt at defining the ruling group which presided over this economic system.[24] In the spring of 1919, certainly, in a lecture delivered to the Moscow Proletkul't, Bogdanov indicated that it was an open question whether the war and revolution in Russia might result in the subjugation of the proletariat to 'some new social stratum'; and in the summer of that year he had argued that the ideas of Alexei Gastev for the 'scientific organization of labour', if applied, would result in the emergence of a 'social group . . . of scientific engineers' (*uchenogo inzhenerstva*); however, in his published work, he never went beyond this hypothesis.[25] The section 'Contemporary Ideals' reappeared in an edition of 1922 of his *Tektologiya*, but without any reference to Soviet conditions;[26] and in 1923, in a new edition of one of his major economic textbooks, Bogdanov went no further in identifying the class basis of the Soviet state than to say that 'The state pursues its New Economic Policy in the interests of the labouring classes [*trudovye klassy*].'[27] In none of his later publications did he elaborate upon this opaque formula.

[23] Ibid.
[24] On Bogdanov's interpretation of the revolution of 1917, see J. Biggart, 'Alexander Bogdanov and the Theory of a "New Class"', *Russian Review* (July 1990).
[25] See A. A. Bogdanov, *Elementy proletarskoy kul'tury v razvitii rabochego klassa* (Moscow, 1920), 48; and 'O tendentsiyakh proletarskoy kul'tury (otvet Gastevu)', *Proletarskaya kul'tura* 9–10 (1919), also in *O proletarskoy kul'ture* (Moscow and Leningrad, 1925), especially p. 326.
[26] A. A. Bogdanov, *Tektologiya: Vseobshchaya organizatsionnaya nauka* (Berlin, Petrograd, and Moscow, 1922), 303.
[27] A. A. Bogdanov, *Nachal'nyy kurs politicheskoy ekonomii* (9th edn., Moscow and Petrograd, 1923), 125.

BUKHARIN'S 'NEW CLASS'

Bukharin, less politically vulnerable than Bogdanov and with less need for circumspection in his diagnosis of trends within Soviet society, was less inhibited in his pronouncements. In his analysis of the danger of cultural counter-revolution, he was, moreover, able to invoke a speech which Lenin had delivered to the Eleventh Party Congress on 27 March 1922 when, referring to those members of the old ruling classes who were advocating an accommodation with the Soviet regime, he had admitted that this 'Change of Landmarks' movement (*Smenovekhovstvo*) expressed the mood of 'thousands and tens of thousands of bourgeois of all sorts and Soviet officials who participate in our New Economic Policy'. Lenin had added the sombre warning that in the history of civilizations it was not always the case that a conquering people imposed its culture upon the vanquished; sometimes, if it possessed a superior culture, the conquered nation would impose its culture upon its conquerers.[28]

For Bukharin, a key role in any such cultural restoration would be played by the technical intelligentsia. Formed under capitalism, the intelligentsia was essentially a social stratum which served the interests of the bourgeoisie.[29] In the Soviet Union they did not believe in socialism or in the planned economy and they tended to view everything that had happened since October as a deviation from the norm. Even those intellectuals who worked in good faith with the proletariat inevitably brought with them the experience of the old regime. The result was that 'these cadres begin to eat away the very substance of the workers' revolution just as a moth eats away a cloth'.[30] The changes which they brought about would be not sudden but incremental. If they had their way, there would not

---

[28] V. I. Lenin, 'Political Report of the Central Committee to the Eleventh Congress of the RCP(b), 27 March 1922', in *Collected Works* (45 vols.; Moscow, 1960–70), xxxiii. 288–99. Cited in Bukharin, 'Burzhuaznaya revolyutsiya', 79, and *Proletarskaya revolyutsiya i kul'tura*, 42–3.

[29] Bukharin, 'Burzhuaznaya revolyutsiya', 72–3. Bukharin's apprehensions concerning the formation of a 'new class' have been noted by S. F. Cohen, in his *Bukharin and the Bolshevik Revolution: A Political Biography, 1888–1938* (New York, 1973; 2nd edn., Oxford, 1980), ch. 5, 'Rethinking Bolshevism'. My own account accords greater importance to Bukharin's 'new-class' theory in his general theory of cultural revolution.

[30] Bukharin, 'Problema kul'tury'.

necessarily be a return to things as they had been; but there would certainly be a movement away from socialism towards some new form of the old class society.[31] In his *Theory of Historical Materialism* of 1921 Bukharin, taking issue with Roberto Michels, had admitted the possibility of 'the excretion of a leading stratum in the form of a class germ (embryonic class)' during the transition to socialism.[32] Now he again conceded that, out of the technical intelligentsia, out of the new NEP bourgeoisie (*podryadchiki, postavshchiki, arendatory*), and even from within the Communist Party, a new ruling class (*novyy klass, gospodstvuyushchiy klass*) might be formed.[33] This was indeed, he warned, the expectation of *Smena vekh*: that the Soviet regime would produce a new bourgeoisie of the American type which would advance under a national flag.[34]

In his first essay (of July–August 1922) Bukharin had envisaged one set of circumstances in which the proletariat would lose this 'battle of ideologies' between the old and the new. The formation of new cadres out of the working class was a necessary preventive measure against bourgeois restoration. However, in cases of extreme backwardness and cultural deprivation these new administrative and managerial cadres would necessarily have to be allocated a greater share of the means of consumption than the average worker. A danger would then arise of estrangement between the masses and that stratum of the command staff which had been promoted out of a working-class milieu. These cadres would be susceptible to cultural assimilation by the more cultured elements of the command staff and might combine with them in forming a new ruling class. Neither working-class origins nor proletarian conscience were sufficient guarantees against this happening and in the Soviet Union the risk of such an outcome would be increased if the regime failed to act against the emergence of new capitalist social groups.[35]

---

[31] Bukharin, 'Burzhuaznaya revolyutsiya', 80; 'Diskussiya', 97.
[32] N. I. Bukharin, *Teoriya istoricheskogo materializma: Populyarnyy uchebnik marksistskoy sotsiologii* (Moscow, 1921), trans., as *Historical Materialism: A System of Sociology* (New York, 1925), 309–11.
[33] Bukharin, 'Burzhuaznaya revolyutsiya', 81; *Proletarskaya revolyutsiya i kul'tura*, 43.
[34] Bukharin, *Proletarskaya revolyutsiya i kul'tura*, 1–8, 33–4.
[35] Bukharin, 'Burzhuaznaya revolyutsiya', 81; *Proletarskaya revolyutsiya i kul'tura*, 43.

In February 1923, in an elaboration of this theme, Bukharin imagined an additional scenario in which the proletariat failed in the construction of socialism. Now, even if the regime provided new cadres in sufficient numbers to replace the old service estate (*sluzhiloe soslovie*), and so pre-empted the first danger, there was a secondary risk that the original cohorts to be drafted into the higher schools would be followed by their children, grandchildren, and great-grandchildren, thereby forming a closed caste which would rule by virtue of its monopoly control over education. Once again, 'even proletarian origins and the most calloused hands provided no safeguard against transformation into a new class'.[36]

'COMMAND STAFF' AND 'IRON COHORT'

Having identified the dangers which lay ahead, Bukharin proceeded to outline his own strategy for cultural revolution, a strategy which he considered distinct from those of Lenin and Bogdanov. In his *Theory of Historical Materialism* he had argued in response to Michels that the emergence of a new class would be 'retarded by two opposing tendencies: first by the *growth of the productive forces*, second by the *education monopoly*. The increasing reproduction of technologists and organisers in general out of the working class itself will undermine [this] possible new class alignment.'[37] In 1922 Bukharin reaffirmed his belief in the efficacy of the educational monopoly:

The cultural struggle is a struggle in the first instance and above all for the formation of administrative and ideological class cadres . . . That class has earned the historic right to rule which proves itself capable of producing from within itself a sufficient quantity of administrators, organisers and ideologues to lead society in a pre-determined class direction.[38]

And in his speech to Moscow Party activists on 9 October:

To form a full complement of cadres, a complete 'command staff' from representatives of the working class in the first instance, and

---

[36] Bukharin, *Proletarskaya revolyutsiya i kul'tura*, 45.
[37] Bukharin, *Historical Materialism*, 309–11.
[38] Bukharin, 'Burzhuaznaya revolyutsiya', 81.

thereafter to draw into the processes of government the broad masses of the working class—this is a matter of first importance. The working class will either resolve it, or, failing to resolve it will regress to capitalism by one route or another.[39]

It was in his programme for the education of the 'command-staff' of the proletariat that Bukharin departed most radically from the theories of Bogdanov. Having provided in his article of July–August 1922 a definition of proletarian culture in its embryonic, 'capitalist', stage of development, Bukharin in his lecture of 9 October 1922 went on to outline what he considered should be the goals of a socialist education during the transition period. These were to be as follows:

1. Reconstruction of the individual psyche. In July–August 1922 Bukharin had written of 'cadres with a developed and solid communist–proletarian world-view and world-feeling [*mirooshchushchenie*], for the feelings play an important social role'.[40]

2. Pragmatism. A combination of Marxist theory with American practicality (*khvatka*) and business efficiency (*delechestvo*).[41]

3. Elimination of the humanitarian bias in education and an increased emphasis upon practical and technical subjects. Engineers and technicians who subscribed to Communist ideals were the most valuable social type (following Bukharin's speech in Moscow a number of students resigned from the Communist University and enrolled in technical college!).[42]

4. Specialization instead of universalism: 'We have to put out of our mind the idea that everybody can do everything. Now we need specialists who perhaps know nothing about other disciplines but who are expert in their own discipline, as the bourgeois specialist used to be.'[43]

[39] Bukharin, 'Problema kul'tury'.
[40] Ibid.; Bukharin, 'Burzhuaznaya revolyutsiya', 80.
[41] Bukharin, 'Problema kul'tury'; *Proletarskaya revolyutsiya i kul'tura*, 37, 48–9.
[42] Bukharin, 'Problema kul'tury'; *Proletarskaya revolyutsiya i kul'tura*, 49–50.
[43] Bukharin, 'Problema kul'tury'.

5. Physical and mental development of the individual and the training of the will.[44]

'BUKHARINISM' AND 'BOGDANOVISM'

How far did Bukharin's theory of cultural revolution derive from that of Bogdanov and how far did Bukharin acknowledge the influence of Bogdanov's ideas upon his own thought? In his emphasis upon the organizing function of ideology Bukharin owed much to Bogdanov. The idea of the intelligentsia as the intermediary controller of ideology, acting on behalf of the ruling class, was also well established in Bogdanov's thought. On the other hand, as we have seen, Bukharin had gone further than Bogdanov in warning that the intelligentsia (neo-bourgeois and proletarian) might metamorphose into a ruling class even under the Soviet regime (though Bogdanov's disciples, the 'Collectivists' and *Rabochaya pravda* had drawn a similar inference from his work).[45]

In a debate with Yakovlev in December 1922 (see below) Bukharin on one fundamental issue openly aligned himself with Bogdanov: it was important, he insisted, to think not in terms of mass (*obshchenarodnoe*) culture but in terms of class culture. Lenin had therefore been mistaken in his 'reply to Bogdanov' in denying the ideological partisanship of the sciences. Besides, the error of the Proletkul't in Bukharin's opinion had been not their attempt to foster the development of working-class culture ('in laboratory conditions', as Yakovlev had put it) but a failure to define clearly the area in which they wished to work. They had created an impression of having far-reaching pretensions and had antagonized other institutions.[46] As late as February 1925, at a Literary Conference convened by the Central Committee of the Communist Party, Bukharin

---

[44] Bukharin, 'Problema kul'tury'.

[45] For a survey of 'new-class' theories in Eastern Europe, see M. Sawer, 'Theories of the New Class from Bakunin to Kuron and Modzelewski: The Morphology of Permanent Protest', in M. Sawer (ed.), *Socialism and the New Class: Towards the Analysis of Structural Inequality within Socialist Societies* (APSA Monography, 19; Australasian Political Studies Association, Sydney, 1978). Bogdanov's distinctive contribution to this body of theory is discussed in Biggart, 'Alexander Bogdanov and the Theory of a "New Class"'.

[46] Bukharin, 'Diskussiya', 122, 124.

reaffirmed his belief in the existence of a transitional 'proletarian' culture and insisted that 'not everything that Bogdanov has written on the subject is mistaken; he has written a great deal that is relevant and correct'.[47]

At the same time, in his speeches and writings of 1922–3 Bukharin on several points of theory both explicitly and by allusion expressed disagreement with Bogdanov. In an article of 1923 he criticized Bogdanov for 'psychologizing' historical materialism by arguing that it was not the physical nature of the instruments of production which constituted the material 'base' of society but rather the technical ability (*umen'e*) acquired by people in employing them.[48] This distinction was important in relation to another point in Bukharin's theory according to which capitalism 'held back' the development of proletarian culture. No mere changes in the economic 'base' would enhance the cultural development of the proletariat: the 'widespread' view of 'some Marxists and semi-Marxists like Bogdanov' that the increasing automation of industry would abolish the divisions between skilled and unskilled labour and combine the work of the manual worker and the technical specialist was mistaken. Certainly, with the increasing complexity of industrial techniques the worker became more skilled; but the specialized nature of these skills perpetuated the division of labour. Nor could the worker apply his increased ability to control machines to the organization of people or of production as a whole. Besides, the technical intelligentsia also increased its competence, thereby maintaining its cultural superiority over the working class:[49]

The worker develops intellectually, the upper classes develop even further, and in so doing they retain their supremacy and their necessary role in the process of social production. One cannot, therefore,

[47] N. I. Bukharin, 'Proletariat i voprosy khudozhestvennoy politiki', *Krasnaya nov'*, 4 (1925), 263–72.

[48] See N. I. Bukharin, 'K postanovke problem teorii istoricheskogo materializma (Beglye zametki)' (1923), in *Ataka: Sbornik teoreticheskikh statei* (Moscow, 1924), repr. in N. I. Bukharin, *Izbranniye proizvedeniya*, ed. G. L. Smirnov (Moscow, 1988), 43.

[49] Bukharin, 'Burzhuaznaya revolyutsiya', 71–3; *Proletarskaya revolyutsiya i kul'tura*, 23.

argue that the working class will attain maturity under capitalism or a higher cultural level than the class which it overthrows.[50]

While there is scarcely any mention in Bukharin's publications of 1922–3 of 'collectivism', it would not be true to say, despite point (5) of his programme, that Bukharin placed greater emphasis on the training of the 'individual', for in February 1925 he acknowledged that 'the anti-anarchic, anti-individualistic, collectivist spirit combines with the militant characteristics of the advancing revolutionary proletariat'.[51] In any case, Bogdanov himself had argued that a collectivist education *should* cater for the needs of the individual through the encouragement of initiative, criticism, originality, and all-round development. What was to be avoided was the use of individuality in the pursuit of personal interest.[52]

Rather the educational programme of Bukharin differed from that of Bogdanov in the following respects:

1. While Bogdanov had certainly provided for the 'education of the educators' in his project for a 'Proletarian University', the educational strategy of the Proletkul't was essentially non-élitist. Conscious of the role of education in creating divisions within the working class, the Proletkul't had attempted to bring education to the workplace (*Rabochaya pravda* had condemned the transfer of able workers from the shop-floor to higher schools (VUZy)). Bukharin, in his proposal for the training of an 'administrative industrial command-staff', provided no safeguards against élitism.

2. Bukharin's emphasis upon specialization in training over 'universalism', his hostility towards the humanities, and his enthusiasm for technicians and engineers contrast markedly with Bogdanov's call for the 'integration' of man. It is not fortuitous that Bukharin's programme for

---

[50] Bukharin, P*roletarskaya revolyutsiya i kul'tura*, 23. Here we could say that Bukharin steers a middle way between the position defended in 1913–14 by Potresov and that of Pletnev (Valerianov), Lunacharsky, and Bogdanov, who in reply had pointed to the effect of industrialization in creating a proletarian subculture. See Biggart, 'Cultural Revolution'.

[51] Bukharin, 'Proletariat i voprosy khudozhestvennoy politiki'.

[52] A. A. Bogdanov, 'Ideal vospitaniya' (1918), in *O proletarskoi kul'ture*, 236.

cultural reconstruction was enthusiastically endorsed in 1924 by the Soviet proponent of 'Taylorism', Alexei Gastev.[53]

3. Where Bogdanov had proposed that a 'universal organizational science' would assist the working class in its study of nature and society, Bukharin entrusted the education of the proletariat to the 'generals of Marxist ideology'. These '*Marxist* historians, *Marxist* mathematicians' were to produce the officers and non-commissioned officers of the new regime, who would in turn train lower-level educators in the 'transformation' (*pererabotka*) of the masses. The objective was the creation of a culture that was 'communist–proletarian'.[54]

4. Whereas Bogdanov envisaged the cultural development of the proletariat taking place outside the Communist Party, for Bukharin, as for Lenin, the Communist Party, the 'iron cohort of the proletarian revolution', was the instrument *par excellence* of the cultural development during the transition period.[55]

Arguably, it was because of these important differences in their educational strategies that Bukharin considered it legitimate during the later 1920s to disguise the extent of his indebtedness to Bogdanov. However, it seems likely that there were other reasons. It was explicit in Bukharin's theory of development that the industrial working class was the ruling class in the Soviet Union; it was implicit in the theory of Bogdanov that it was not. Whereas Bukharin's theory provided a programme for the Party in power, Bogdanov's could provide a platform for political opposition. Even in the period when he was most influenced by Bogdanov's ideas, Bukharin had felt it necessary to condemn 'Bogdanovist' opposition groupings (as in the

---

[53] A. Gastev, 'Shatkunovskaya kak metodika', *Krasnaya nov'*, (1924), cited in K. E. Bailes, 'Alexei Gastev and the Soviet Controversy over Taylorism, 1918–1924', *Soviet Studies*, 3 (1977), 387. Gastev cites Bukharin's speech to the Moscow Party organization of 9 Oct. 1922, 'Problema kul'tury'.

[54] Bukharin, *Proletarskaya revolyutsiya i kul'tura*, 53.

[55] N. I. Bukharin, 'Zheleznaya kogorta revolyutsii', *Za pyat' let, 1917–1922: Sbornik*, (Moscow, 1922); repr. in Bukharin, *Izbrannye proizvedeniya*, 38. This article provides an early example of the contribution of Bukharin to the cult of the Communist Party and to the cult of Lenin.

episodes of the 'Collectivists' and of *Rabochaya pravda*). Indeed, Bukharin publicly denounced *Rabochaya pravda* only weeks after expounding his own 'neo-Bogdanovist' ideas before a Party meeting in Petrograd.[56] Later in the 1920s Bukharin remained sensitive to the political implications of Bogdanov's ideas. Writing in 1926, he described the 'Bogdanov—Bazarov' theory of cultural revolution as one which favoured an extended period of capitalist development in view of the alleged unpreparedness of the proletariat for the complex ta k of socialist planning.[57] For Bukharin, any theory that the proletariat, 'the exploited and economically, politically, and culturally oppressed class', would 'ripen' under any capitalist system was 'utterly wrong'. Harking back to his writings of 1922–3, he accused Bogdanov and Bazarov of failing to understand the 'difference in principle between proletarian and bourgeois revolutions'; it was the 'period of transition' which enabled the cultural ripening of the proletariat.[58] This was not all: a theory of 'bureaucratic degeneration (the technico-intellectual bureaucracy, the "organizing" caste)', was now 'held by the combined opposition'. Drawing a veil over his own earlier apprehensions, Bukharin now accused Bogdanov of having invented this theory of 'inevitable' degeneration.[59]

'BUKHARINISM' AND 'LENINISM'

One year after Lenin's death, during a Literary Conference convened in February 1925 by the Central Committee of the

---

[56] See N. I. Bukharin, 'Vliyanie NEPa i "uklony" v rabochem dvizhenii', *Pravda*, 25 Mar. 1923. Bukharin had addressed a Party meeting in Petrograd on 5 Feb. 1923.

[57] N. I. Bukharin, 'O kharaktere nashei revolyutsii' *Bol'shevik*, 19–20 (1926); trans. as *Building p Socialism* (London, 1926), 5, 8, 14–17.

[58] Ibid. 18.

[59] Ibid. 32, 47. Throughout, Bukharin cites from A. A. Bogdanov, *Voprosy sotsializma* (Moscow, 1918) and from V. Bazarov, *Na puti k sotsializmu* (Kharkov, 1919). In neither of these works does the author allege that the Soviet regime is led by a 'new lass', but during the later 1920s Bogdanov's detractors frequently held such an allegation against him. According to St. Krivtsov, Bogdanov, 'after the war developed the theory of a peaceful super-imperialism presided over by a new class—the technical intelligentsia' ('Pamyati A. A. Bogdanova', *Pod znamenem marksizma* 4 (1928), 185).

Party, Bukharin criticized the efforts of the literary critic Vardin posthumously to enlist Lenin in the camp of the cultural Left. Implicitly accepting his own inclusion in this category, Bukharin insisted that there were 'two questions out of all of those upon which Vladimir Il'ich and I disagreed and on which I remain in disagreement with him: these are the questions of proletarian culture and of state capitalism'.[60]

Elsewhere, I have argued that Lenin used the pretext of the appearance in *Pravda* on 27 September 1922 of an article by Pletnev on the subject of 'proletarian culture' in order to criticize what he considered to be the very similar ideas of Bukharin. As Bukharin reminded a literary conference convened by the Central Committee in February 1925: 'Vladimir Il'ich disagreed with my conception of proletarian culture. . . . He sent me memoranda and even enlisted the aid of Yakovlev.'[61] It seems likely that in the first draft of the article which Lenin commissioned from Yakovlev direct criticisms were made of Bukharin, for as Bukharin recalled, 'I issued an ultimatum to the effect that, if he insisted on the first draft of Yakovlev's article, I would myself publish the sharpest possible reply. Vladimir Il'ich then persuaded Yakovlev to remove a whole series of comments.'[62]

An exhaustive account of Lenin's theory of cultural revolution need not be given here; the subject has been usefully dealt with by Claudin-Urondo and Sochor.[63] It must be borne in mind that, as the Civil War ended, Lenin was anxious to direct the energies of the Communist Party away from what he considered to be utopianism and towards the practical tasks of economic reconstruction. In a speech to the All-Russian Conference of *Guberniya* and *Uezd* Political Educational Workers (*Narobraz*) on 3 November 1920 he had declared that:

Propaganda of the old type is useless and describes and illustrates what communism is. This kind of propaganda is now useless for we

[60] Bukharin, 'Proletariat i voprosy khudozhestvennoy politiki', 263. On the disagreement between Lenin and Bukharin over 'state capitalism', see H. Ray Buchanan, 'Lenin and Bukharin on the Transition from Capitalism to Socialism: The Meshchersky Controversy, 1918', *Soviet Studies*, 28 (1976), 66–82.
[61] Bukharin, 'Proletariat i voprosy khudozhestvennoy politiki', 365.
[62] Ibid.
[63] See C. Claudin-Urondo, *Lenin and the Cultural Revolution* (Sussex, 1977); and Sochor, *Revolution and Culture: The Bogdanov–Lenin Controversy*.

have to show in practice how socialism is to be built . . . All our propaganda must be based on the political experience of economic development . . . Our main policy must be to develop the state economically so as to gather in more puds of grain and mine more puds of coal . . . There must be less fine talk for you cannot satisfy the working people with fine words.[64]

It is against this background that we should understand Lenin's proposal of 8 December 1920 for an 'All-Russian Bureau of Production Propaganda' under the All-Union Trade Union Council and his recommendation on 20 December 1920 that *Pravda*, *Izvestiya*, and all newspapers of the Russian Republic should direct their attention to production rather than politics.[65] It is against the same background (allowing also for Lenin's intellectual antipathy for Bogdanov) that we should understand his hounding of the Proletkul't and the adoption by that organization in December 1920 of the 'Production Platform' which made the improvement of labour productivity one of its principal objectives.[66] At the outset of the NEP Lenin's theory of development was uncompromisingly 'economistic'. It also addressed the needs of the population as a whole rather than those of the working class in particular. It was only during the debate of 1922, as Lenin confronted the threat of bourgeois restoration, that the idea of culture entered into his thinking in any significant way. It was this reappraisal which produced, in Lenin's last writings, the idea of institutional safeguards against the degeneration of the state and the emphasis upon 'co-operation'.

When Yakovlev's article was finally published it did contain two references to Bukharin but these were of an innocuous nature; the two leaders had agreed not to advertise their differences in the press.[67] At a Party meeting especially convened

[64] Lenin, *Collected Works*, xxxi. 371–2.

[65] Ibid. xlii.

[66] Minutes of the Central Committee of the Proletkul't, 16–20 December 1920, TsGALI, f.1230.1.7. For the programme as adopted, see 'Ideologiya, politika i taktika Proletkul'ta', *Byulleten' 2-ogo Vserossiyskogo S"ezda Proletkul'tov*, 2 (21 Nov. 1921), 73–8.

[67] Ya. Yakovlev, 'O proletarskoy kul'ture i Proletkul'te', *Pravda*, 24, 25 Oct. 1922. In later textbook editions of this article all references to Bukharin were deleted, as was a list of the theatrical repertoire of the Proletkul't, ridiculed by Yakovlev as belonging to the culture of the past. See, e.g., the 3rd augmented

by Yakovlev on 16 December 1922, however, Bukharin did not conceal the fact that he as much as Pletnev or Bogdanov had been the target of Lenin's criticism, and on this occasion and in a speech delivered in Petrograd on 5 February 1923 he defended his programme for cultural revolution at length.

According to Bukharin, the article of Yakovlev expressed a view 'shared by a significant number of Party comrades' that the Soviet regime could not afford to adopt long-term perspectives but should concentrate on the fundamental task of eradicating backwardness. Lenin, for example, took the view that the needs of the millions for literacy and elementary education should take precedence over all other considerations, and Yakovlev in the debate of December 1922 argued that culture should be understood as 'popular culture' (*obshchenarodnoe*).[68] However, for Bukharin this was a simplistic view of the task in hand. For one thing, to argue that all resources should be directed towards the mass of the people (*narod'*) was to disregard the interconnectedness of sectors of the economy (the regime, he reminded his audience, had been guilty of this in the past). But, apart from this, one had to offer something more than literacy to prospective cadres who demanded guidance along the path of cultural development. The needs of the most able groups of a highly differentiated working class could only be catered for in institutions such as the workers' faculties (*Rabfaki*), the Sverdlov University, and the Institute of Red Professors.[69]

Bukharin then turned to an issue which had been at the centre of his disagreement with Lenin in October 1920 when the Politburo had debated the status of the Proletkul't. Whereas Lenin tended to view certain disciplines as 'value free' and had argued that in respect of these disciplines the 'assimilation of bourgeois culture' should take precedence over the 'invention of a new proletarian culture', Bukharin, like Bogdanov, denied the neutrality of the sciences, natural or social, and was wary

edn. of *V. I. Lenin o literature i iskusstve* (Moscow, 1967). By the 7th edn. (Moscow, 1986), which is said not to differ from the 6th edn. (Moscow, 1979) the theatre repertoire had been reinstated, though not the references to Bukharin.

[68] Yakovlev, 'Diskussiya', 110, 117.
[69] Bukharin, 'Diskussiya', 33.

of a strategy of 'total assimilation'. Considering that the methods of all the sciences were inextricably bound up with the research strategies which they adopted or were prescribed, Bukharin wished to abolish the hegemony of the bourgeoisie in all branches of knowledge.[70]

In an attempt to resolve this disagreement, Bukharin suggested that the category 'culture' be divided into two sub-categories: material culture or the economic base, comprising techniques, the means of production in all their interrelationships and the everyday habits and customs of people (*tekhnika ob"edinennoy zhizni, byt*); and spiritual culture, the means of representation or cognition (*sposob predstavleniya*)—in Marx's expression, the 'Vorstellungsweise': the ideological expression of a particular system of production relations. This latter aspect of culture should be recognized as being as important as the former.

It was, therefore, incorrect to argue, as did Kautsky and the Austrian Marxists (by implication, also Lenin), that a proletarian revolution consisted merely in the transfer of control over production processes and of the apparatus of power from the bourgeoisie to the proletariat. This was to ignore the role of the means of cognition, in which sphere there must also be discontinuity. The bourgeois educator was a 'means of production for the reproduction of bourgeois culture', a 'living machine radiating the energy of bourgeois culture'.[71] The proletarian revolution witnessed the demise of the world view of the bourgeoisie (its conception of science, its moral norms, and the entire domain of its spiritual culture) and introduced a completely different system of values. A necessary precondition of such change was the breaking of the stranglehold of the bourgeoisie over higher education (*vysshaya shkola*).[72]

FROM LENIN TO STALIN

Bukharin could later legitimately claim that Lenin had changed his views to take account of his own. As he declared in February 1925:

---

[70] See also J. Biggart, 'Bukharin and the Origins of the "Proletarian Culture" Debate', *Soviet Studies*, 39 (1987), 233.
[71] Bukharin, *Proletarskaya revolyutsiya i kul'tura*, 37.
[72] Ibid. 37; 'Problema kul'tury'.

It is fair to say that Vladimir Il'ich clarified his position on state capitalism in his last writings on co-operation. Previously he had argued that we had no socialism at all or at most a small island of socialism in the midst of state capitalism and that even that small island was shrinking in size. But subsequently he conceded that we were growing stronger. What he seemed to be saying was: 'Well, if our comrades are told that we have a socialist system already in existence they simply won't get on with building socialism so they will have to be taken down a peg and be told—"Please, no bombast. We have no socialism at all."' This is the approach we should adopt in the very important matter of educating our cadres. . . . I personally do not agree with his theoretical position, but I do associate myself with his practical recommendations.[73]

During the later 1920s, as the official ideology of 'Leninism' developed (Bukharin played an important part in its formulation), and as a reverential attitude to the legacy of Lenin, however defined, became a prerequisite of political survival, Bukharin refrained from advertising their differences.[74] Rather, after Lenin's death, he took care to single out those aspects of Lenin's theory which he found congenial and to ascribe to Lenin conceptions of cultural revolution which were in fact his own. In 1924, in a speech delivered to the Communist Academy, Bukharin included amongst five theoretical problems which Lenin had identified as being in need of solution the problems of the 'growing into socialism' and the 'cultural problem'. Associating himself with the programme for peaceful development 'along evolutionary lines' which Lenin had outlined in his last writings, and especially in his article on co-operation, Bukharin warned that any 'third revolution' against this conception of the proletarian dictatorship would result only in counter-revolution and restoration. At the same time, Bukharin took care to include his own priorities in his definition of 'Leninism': in the development of culture Lenin had stressed the need to enlist the aid of bourgeois specialists; however, he had also stressed the need for Communist education and the need to 'combine' (*sochetat'sya*) proletarian culture with the culture of the past.[75]

---

[73] Bukharin, 'Proletariat i voprosy khudozhestvennoy politki'.
[74] His obituary of Bogdanov referred to Lenin as a 'leader of supreme genius' (*Pravda*, 8 Apr. 1928).
[75] N. I. Bukharin, 'Lenin kak marksist' (a speech at the Communist

In 1928, on the fourth anniversary of Lenin's death, seven years into the 'transition period' and on the eve of Stalin's break with NEP, Bukharin took stock of the cultural achievements of the Soviet regime, applying the measure of 'Leninism' as he understood it.[76] Deriding past and present critics, and their fears of the 'sinister Communist iconoclasts', Bukharin accused the 'better dressed and perfumed diplomats of the most Christian states with their lisping talk, their kid gloves, and their "noble" anxiety for God and culture' of presenting a greater threat to civilization. Far from having brought about the destruction of culture, the 'Communist iconoclasts' were now 'outdoing all others in extending culture to an enormous mass of people, creating a tremendous cultural movement of the masses'.[77] Citing Lenin's last writings, in which he had redirected policy away from the political struggle towards 'peaceful and organizational "cultural" work', Bukharin reminded his audience that achievements in this sphere should be judged not only in terms of the growth of socialist industry and transport, of the 'commanding heights' of the economy, but also in terms of the 'remodelling of the masses, the reformation of their nature, and in particular the re-forming of the proletariat'.[78] Lenin, he claimed, had regarded this remodelling of the masses as 'the most essential problem confronting our Party'. In his last writings he had argued that the cultural revolution should be brought about by a reforming of the state apparatus and by 'cultural work amongst the peasants' (here Bukharin quotes from Lenin's 'On Co-operation' (1923)). However, if we read these lines again and again we are involuntarily prompted to ask: 'And what about the working class?' Bukharin noted that a superficial critic

Academy, 17 Feb. 1924), *Vestnik Kommunisticheskoy Akademii*, vii (1924), 59, 61. In this section I disagree with Stephen Cohen, who considers that Bukharin and Lenin had a common understanding of NEP by 1924 (see Cohen, *Bukharin and the Bolshevik Revolution*, 153).

[76] This speech was extensively published under the title 'Leninizm i problema kul'turnoy revolyutsii' in both *Pravda* and *Izvestiya*, 27 Jan. 1928, and in *Narodnoe prosveshchenie*, 2 (1928), and *Narodnyy uchitel'*, 1/2 (1928). I have used the translation published in *International Press Correspondence*, 7, 8, 9 (1928).

[77] Ibid. 7 (1928), 159.

[78] Ibid.

might suggest that there was here some 'deviation in the direction of the peasantry'.[79] However in speaking of the reforming of the state apparatus Lenin had naturally understood this to be 'in close alliance with the cultural rise of the working class', for 'our state is the most comprehensive organisation of the working class'. If, therefore, one asked the question along what lines the state apparatus should be reformed, the answer must be

along the lines of a struggle against bureaucracy, the education of the working masses, the instruction of the working masses in the art of administration. . . . When the predominant mass of the working class is firmly established at the tillers of the administration, bureaucracy and bureaucratism will die a natural death. The improvement of the cultural level of the workers is therefore a presumption for the actual improvement of our state apparatus.[80]

Bukharin's reconciliation of Lenin's theory of cultural revolution with his own was ingenious. He made no effort in his speech to conceal that 'for Lenin it was the mass that stood in the centre of the entire system' and he recalled the debate of 'many years ago' when Lenin had pitted all his energy against the 'errors in our ranks'.[81] He asked the question whether Lenin's programme was being fulfilled and found that there had undoubtedly been progress in raising the general cultural level of the peasantry, of the working class, the nationalities, and of women. At the same time, he noted 'some satisfactory results as regards the formation of our working cadres. . . . We are already beginning to form special cadres of our own technicians . . . cadres of fairly experienced administrators . . . men of the working class . . . who have acquired tremendous experience and a certain theoretical schooling.'[82]

[79] cf. Stalin: 'Some think that the fundamental thing in Leninism is the peasant question . . . This is absolutely wrong. The fundamental question of Leninism . . . is not the peasant question but the question of the dictatorship of the proletariat' ('The Foundations of Leninism', Lecture delivered at the Sverdlov University, Apr.–May 1924, in J. V. Stalin, *Works* (13 vols.; Moscow, 1952–5), vi. 126). Stalin made the same point, this time against Zinoviev's definition of Leninism, in 'Concerning Questions of Leninism' (9 Feb. 1926), *Works*, viii. 14, 16, 18.

[80] 'Leninizm', *International Press Correspondence*, 7 (1928), 160.

[81] Ibid.

[82] Ibid. 8 (1928), 184.

On the point of 'theoretical schooling', or the partisanship of knowledge, Bukharin also reinterpreted the argument of Lenin to suit his own purposes. Lenin, he insisted, had by no means intended that the culture of the bourgeoisie should be taken over 'in its entirety and without restrictions'. For Lenin:

Our peaceful organizational and cultural work is by no means in itself a 'peaceful' activity but only another form of the class struggle of the proletariat, of the fight for socialism. Even when Lenin told us that we must 'build up socialism with the hands of our enemies' or maintained that 'one good bourgeois specialist is better than ten bad Communists', he was speaking of nothing else than this very class struggle to be carried on by special methods.[83]

Since Lenin's death the Soviet regime had witnessed a 'scientific revolution' which was affecting not only the social sciences, 'in which Marxism has already for many years occupied a commanding position', but also the natural sciences:

We already have a number of prominent biologists who enthusiastically discuss Marxian dialectics and their application to biology. Physics, chemistry, and physiology are included in the same current, as also are reflexology, psychology, and pedagogics. There is even a society of mathematicians dealing with the problems of Marxism in relation to mathematics. . . . Marxism, which fought originally with arms and with political propaganda, is now extending its work to the entire cultural front and is penetrating into every apartment of the cultural edifice, even into the 'holy of holies' of former cultures with a view to remodelling everything according to its own example . . . the same process is also noticeable in art.[84]

The concluding note of Bukharin's review of the cultural revolution by 1928 was optimistic but not complacent. Bourgeois science and the civilian and military economies of capitalism were still strong. The Soviet Union was 'destined for a long time to live under the shadow of imperialism'. The post-war crisis had not been overcome: 'On the horizon we see the indications of further catastrophes.' No more than in 1922–3 could the Soviet regime ignore the struggle on the ideological front where 'our opponents . . . speculate on our technical and

[83] Ibid. 183.
[84] Ibid. 184.

economic backwardness, our lack of culture'.[85] In these circumstances it was all the more imperative 'even more speedily
than in other respects to overcome the period in which the
"old" has already been destroyed without the "new" yet
having been constructed. . . . We must make greater haste in
getting over the intermediate stage between the eradication of
the old and the introduction of the new.'[86] In respect of the
masses, public health care must be extended and the fight
against alcoholism and syphilis intensified; the skills of economic management must be conveyed to the peasantry, for
'even, within the limits of the ordinary budget of a peasant
farm, there is the possibility of very considerable progress';
there must be a provision of amenities such as public baths,
bakeries, laundries, schools, and libraries, and the development of leisure through clubs, the cinema, and radio.[87] However, none of these tasks could be executed 'if our cadres are
not improved to the utmost'. There was still 'an undeniable
lack of culture in our administrative cadres and even among
our members of the Party'. Cadres displayed a deficiency
of 'special knowledge'; there were 'few technicians with a
medium degree of qualification'; technically unqualified Party
members were often 'unable to fulfil their political functions
in the Party'. As far as the higher leading cadres were concerned, they had still far to go in finding the correct blend of
revolutionary enthusiasm and 'Americanism'.[88]

For Bukharin, therefore, in 1923 and 1928, as much as for
Stalin in 1929, 'cadres' and ideology were the principal levers
to be employed by the Communist Party in the engineering
of social change.[89] To draw this conclusion is not to ignore the
importance which Bukharin attached to the growth of civil
society (*Sovetskaya obshchestvennost'*).[90] It is no doubt true that

[85] Ibid. 7 (1928), 159.
[86] Ibid. 9 (1928), 209.
[87] Ibid. 210.
[88] Ibid.
[89] In 1929 Stalin identified socialist construction with the tasks of 'a) enlisting
tens of thousands of Soviet-minded technicians and experts for the work of
socialist construction; b) of training new Red technicians, Red experts from
among the working class' (see 'A Year of Great Change' (3 Nov. 1929), in
Stalin. *Works*, xii. 130).
[90] See Cohen, *Bukharin and the Bolshevik Revolution*, 145.

he counted upon the emergence of 'hundreds and thousands of small and large rapidly expanding voluntary societies, circles, and associations' to provide a ' "transmission mechanism" through which the Party could influence, and be influenced by, public opinion'. No doubt, too, he hoped that such social institutions would check the expansion of the bureaucratic state.[91] At the same time, Bukharin reserved for the Communist Party, its 'command staff', and its social doctrine a privileged and inviolable status in relation to all other social institutions; and his approval of 'mass initiative at the local levels' did not extend to factional opposition within the Party. That Bukharin's political thought after 1921 was more pluralist and more gradualist than it had been during the period of War Communism is certainly arguable. Even so, he remained the theorist of what became the Stalinist cultural revolution 'from above'.

[91] N. I. Bukharin, 'Zadachi vypusknika-Sverdlovtsa', *Zapiski Kommunisticheskogo universiteta 'meni Ya. M. Sverdlova*, ii (Moscow, 1924), 225–9; repr. in *O rabkore i sel'kore: Sat'i i rechi* (2nd edn., Moscow, 1926).

8

Bukharin and Science Policy

Robert Lewis

THE Revolution of October 1917 brought to power in Russia a regime strongly committed to the idea that science and technology could transform society. At one time or another all the main Soviet leaders referred to the importance of the natural sciences and technology and stressed the scientific basis of the new society. At a time when the pressures on his time were enormous, Lenin took a close interest in scientific matters. His 'Draft of a Plan of Scientific and Technical Work'[1] is widely cited in discussions of Soviet science, and he gave constant encouragement to younger revolutionaries who had the task of formulating a science policy for the new state.[2]

Of all the Bolshevik leaders, Bukharin was to be the most closely involved in the analysis of science and in science policy. In part, this was a consequence of his interest as a Marxist in the relationship of science to society. But it also reflected a practical commitment to the vital importance of science in building the new socialist state. In his enthusiasm for science, he once offered to make available to the physicist George Gamow all the electric power of Leningrad, if it would assist him to make a research breakthrough in nuclear physics.[3] However, to an extent, the quantity of Bukharin's writings on science and technology, and the depth of his involvement in science policy-making, were the result of his political defeat at the end of the 1920s. Thereafter, he became directly involved in Soviet science policy at a key moment in its development. Hence there are two strands to this discussion of Bukharin and

---

[1] V. I. Lenin, *Polnoe sobranie sochinenii* (5th edn., 55 vols., Moscow, 1958–65), xxxvi. 228, 231.

[2] In particular N. P. Gorbunov; see, e.g., *V. I. Lenin vo glave velikogo stroitel'stva* (Moscow, 1960), 178; *Novyymir*, 8 (1964), 278–9.

[3] A. Kramish, *Atomic Energy in the Soviet Union* (Stanford, Calif., 1959), 13.

science: Bukharin the theorist and Bukharin the politician. The resulting interplay of 'theory' and 'practice' clearly had an important influence on Bukharin's views on the role and organization of science in the Soviet Union.

BUKHARIN ON SCIENCE

Although we cannot here discuss Bukharin's social philosophy in detail, it is against his general analysis of economy and society that his view of science has to be placed. For a dialectical materialist, such as Bukharin, scientific laws were formulae reflecting objective facts, and scientific activities were based in social relationships.[4] Theory is linked to practice, but 'their unity develops on the basis of the *primacy of practice*'. The sciences, in their development over time, '"grow" out of practice, the "production of ideas" differentiates out of the "production of things"'.[5] This viewpoint naturally led Bukharin to criticize those who considered that there was 'pure' science and that it was possible to devote oneself to 'science for science's sake'.[6] He was frequently to couple the term 'fetish' with the notion of pure science, and to link this position with what he perceived as an atomizing of science under capitalism. For example, in his paper to the Second International Congress of the History of Science and Technology in London in 1931 he wrote:

The fetishing of science, as of other phenomena of social life, and the deification of the corresponding categories, is a perverted ideological reflex of a society in which the division of labour has destroyed the visible connection between social function, separating them out in the consciousness of their agents as absolute and sovereign values. Yet any—even the most abstract—branch of science has a quite definite vital importance in the course of historical development. Naturally, it is not a question of the *direct* practical importance of *any* individual principle—e.g. in the sphere of the theory of numbers, or the doctrine of quantities, or the theory of conditional reflexes. It is a question of

---

[4] See, e.g., N. I. Bukharin, 'Nauka i SSSR', *Bol'shevik*, 17 (1927), 14.
[5] N. I. Bukharin, 'Theory and Practice from the Standpoint of Dialectical Materialism', in N. I. Bukharin *et al.*, *Science at the Cross Roads* (London, 1931; 2nd edn. 1971), 15 (with prefaces by G. Werskey and J. Needham).
[6] Ibid. 20; Bukharin, 'Nauka i SSSR', 14.

systems as a whole, of appropriate activity, of *chains* of scientific truths, representing in the *long run* the theoretical expression of the 'struggle with nature' and the social struggle.[7]

For Bukharin science in the capitalist world was in a blind alley (*tupik*). The disunity of approach which existed meant that the various branches of natural science were becoming increasingly isolated from each other.[8] To adopt a socialist organization of society based on the principles of dialectical materialism was to give all the sciences a unity of method. The opportunities for and demands on science under socialism were immense. The new common philosophical core would enhance the possibility of developments across disciplinary boundaries. The end of private property in industry meant the end of private property in science and would greatly raise the effectiveness of science. Education would lose its class basis with a consequent large-scale widening of the pool of talent on which science could draw.[9]

While Bukharin may have written of the sciences growing out of practice, he did not see the relationship between the theoretical and applied sciences as totally unidirectional. He considered that theoretical problems could and did generate other theoretical problems and that the solutions to theoretical problems 'sometimes fertilise a number of hierarchically lower branches of science, and through technology penetrate into technique—consequently into the direct practice of material labour, transforming the world'.[10] Thus 'science *actively* "has a feedback effect" on the existing technical structure'.[11] This view of the relationship between theory and practice has a strong influence on Bukharin's approach to problems of science policy.

BUKHARIN AND SCIENCE POLICY

At the end of May 1929 Bukharin was put in a position to have a more direct impact on science policy-making, when he was

[7] Bukharin, 'Theory and Practice', 20–1.
[8] N. I. Bukharin, *Etyudy* (Moscow and Leningrad 1932), 254–5; 'Nauka i SSSR', 13–14.
[9] Bukharin, 'Nauka i SSSR', 14, 18; *Za industrializatsiyu*, 17 Dec. 1930.
[10] Bukharin, 'Theory and Practice', 26.
[11] Bukharin, *Etyudy*, 277.

appointed head of the Scientific and Technical Administration (STA) of the Supreme Economic Council (*Vesenkha*) of the USSR.[12] At the time this post could be seen as a temporary resting place for leaders whose star was waning. Kamenev had been the previous head, and in 1925 the task of overseeing the STA's predecessor, the Scientific and Technical Department, had been one of the three jobs given to Trotsky after his removal from the post of Commissar of War.[13]

In the late 1920s the STA was the key science policy organ of the Soviet state. In 1928 *Vesenkha's* research organizations were absorbing about one-third of the Soviet Union's total expenditure on science. Besides administering research institutes and laboratories, the STA was deeply involved in drawing up technological policy for the first five-year Plan in geological surveying, standardization, and other fields. The 'unreformed' Academy of Sciences had a scientific staff only one-third as large as *Vesenkha* and was still largely divorced from science policy decision-making. Research in the universities and research institutes of the education sector was underfunded and becoming increasingly squeezed by the pressures of teaching.[14]

In all, Bukharin was to head the Research and Development section of the central administration of *Vesenkha* and subsequently (from 1931) the Commisariat for Heavy Industry for five years until his partial and short-lived 'rehabilitation' in 1934. Further, unlike his two famous predecessors, who apparently treated their duties largely in 'ceremonial' terms, Bukharin was to play a very active role in the administration of and policy-making for industrial Research and Development. Indeed he was soon deeply embroiled in a debate within *Vesenkha* about the administrative structure for research which would best meet the changing demands of the economy and fit most sensibly into a revamped administrative structure for industry as a whole.[15] The goal of the proposed changes was to orientate the central apparatus of *Vesenkha* more towards

[12] *Prikaz VSNKh SSSR*, 795 (31 May 1929).
[13] R. Lewis, *Science and Industrialisation in the USSR* (London, 1979), 45, 51.
[14] R. Lewis, 'Government and the Technological Sciences in the Soviet Union: The Rise of the Academy of Sciences', *Minerva*, 15/2 (1977), 186–9.
[15] The following paragraphs draw on Lewis, *Science and Industrialisation*, 37–54.

planning and co-ordination by establishing 'associations' (*ob''edineniya*) to control the individual branches of industry. The formation of these new large industrial organizations raised the important question, whether *Vesenkha's* research institutes should continue to be centrally administered or should become part of the branch associations. Further, what consequences would any change have for the role and status of STA itself? Such issues were not new. Running all through discussions of industrial research policy in the 1920s was a thread which has continued to reappear as a subject of debate in the Soviet Union—the relations between research and development organizations and industry, and, in particular, the form of the most effective structure for industrial research. The key questions were: how far should research and development organizations be removed from the day-to-day pressures of industry? Would largely independent organizations tend to ignore the needs of industrial development for the delights of the ivory tower? The debate on these issues was to mirror earlier discussions in the mid-1920s, when it was argued by some members of *Vesenkha*, and in particular by Piatakov, at the time a deputy head, that industrial research and development should be decentralized, by entrusting the control and finance of the research institutes to the trusts which were the major form of industrial organization. On that occasion Dzerzhinsky, head of *Vesenkha*, strongly supported the idea of a central science policy organ in industry and stressed that the research institutes needed independence. He considered that, if control of research and development passed to the trusts, initiative would be stifled and research potential scattered to the four winds. This intervention effectively ensured the survival and indeed subsequent enhancement of *Vesenkha's* science policy organ.

In 1929 it was Bukharin who was to pick up this torch and urge that the major industrial research institutes should maintain their independence. At the beginning of September the *Vesenkha* commission dealing with the reorganization of the industrial administration is reported to have proposed that *Vesenkha's* research institutes should be administratively subordinate to the associations. At a meeting of the Presidium of *Vesenkha* which reviewed these proposals, Bukharin argued

against this view. He stated that any decentralization of research resources might produce some short-run benefits, but
that the adoption of such a policy basically meant the use of
research and development personnel to meet a shortage of
middle-level technical personnel. The consequence would be a
running-down of the research and development activity which
was vital for successful long-term industrial development. However, the press report of the meeting implies that Bukharin
was in a minority, with speakers such as Mezhlauk (deputy
chairman of *Vesenkha*) and Likhachev (head of the Moscow
car plant which now bears his name) forcefully taking the
view that, under the existing structure, science was too
divorced from industry. The final recommendation was to
some extent a compromise between these two positions. As
regards *Vesenkha*'s research organizations, it proposed that,
while narrowly specialized institutes would be controlled by
the relevant association, those which did work of relevance to
more than one branch of industry or to industry as a whole
would remain under the STA. At the same time it appeared
that the status of the STA with regard to its wider functions
of technological policy-making and co-ordination was to be
enhanced. In the words of Kuibyshev, head of *Vesenkha*, it was
to be converted 'into the headquarters [*shtab*] of the scientific
and technical leadership of industry'. It was to comprise one
of the two top-level departments with *Vesenkha*.[16] In fact, its
suggested role had many parallels with that to be given to the
State Committee for Science and Technology in the 1960s.

   In spite of the fact that the reorganization proposals were
then approved by Gosplan in mid-September, Bukharin continued to fight for the retention of all research institutes under
the STA. At the Sixth Plenum of *Vesenkha* in October he again
attacked the proposed break up of the STA's research and
development system. The STA could only become the desired
headquarters of technological development, if it had a strong
network of research and development organizations directly
under its control.[17] The STA colloquium had produced a set of

---

[16] The Planning and Economic Administration was, as its title suggests, to
look after questions of industrial planning and economic management.
[17] *Ekonomicheskaya zhizn'*, 13 Oct. 1929; *Pravda*, 14 Oct. 1929.

theses for this meeting on STA and the reorganization of industry. This document, which bears unmistakable signs of having been largely written by Bukharin, argued that, if the Soviet Union was to catch up and overtake the capitalist world economically, it would have to catch up and overtake it in science and technology, and that work on broad theoretical problems was an essential investment in the future; they provided 'fixed capital' for continuing economic growth. Indeed, all science was in one way or another linked with the process of material production. The STA considered that its research institutes were the most important of all its constitutional parts. The document agreed that industry needed 'central' and factory laboratories but considered that they should not be formed by making use of the resources of the existing institutes.[18]

However, by this time it was becoming 'open season' on Bukharin. Two weeks later, in an article in the *Vesenkha* newspaper entitled 'On the Pretensions of the Technical Intelligensia and the Theses of the STA',[19] the STA's theses were subject to a stinging assault. The main thrust of the remarks was that the STA represented a technocratic deviation. Its document marked an attempt by technical specialists to gain independence from the factory and the working class. This represented a right-wing, social democratic view of society, which the author coupled with Hilferding's revisionist ideas on organized capitalism.

Markov also denounced Bukharin's sophisticated view of the relationship between theory and practice, theoretical and applied research and industry. In Markov's world, science was firmly in the superstructure, with no ability in itself to influence the world of production: for him, the level of world science is clearly a function of the level of world production. It was nonsense to talk of the need to catch up and overtake capitalism in science as being a precondition of achieving this end economically.

With the attacks on Bukharin growing before his removal

---

[18] *Torgovo-promyshlennaya gazeta*, 12 Oct. 1929.
[19] Vl. Markov, in *Torgovo-promyshlennaya gazeta*, 26 Oct. 1929; the delay suggests that it was a carefully prepared attack.

from the Politburo in November 1929, the battleground over science policy row also started to shift. It seems likely that even an enhanced department of a commissariat began to be seen in some quarters as too important a power base. The very existence of the STA itself was now under threat.

The published theses of the Central Control Commission and the Workers' and Peasants' Inspectorate on the industrial reform discussed in detail the new administrative structure for each branch of industry, but there was nothing on the future structure of *Vesenkha*'s central apparatus. At the Central Committee, Kaganovich strongly attacked a document which Bukharin had circulated on the reorganization of industry and the role of the STA, raising like Markov the spectre of a technocratic deviation.[20] When the reorganization was finally agreed, the new-look, high-powered STA had disappeared. Responsibility for science was to be rested in a sector of Planning, Technical, and Economic Administration and the status of Bukharin within *Vesenkha* was correspondingly reduced. His one success was that between one-third and one-half of *Vesenkha*'s research institutes remained under central control.

The early 1930s were a period of almost continual change in the industrial administrative structure, as the leadership sought to find the most appropriate structure to cope with the strains of the industrialization drive. At the same time they were years of rapid expansion and change in the Soviet research and development network. Until his departure in 1934 Bukharin remained true to his view of the relationship between theory and practice and pressed the need for a strong research and development base outside the branch-administrative structure. However, the intervening years saw a decline in the importance of central controlled research institutes in the industrial research and development systems.[21]

BUKHARIN AND THE PLANNING OF RESEARCH

The years during which Bukharin headed the research and development apparatus of *Vesenkha* were also the years which

---

[20] *Bol'shevik*, 2-4 (1929), 64, 70.

[21] See, e.g., 'Nauchno-tekhnicheskoe obsluzhivanie promyshlennosti' *Sotsialisticheskaya rekonstruktsiya i nauka*, 3 (1934), 19.

saw the issue of the planning of research pushed to the forefront. For Bukharin, the scientific approach to the economy and society which gave rise to the development of a planned economy also pointed to a planned approach to science itself. In his 1927 article on 'Science and the USSR' he was to write that 'planned scientific work, socially organized, is the *new* principle which is quite fundamentally linked to *socialism's* planned economy'.[22] Within *Vesenkha* the first steps towards planning industrial research were being taken at this time. A debate was initiated in the journal of Gosplan, *Planovoe khozyaystvo*, on the application of planning to science. This soon spread to other publications. The participants tended to agree that, in spite of its complex nature, science could and should be planned. But there was a clear divergence between pro-planning scientists and planners about the approach. The former generally appeared to see the role of central-planning organs as the co-ordination of plans produced by the research establishments themselves; the latter foresaw a greater degree of central direction.[23] However, it seems most likely that such discussions will have left many if not most scientists untouched or unimpressed.[24]

This debate proved to be part of a compaign aimed at winning support for the principle that the country's scientific research effort could be planned. The climax of this campaign was the calling of the First All-Union Conference on the Planning of Scientific Research by the STA's replacement the Scientific Research Sector of *Vesenkha*, and Gosplan. Bukharin, as head of the former organ, made the opening keynote address, and, in his three-hour speech, he produced the most detailed statement which was offered on the various methodological questions involved in any attempt to plan science.[25] On the other hand, his remarks were somewhat rambling, and he did not present a fully worked-out approach for the plan-

---

[22] Bukharin, 'Nauka i SSSR', 14.

[23] Lewis, *Science and Industrialisation*, 80–1.

[24] See, e.g., M. N. Pokrovskiy's remarks to the Fifteenth Party Congress, *Pyatnadtsatyy s"ezd VKP(b): sten. otchet.* (Moscow, 1962), ii. 1136; S. I. Kaplun, 'O planirovanii nauchno-issledovatel'skoy raboty. Na odnom iz bol'nykh uchastkov', *Planovoe khozyaystvo*, 3 (1930), 83.

[25] It was reprinted in Bukharin, *Etyudy*, 236–305.

ning of research. On occasions he appears to have had problems in relating the possible approaches to planning which
were being discussed to his underlying view of the relationship
of science and society. He also took the opportunity to attack in
Aesopian language the rigid control economic planning which
was in the process of being established in response to the
stresses and strains of the first five-year plan and the Stalinist
view of centralization. Nevertheless, it remains one of the most
comprehensive attempts to grapple with the issues raised in
any attempt to plan science.

Bukharin basically addressed three questions: 'why plan?',
'what to plan?', and 'how to plan?' In answering the first
question, his aim was to win over the waverers to support the
possibility of planning. His approach was to turn the question
on its head and answer four objections made by scientists
to the idea of planning. He then went on to point out that
even bourgeois societies recognized the need to plan scientific
activities. He took geology as his example and argued that
there were no differences of principle in the approach adopted
in geology from that adopted in other areas of science.[26]

The objections to planning which he discussed were: first,
that science was an intensely personal activity. His response to
this was that such a view of science was now obsolete. One
only had to look at the large well-organized laboratories which
now provided the scientific underpinning of capitalism. The
second argument was that scientific research was an intensely
creative activity, which significantly depended on intuition.
Bukharin's reply was that such leaps of intuition were based
on a solid accumulation of information, and, while it was
impossible directly to plan intuition, it was possible to plan the
rational and solid basis which underlay it; this in the last
analysis was the crucial factor. Thirdly, there was the criticism
that the planning of science by leaning towards a collective
approach unduly constricted especially gifted researchers. This
objection, he claimed, was based on a misunderstanding of
the nature of the collective. The collective did not destroy
personality; on the contrary a well-organized collective increased the opportunities for a talented scientist. Fourthly,

[26] Ibid. 267–73.

people suggested that a plan destroyed the freedom of research. This, he agreed, was in one sense true. Soviet plans for science had the reconstruction of the country as their goal; there would be no room for 'idealistic philosophy, anti-Marxist historical doctrine, teleological views, "occult sciences", mystic systems, malicious imperialist doctrines, fascist political theories, economic doctrines which are apologies for capitalism'.[27] Since the objective interests of science coincide with the interests of the development of socialism, this restriction on scientific work was justified. Such a statement will not have been found convincing by many of the old guard of Soviet science; nor will the fact that he ended his discussion of this issue with the sentence: 'The plan is the most powerful weapon of the class policy of the proletariat on the research front.'[28]

The objections which Bukharin dealt with in this way were mainly concerned with attempts directly to control the research projects on which scientists work. This was not the only feature of science which was seen as 'plannable'. Indeed, Bukharin went on to catalogue the aspects of the country's research activities which should be planned.[29] Most scientists were likely to have little objection to many of the features, as control over them was already largely out of the hands of scientists everywhere, with developments subject either to state or to a mixture of state and private control. He saw six parts to a comprehensive plan of science: (i) the share of the national cake to be devoted to research, (ii) research topics, (iii) the construction of research facilities, (iv) the geographical distribution of research facilities, (v) expenditure, (vi) staffing.

It was the second item on this list to which he devoted most attention and which, indeed, as we have seen in our discussions of his remarks on 'why plan?', provides the real focus of his whole speech. The planning of research work was, in Bukharin's words, 'the most important, the most difficult and decisive constituent of planning'.[30] He went on to discuss the issue in terms of society's demands on science. It was easy to

---

[27] Ibid. 270.
[28] Ibid. 273.
[29] Ibid. 275–91.
[30] Ibid. 275.

draw up a list of immediate needs on the part of the economy;[31] there were at that time a whole number of problem sectors. Similarly, there were many less immediate but still urgent problems which science had to solve. It should also be identifying such problems itself without waiting to be asked, indeed it should be preventing their appearance. At a further remove the annual and five-year economic plans should be closely linked with and serviced by the research and development network. Finally there was longer-term work. For Bukharin one of the most sensitive issues was the relationship between today's and tomorrow's topics, or—to use terms which he, perhaps consciously, avoided—theoretical and applied research. He could give no guidance as to how the correct balance would be found but clearly he feared the longer-term losses to the economy of a system of planning which squeezed out longer-term work, and on this occasion too he spoke of the great need for research institutes, which had the opportunity to pursue important theoretical problems. He stressed that it was certainly not correct to suggest that all the current problems should be completely solved before longer-term problems were attacked.

Bukharin considered that one of the chief faults of such planning as already existed was the lack of co-ordination among the different research systems in the country. This meant that the country was not getting the benefit of an interchange of ideas amongst the scientific disciplines or between the different sectors of the economy. This naturally led him to discuss the issue of parallelism. One of the strengths of the Soviet research and development system was seen in the absence of the barriers between factories and scientific organizations which resulted in wasted resources in the West. In the Soviet Union lack of proper channels of communication was resulting in waste of resources. There were, however, according to Bukharin, two exceptions to the 'parallelism is bad' rule. First, when there are in existence a variety of methods (conceptual or technical) for solving a problem. Secondly, he suggests, somewhat surprisingly, that, when a *quick* solution to a task

---

[31] In a neat analogy Bukharin used the phrase 'scientific and technical first aid' (*skoraya nauchno-tekhnicheskaya pomoshch'*).

has to be found, the work should not be entrusted solely to a single research institute. He felt that a 'monopoly' approach would mean a 'bureaucratic slowdown' (*byurokraticheskoe tormozhenie*) in useful work. Whether this is a veiled criticism of the policy of establishing one large specialized research institute for each branch of industry is not clear.

When Bukharin discusses *how* scientific research should be planned,[32] it becomes apparent that he saw the developing central-planning system as inappropriate for science and that he was siding with the scientists' rather than the planners' view of planning. He began by stating that the methods of planning had to be thought out in a thorough way. The main problems all stemmed from the fact that science was a creative activity which contained a large number of unknowns. He was against any mechanical transfer of planning methods from one area to another. In any planning system you had to take account of the fact that in any sensible approach there was no possible way to establish rigid deadlines such as could be done for industrial production: 'it is laughable to say: please split the atom by 28 September 1940'. However, for Bukharin, this was not an argument against planning, but an argument against 'backward, bureaucratic, and bungled' (*poshekhonsko-byurokratichesko-golovotyapskiy*) planning.[33] Further, a creative scientist will discover new interesting lines of research, unexpected possibilities, and clearly there should not be a system which forbids the exploitation of fruitful opportunities 'only because they were not earlier included in a plan'.[34] To cope with such developments each research establishment's plans should have a certain amount of reserve time which could be used to take advantage of such opportunities. Loren Graham suggests that this would be looked on as the scientists' 'private plots'.[35]

The measurement of plan success was also problematic. In research you sometimes suffered failures. It was possible to work for a year and achieve nothing. However, it would be

[32] Bukharin, *Etyudy*, 291–302.
[33] Ibid. 292.
[34] Ibid.
[35] L. R. Graham, 'Bukharin and the Planning of Science', *Russian Review*, 23/2 (1964), 144.

completely absurd to record the result of this year of exploration as a large o, for it marked a state in a learning process
which would end in ultimate success. Failure to allow in a
planning system for this 'research risk' would inevitably result
in conservatism and the stifling of initiative. The right to take
risks had to be particularly noted and secured. It thus naturally
followed that he turned to a criticism of bibliometric methods
of measuring research output. Sensible assessment involved
questions of quality. Systematic work on this question of
research effectiveness, he said, still needed to be done.

Bukharin clearly had in mind those authors who advocated a
stricter and more mechanical planning system which reflected
more closely he industrial planning system. He went on
to state that the special characteristics of science which he
had listed made the bureaucratic distortion (*byurokraticheskoe
izrashchenie*) of planning an especially strong danger. He cited
the authority of Lenin as support for his insistence that the
bureaucratic approach had to be nipped in the bud. It would
alienate many scientists who were sympathetic but who could
be scared off by 'bungled "planning"'.[36]

It was not surprising, in the light of these remarks, that
Bukharin saw the central authorities as playing only a limited
role in establishing what was to be done 'on the shop-floor' in
the laboratory The basic general principle had to be that only
the most general problems were produced at the top—the chief
directions of work, the largest tasks, particularly urgent work.
However, having apparently given scientists a great degree of
freedom, he immediately went on to insist that planning must
provide for the closest link of research with practice. He considered that this was 'the chief and basic guiding principle
of all planning'.[37] Consequently the plans of the branch industrial research institutes were to be based on the plans of the
relevant industrial branch, but at the same time they had to
go beyond those plans and provide for the future. A further
input into the planning process was to come from an array of
scientific meetings and conferences. Amongst other things
these were to be forums for the exchange of information, the

[36] Bukharin, *Etyudy*, 294.
[37] Ibid. 295.

exploration of problems emerging on the boundaries of disciplines and for reviewing developments in foreign science and technology.[38] Again Bukharin was quick to stress that

> these meetings must be free of any element of bureaucracy, administrativeness [*administrirovanie*], control by state functionaries [*chinovnich'ya opeka*]. He hoped that the combination of these three approaches would produce plans that were 'real plans, but not a list of topics; a system, but not a mechanical agglomeration of questions'.[39]

But then, to confuse the issue, Bukharin added a rider that the plan should also find a way of including and funding individual researchers' pet projects, especially those of the most prestigious scientists.

Bukharin never further developed the issues which he raised on this occasion, and the overall pressures of the Soviet planning system overwhelmed any possibility of a sophisticated approach to the planning of science. Indeed some of the fundamental problems of planning Soviet science remained unsolved. There was a Second Planning Conference at the end of the following year, but this was concerned solely with assessing the proposals of research work in heavy industry. Bukharin's report on that occasion was not so much concerned with analysing the developments in planning as with listing the technical developments of the first five-year plan and reviewing the country's mineral resources. He was to claim that the idea of research planning had been sufficiently introduced into the minds of research workers and there was now no need to prove either the logic or the necessity for planning. However, the tenor of his remarks showed that little progress had been made towards the planning of research on the general lines which he had propounded. The central bodies responsible for research were basically involved solely in the distribution of resources. There had been no serious study of how research institutes operated. The one thing that the various elements of summary research plans had in common was not some overriding idea of cooperation between

---

[38] Ibid. 297.
[39] Ibid. 298.

institutes and production, but simply the binding which held them together.[40]

In neither of the two areas on which we have focused our attention is it possible to consider Bukharin 'successful'. He was unable either to achieve the administrative system for research and development which he considered most appropriate, or to push the research planning in the direction which he proposed. What we have seen is that the positions which he adopted and defended are based on his more sophisticated view of the fundamental relationship between theory and practice. For Bukharin, it was 'utterly absurd to conceive of the socialist principle of physical and scientific labour, the socially organized union of theory and practice *only* in the form of isolated "orders" [*zakazy*] going from factories to scientific laboratories'.[41]

However, as a consequence he found himself adopting a position on the role of science and technology which was in some aspects closer to that of the engineers and scientists who were attacked at the end of the 1920s for their independent technocratic views, than to the developing Stalinist view which became the ruling ethos of the 1930s industrialization drive.[42] Writers such as Markov could certainly find enough similarities to tar him with the same brush.

As we have seen, much of the strain in Soviet science policy during these years centred on the balance between 'short-termism' and research for the longer perspective. Indeed, this was to remain a key problem for the Soviet research and development system. We have seen that Bukharin addressed the theoretical and practical concerns underlying this policy dilemma in much of his writing. He summed it up perhaps most elegantly during his speech to the 1931 Conference on planning research:

---

[40] N. I. Bukharin, 'Tekhnicheskaya rekonstruktsiya i tekushchie problemy nauchno-issledovatel'skoy raboty', *Sotsialisticheskaya rekonstruktsiya i nauka*, 1 (1933), 24–7.

[41] Bukharin, 'Nauka i SSSR', 15.

[42] On this, see K. E. Bailes, *Technology and Society under Lenin and Stalin: Origins of the Soviet Technical Intelligentsia, 1917–1941* (Princeton, NJ, 1978), 69–121.

We have *to carry out a struggle on two fronts,* both against an old academism, a conservative love of abstraction, concern for the problems of an exclusively remote type, against distancing oneself from the noise and din of life and the 'evils of today'; and against a trivial, hair-splitting, narrow-minded attitude to science, when 'the great theoretical interest', about which Engels spoke, and which Lenin supported, is lost, when we lose sight of the wood for the trees . . .[43]

Unfortunately, in the last analysis, in the struggles and strains of the 1920s and 1930s, he was no more successful than any other of his contemporaries in establishing how the correct balance might be achieved.

[43] Bukharin, *Etyudy,* 280.

9

Bukharin and Beyond

A. Kemp-Welch

TWO somewha contradictory theses have been advanced in this book. On the one hand, Bukharin has been treated by his recent Soviet interpreters as a part of contemporary political argument, a former political leader whose legacy can be restored or redeployed on behalf of perestroika. Thus, ideas could be advanced through his agency about the compatibility of socialism and the market, of Marxism and intellectual or cultural autonomy, and, above all, of the combination of social, cultural, and other freedoms in the context of political monopoly. This may be myth-making but it is not new. Ever since the 1920s the notion of 'Bukharinism' as a model, however putative, of a non-Stalinist path to socialism has exerted a powerful influence on both the left and the right of the political spectrum. The argument resurfaced during the Khrushchev period as part of a continuing debate between the friends and foes of change. It should also be noted that Bukharin's own intellectual trajectory confirms this interpretation. Even fervent admirers would admit that, after 1921, he offered no systematic exposition of his ideas, wrote no sustained treatises, and did not attempt a general explanatory theory of politics or the social sciences. His subsequent contributions to the Marxist canon cannot be compared to the innovations of Gramsci, or even, perhaps, of Lukacs. Post-1921 Bukharin became primarily a publicist, an indefatigible propagandist of ideas, fertile and compelling, to a wide circle of pupils and admirers at home, and of fundamental importance—between the *ABC of Communism* of 1919 and the Comintern theses of 1928, when he was finally overturned by Stalin—to well-wishers of the Soviet experiment abroad.

On the other hand, as contributors to this volume have confirmed, there is an intrinsic interest in his ideas. This tran-

scends the more obviously appealing features of his thought—
the moderate path he sought towards a more civilized human
condition. There are certainly powerful counter-arguments to
consider about the political monopoly within which Bukharin
thought that humane socialism could be attained. But even
'instrumentalists' tend to concede that his ideas have substantive intellectual content. They cannot be resurrected simply
as the more or less redundant memorabilia of an Old Bolshevik
who once held, and then lost, power. An alternative, 'in-
tellectualist', approach to the re-examination of his ideas
recognizes that they do lead to central theoretical issues of
politics, economics, and international relations. In what follows
we attempt one further exploration, whose resolution perhaps
requires rather more than Bukharin himself, in his day, could
offer. We try to examine Bukharin, and his intellectual ability
and equipment, when applied to the greatest political challenge
he himself faced: the advent of Stalinism, which removed him,
without much difficulty, from the political stage.

Bukharin was not afraid to raise, and comment sharply
upon, systemic questions. From the early days of the New
Economic Policy (NEP) he was ready to criticize the consequences of 'War Communism', the system he had until
recently supported, and at the end of the 1920s he offered a
thoroughgoing critique, even a polemic, against a Stalinist re-
enactment. Of course, Bukharin was never able to publish a
full analysis of Stalinism. To do so he would have had to
emigrate, an opportunity he rejected in the spring of 1936.[1] But
statements to those he still trusted, such as Boris Nicolaevsky
and his wife Larina, as well as more-or-less Aesopian utterances
at cultural gatherings, especially during 1934, show that he
continued to agonize over the phenomenon, to canvass pal-
liatives, and even to offer tentative solutions. As long as Party
archives are closed to independent scrutiny, much of the
material for reconstructing his account remains obscure. But
there are now promising signs that such evidence is extant and
that it will be placed in the public domain.[2] The following

---

[1] Interview with Anna Larina, Bukharin's widow, Moscow, Aug. 1988.

[2] T. Edmonds, 'Recent Developments on the Historical Front: Excerpts from
an Interview with Viktor Petrovich Danilov' *Slavic Review* 50/1 (1991), 150–6.

sketch should thus be regarded as no more than preliminary to such a fully-documented account. We attempt an overview in two sections: one concerned with the defeat of the 'Right Deviation', and the other considering Bukharin's ideas, so far as they can be discerned despite censorship, in political defeat.

THE RIGHT DEVIATION, 1928–9

Bolsheviks had railed against bureaucracy at every Congress. By general consent, it was a baneful development, to be avoided at all costs. But few members were willing to accept Trotsky's warning, set out in *The New Course* (1924), that the Party's revolutionary spirit, characteristic of its old guard, was being driven out by a new tendency, 'threatening to detach the leaders from the masses, to bring them to concentrate their attention solely upon questions of administration, of appointments and transfers, of narrowing their horizons'.[3] Yet, Trotsky noted, this incipient bureaucracy, while conservative in essence, was capable of a certain dynamism, satisfying various needs: stability, security, and order. When backed by unlimited power, he noted prophetically, it could be a most powerful engine for reshaping society. However, in the early 1920s Trotsky's was a lone voice still agonizing over the contradiction between his critique and a determination to be loyal to Bolshevism. 'None of us wishes to be right, or can be right, against his Party. Ultimately, the Party is always right.'[4]

By the end of the decade Bukharin had come to accept the analysis almost in its entirety. He told Kamenev that the Party and state had merged, had become 'étatized', and that 'this was the greatest misfortune'.[5] Yet he was caught in a political trap of his own making. As Stephen Cohen points out,

Bukharin had come to share most of Trotsky's criticisms of the party's internal regime. Unlike Trotsky, however, having sanctioned its development he was its prisoner. His dissent and accompanying pleas for the tolerance of critical opinion in 1928–9 were regularly rebuffed with quotations from his own, earlier sermons against the

[3] L. D. Trotsky, *Novyy kurs* (Moscow, 1924), 13.
[4] *Trinadtsatyy s"yezd VKP(b). Mai 1924 g.: sten. otchet* (Moscow, 1924), 165.
[5] Kamenev's report to Zinoviev is available in the Trotsky Archives at the Houghton Library, Harvard University: T. 1897.

Left's 'factionalism', and his attacks on Stalin's 'secretarial regime' with derisive jeers: 'Where did you copy that from? . . . From Trotsky?'[6]

Anguished statements to the Party, preserved in the Trotsky Archives, show Bukharin grappling with this, hitherto unforeseen, development. His speech to the July Plenum of 1928 strove against interruptions, including a sardonic aside from Stalin, to make the necessary connections. The issue of forced grain requisitioning could not be treated in isolation. There was a political economy of 'extreme measures', which, in turn, would lead to a terrible social devastation. He concluded his peroration thus: 'The problem of forcible grain requisitioning is part of the problem of our state apparatus and of the struggle with the bureaucratization of that apparatus.'[7] Failure to find a satisfactory resolution to the grain problem, would, sooner or later, render impossible the resolution of the wider problems of political power.[8]

On 30 September 1928 he made a public analysis of power in the state apparatus. He told readers that the over-rapid elimination of small-scale production had resulted in the creation of a 'gargantuan administrative body'. Likewise, destruction of individual farming meant that peasants were forced to produce and sell solely through the state, with an accompaniment of massive centralized control. He warned that, 'Under absolute monopoly it is easy to become rigid and bureaucratic.' The 'pores of our gigantic apparatus' harboured 'elements of bureacratic degeneration, total indifference to the interests of the masses, their well-being, their material and cultural interests'.[9] Into such a body, 'people who are looking for reforms are never admitted'. They are replaced by 'red tape, paper work, an extraordinary waste of ink'. More damaging still, state employees are primarily motivated by coercion and cynicism: 'There are officials, "at your service", who are

---

[6] S. F. Cohen, *Bukharin and the Bolshevik Revolution: A Political Biography, 1888–1938* (New York, 1973; 2nd edn., Oxford, 1980), 325.

[7] T. 1901.

[8] Ibid. 10.

[9] N. I. Bukharin, 'Zametki ekonomista (K nachalu novogo khozyaystvennogo goda)', *Pravda*, 30 Sept. 1928; trans. in N. I. Bukharin, *Selected Writings on the State and the Transition to Socialism*, ed. R. B. Day (New York, 1982), 301–30.

willing to produce any kind of plan, even to work out a super-industrialist plan, only to laugh at us tomorrow in their own "closed circle" and walk hand in glove with our opponents the day after tomorrow.'[10] Although ostensibly directed at capitalism, these epithets had plenty of applicability to Soviet society, as Bukharin made clear by referring to them as 'problems now on the Soviet agenda'. They work well as a description, then and later, but are less satisfactory as an explanation of how such phenomena came into being. Bukharin points out that centralization leads to bureaucracy with all its attendant baggage: mismanagement, waste, a stagnant economy. But this does not account for a bureaucracy's arising in the first place.

Bolshevism, like Marxism itself, lacked a complete analysis. Indeed, there had been precious little from the founding fathers. The young Marx did write an extended *Critique of Hegel's Philosophy of Right* (completed 1847, first published 1927), and in an attendant article condemned Hegel's notion that a state bureaucracy could embody the general good of its citizenry. To his idealization of the Prussian system he retorted, 'wherever bureaucracy is a principle of its own, where the general interest of the State becomes a separate, independent and actual interest, then the bureaucracy will be opposed to the "corporations" or particular sections'.[11] The state, far from being universal as it claims, expresses an interest of a particular kind. In his famous attack on Dühring, Engels adds the thought that a bureaucracy cannot constitute an independent power because it acts in the particular interests of a social or economic grouping.[12] The comforting assurance that this had not happened in Soviet Russia—shared by Trotsky until the mid-1930s—blinded the Bolsheviks to other sources of bureaucratic power. What they did not comprehend in theory, they could not combat effectively in practice.

By November 1928 Bukharin realized that his arguments and his supporters were being suppressed by machine politics. He dispatched an 'ultimatum' to Stalin at this point:

[10] Ibid. 328–9.

[11] Cited by L. Kolakowski, *Main Currents of Marxism*, trans. P. S. Falla (3 vols.; Oxford, 1978), i. 124.

[12] See S. Avineri, *The Social and Political Thought of Karl Marx* (Cambridge, 1968), 48–52.

1. All Politburo members to guarantee that contentious and complex questions of economic policy and policy in general are discussed beforehand, collectively, and with an appropriate degree of tolerance. This to apply particularly to Monday meetings of the Politburo.

2. To ensure, by means of a Central Committee directive to all Central Committees of the national republics, *oblast*, *krai*, and *gubernia* Party organizations, that the Central Committee circular 'On Self-Criticism' is carried out in full, including that point in the circular which condemns the labelling of deviations and speaks in favour of the comradely character of debate, etc.

3. To publish a critique in *Pravda* of the incorrect methods of conducting the campaign of struggle against the right danger (the mistakes of *Komsomol'skaya pravda*, resolution of local Party organizations published in *Pravda* number 262, etc.).

4. By inserting similar articles in the central Party organ, to conduct a decisive struggle against groundless speculation about political disagreements in the Politburo.

5. To instruct the Press through the *Agit-prop* department of the Central Committee that it must not confine itself simply to recording adopted resolutions, but must guarantee observance of the norms mentioned in point 2 above, and guarantee business-like discussions, without attaching labels, of all complex questions of the country's economic, political, and cultural life.

6. In the course of resolute serious ideological work on overcoming 'right deviations', and conciliatory attitudes towards them, to cease drawing 'organizational conclusions' in the Moscow Party, and to stop the hounding of Uglanov and other comrades.[13]

In these paragraphs Bukharin comes to the heart of the political issues. The struggle against Stalinism was being lost behind the scenes by insinuation and innuendo, by disinformation which pre-empted rational arguments, and through introduction of the vague, but damaging, charge of 'right deviation'.

---

[13] Quoted by F. M. Vaganov, 'Pravyy uklon v VKP(b) i ego razgrom', doctoral dissertation (Moscow, 1970).

The Moscow Party was a test case. Once Bukharin proved unable to defend his supporters in the capital, those in the provinces melted away.[14] Stalin followed by mopping up elsewhere. The extent of the purge is shown by Bukharin's other demands:

7. To sack the editor of *Komsomol'skaya pravda*, Comrade Kostrov, and print the reasons for his dismissal in the Press.

8. To sack the editor of *Krest'yanskaya gazeta*. To bring the cartoonist of *Pushka* to account; if he is not a Party member, to arrest him; if he is, to bring him before a Party court. To reprimand the representative of *Glavlit* (the censorship) severely.

9. To release Krumin and Savelev from editorial duties with *Pravda*.[15] To replace them with N. L. Meshcheriakov and A. D. Zaitsev.

10. To make public the reprimand to the new Party committee of the Krasnaya Presnya *raion*, for the paper aimed against Comrade Sol'ts and for the information bulletin (*svodka*) of 29 October 1928.

11. To make public the reprimand to comrade Khitarov, as leader of the Communist Youth International, for his speech to the party cell of that body, supporting Trotskyist slander against the leadership of the central Party. To publish the reprimand in *Pravda* and the foreign Press.

12. To publish the decision of the Central Council of Trade Unions, based on debates within its Party cell, in *Pravda* and *Komsomol'skaya pravda*, giving detailed refutation of articles they had printed.

13. The Central Committee to repudiate the reference in *Rabochaya Moskva* to the sacking of Uglanov.

14. To instruct Comrade Bukharin to write an answer to his opponents with an explanation of points about the

---

[14] The best account remains R. V. Daniels, *The Conscience of the Revolution: Communist Opposition in Soviet Russia, 1917–1929* (Cambridge, Mass., 1960), 337–44.

[15] Stalin's replacements for Bukharin supporters Astrov and Slepkov. See R. C. Tucker, *Stalin as Revolutionary, 1879–1929* (London, 1974), 411.

tempos of industrialization and so on, draft of this to be approved by the Politburo.

15. To recall Neumann (the Comintern delegate) from Germany and repudiate the speech by Thalmann to the Sixth Congress of the Comintern.

16. To write a letter from the Central Committee, through the Comintern, to all parties of the Comintern about the state of affairs in the leadership of the Party, with order that 'specific measures' must cease.

17. To restore Comrade Sapozhnikov to the board of *Revolyutsiya i kul'tura*.

In this document, found in Central Party Archives by F. M. Vaganov,[16] we see the outcome of the atrophy of inner democracy. Bukharin the theoretician was being routed by Stalin's control over the Party's political and ideological administration. He incorporated the point into his analysis of Stalinism. Strengthening the state apparatus, he now declared, would produce a hybrid modernization whose headlong rush to build anew might merely re-create the old. He called this, in a charge that rankled, 'barracks socialism', based on 'military–feudal exploitation of the peasantry'.[17] His prognosis was gloomy, seeming to confirm Engels's warnings about the authoritarianism of a Party that took political power too early and in social isolation. However, by early 1929 Bukharin had lost the debate.

Stalin's victory has been widely discussed in the Western literature. The primary political reason, as we have seen, was his manipulation of the Party through its apparatus, which enabled him to remove all potential opponents by 'administrative measures'. Almost the entire Bukharin 'school' was dispersed during 1928–9.[18] The second was his appeal to millennial aspirations that NEP frustrated. Since 1921 the Party's policy had been a compromise, a mixed economy, private farming, conciliation of 'bourgeois specialists', and a

---

[16] Vaganov, 'Pravyy uklon'.

[17] Cited by Rudzutak, *Shestnadtsatyy s"yezd VKP(b): sten. otchet* (Moscow, 1930), 200.

[18] The dispersal of the Bukharin school is discussed by P. Ferdinand, 'The Bukharin Group of Political Theoreticians', D.Phil. thesis (Oxford, 1984). Only Stetsky remained, having capitulated to Stalin (see Cohen, *Bukharin and the Bolshevik Revolution*, 308).

prospect for socialism that would take years and years. Stalin's policies promised action at last; the fortress-storming spirit that had made the Revolution was relevant again. More than history was involved here: to young Party members and Komsomols the campaign to collectivize was not just 'War Communism' re-enacted; this was their Civil War, the one against the peasantry.[19] Recent Soviet analyses, such as the important article 'Stalin died yesterday' by M. Gefter,[20] expand this theme. Gefter suggests that Stalin deliberately advanced policies, such as those increasing class tensions, to make *his* leadership more essential. Waging a war against a large part of his own people, eliminating alternative policies and advocates of alternatives, using the methods and languages of military campaigns, fronts, and bridgeheads, creating the atmosphere of a beleaguered fortress menaced by spies and saboteurs, were all part of the act. This procedure is quite familiar to economists: 'Say's Law'—that supply creates its own demand.

The further reason for Stalin's victory was the career prospects that Stalinism opened up. Long accustomed to noting his skill in political manipulation, scholars have been slow to recognize Stalin's talent for social engineering.[21] Quite unlike the 'ideal type' of a totalitarian tyrant emancipated from the society he governed, Stalin astutely harnessed social forces to his rule. This took place in stages. First to be taken up were 'proletarian' activists and iconoclasts during the years 1927–9. Then, in 1931, they were rejected in favour of older specialists, whose former positions and status were restored on condition that they turned their skills over to the planned economy. Stalin's new regime stressed higher educational qualifications and provided the new technical intelligentsia with financial reward above that received by the remainder of the population. Such privileges reinforced a sense of loyalty, often unquestioning, to the Stalinist system. Thus, beneath the dominant

[19] L. Viola, *The Best Sons of the Fatherland: Workers in the Vanguard of Soviet Collectivization* (Oxford, 1987). See also J. Hughes, *Stalin, Siberia and the Crisis of the New Economic Policy* (Cambridge, 1991), ch. 5.

[20] M. Gefter, 'Stalin umer vchera', *Rabochiy klass i sovremennyy mir*, 1 (1988).

[21] Pioneering works were K. E. Bailes, *Technology and Society under Lenin and Stalin: Origins of the Soviet Technical Intelligentsia, 1917–1941* (Princeton, NJ, 1978), and S. Fitzpatrick, *Education and Social Mobility in the Soviet Union, 1921–1934* (Cambridge, 1979).

personality lay a 'new middle' of society upon which Stalin secured his rule.

Bukharin did not fully analyse this development, though his insistence later in the 1930s on the vital role of the intelligentsia contained some pointers. As ever, theory was his *métier*: one looks in vain for fieldwork on social structure or class different-iation. Of course, we have his handbook on sociology, *The Theory of Historical Materialism* (1920) which conceives of society as a huge system, striving for balance between its disparate el-ements. In the subsequent struggle with the 'Right', Bukharin was accused of 'mechanism', and an 'eclectic, abstract con-ception of the development of human society, a society out-side time and space, without classes and socio-economic processes'.[22] It was further alleged that his equilibrium theory was contrary to the 'Marxist–Leninist characterization of the transition period, and a revolutionary re-education of the old and creation of a socialist society'.[23] The result, critics charged, was a naïve reductionism, 'relegating all matters to the technical task of co-ordinating people as "living machines"' Hence, his was an 'anti-Leninist' view of class struggle and proletarian dictatorship.[24]

But, in a masterly chapter, Stephen Cohen defends Bukharin,[25] and shows that he was far from adopting the rigid determinism that this implies. Consequently, he is caricatured when contrasted with the later Stalinist 'voluntarism' on this score. Bukharin's account gives plentiful material to those who would resist the dogmatic version of Marxist orthodoxy that superstructure is determined by base. Hence the elements of a society consist of persons and ideas, not merely things, and its existence presupposes a certain balance between them. Follow-ing a disturbance, society will move towards a new equilibrium that may be achieved either through 'a gradual adaptation of the various elements in the social whole [evolution]', such as the intermediate stages of capitalism which Marx had dis-covered, or through 'violent upheaval [revolution], as when,

---

[22] Vaganov, 'Pravyy uklon'.
[23] Ibid.
[24] Ibid.
[25] Cohen, *Bukharin and the Bolshevik Revolution*, ch. 4.

for instance, capitalism comes to an end'.[26] Bukharin's own preference for evolution became the central feature of his social thought. Above all, there should be no 'third revolution'.[27]

BUKHARIN IN DEFEAT, 1930–7

Stalin's 'third revolution' strengthened the Soviet state to the utmost. Far from 'withering away', it swelled up, making the Leviathan[28] again seem pertinent, perhaps even more than Bukharin imagined. Hobbes's formal approval of arbitrary rule conjures up the terrifying nightmares of twentieth-century totalitarianism. But Hobbes also commended fair and lawful government directed to the common interest. Chapter Thirty of *Leviathan* sets out a formidable catalogue of duties which 'the OFFICE of the Sovereign Representative' must undertake, including concern for the safety and prosperity of the people, good necessary and perspicacious laws, equality of justice and taxation, and the duty 'to choose good counsellors; I mean such'.[29] Of course, Hobbes's preference for good government sits uneasily with the remainder of his political theory, in particular its recommendation of unconditional authority. We are bound to wonder what guarantee there is that rulers will uphold the principles Hobbes himself is so eager to sustain.

One possible interpretation of the 'relaxation' in Soviet politics of 1933–4 is an attempt to institute such guarantees. Do the rumblings in the corridors and the votes cast against Stalin at the Seventeenth Party Congress[30] indicate a drive towards reform? On the basis of a close reading of Kirov's speeches during the period, Benvenuti has identified a series of inter-related propositions. These amount to a call for 'legality', a less arbitrary administrative system, and an end to punitive measures, particularly in the countryside. There were pro-

---

[26] N. I. Bukharin, *Historical Materialism*, 242–62.

[27] The earlier revolutions were regarded as either 1905 and 1917, or February and October 1917.

[28] See Ch. 5, above.

[29] For Hobbes's reply, see D. Baumgold, *Hobbes's Political Theory* (Cambridge, 1988), 103–16.

[30] The vote was reported in R. Medvedev, *Let History Judge: The Origins and Consequences of Stalinism* (New York, 1971), 156; also A. Antonov-Ovseyenko, *The Time of Stalin* (New York, 1983), 80–3.

posals for reforms of kolkhoz administration, notably abolition of the hated political departments of machine tractor stations, and of the State Political Administration (OGPU), both of which took place during 1934.[31] The existence of a 'Kirov tendency' is unproven.[32] However, we have some rather less than Aesopian addresses to the public through *Izvestiya*, which Bukharin edited. He wrote, for instance, of discouraging aspects of 'the gigantic state apparatus' which betrayed tendencies towards 'bureau-pathology' and took upon itself the task of 'planning' society as a whole, strangling initiative and group or individual endeavours.[33] The point was illustrated by a quotation from Saltykov-Shchedrin on the 'Tsarist bureaucracy'. Although we cannot judge with certainty the full validity of the first version of *The Letter of an 'Old Bolshevik'* (thought to be partly based on conversations between Nicolaevsky and Bukharin), it does suggest a struggle continuing behind the scenes, either against Stalin or at least with different tendencies vying for Stalin's ear.[34] One of the paradoxical outcomes was the decision to prepare the 1936 constitution, partly written by Bukharin.[35]

A second set of remedies for Stalinism was also canvassed. As we saw in Chapter 8, Bukharin took charge of the Scientific and Technical Administration of the Supreme Economic Council (*Vesenkha*). This posting, often the quiet pasture of ex-leaders on their way down (such as Trotsky), was taken on by Bukharin with exuberant enthusiasm.[36] The delegation he led to London (after a slight delay while the plane returned to

[31] F. Benvenuti, 'Kirov in Soviet Politics, 1933–1934' (CREES Discussion Papers, 8; University of Birmingham, 1977).

[32] D. A. Volkogonov merely states that nothing was found in the archives (*Stalin: Triumph and Tragedy*, trans. H. Shukman (London, 1991), 208). This squares not at all with evidence presented by R. Medvedev, *Khrushchev* (Oxford, 1982), 83–4.

[33] N. I. Bukharin, 'Krizis kapitalisticheskoy kul'tury i problemy kul'tury v SSSR', *Izvestiya*, 6, 18 Mar. 1934.

[34] The whole 'Letter' is disparaged as 'spurious' by J. Arch Getty, *Origins of the Great Purges: The Soviet Communist Party Reconsidered, 1933–1938* (Cambridge, 1985), 215.

[35] Getty, however, suggests that Bukharin's role was limited ('State and Society under Stalin: Constitution and Elections in the 1930s', *Slavic Review* 50/1 (1991), 22).

[36] See also L. Graham, 'Bukharin and the Planning of Science', *Russian Review*, 23/2 (1964), 135–48.

Moscow to collect Bukharin's forgotten paper) made a lasting contribution to the study of the history of science.[37]

Bukharin in this period began to regain some of his standing as a premier intellectual, both within the Party, and also reaching out to a wider circle within the intelligentsia as a whole. His editorship of *Izvestiya*, from February 1934 to mid-1936, provided a forum and a meeting-place for the exchange of ideas. He offered, for instance, a series of reflections on culture, which deplored low Soviet standards. Addressing the literary intelligentsia, he complained that much contemporary writing remained hackneyed, vulgarized, and provincial. Instead, he sought an enlargement of 'cultural horizons' beyond the perspectives of the 'seminarist' he found so regularly in Soviet *belles-lettres*. Soviet writers, then becoming accustomed to the soothing platitudes of socialist realism, were astounded to hear their efforts measured unfavourably against international achievements. As one protested, they were unaccustomed to such Alpinism.[38]

Underlying this analysis was a concern shared with Gorky[39] that the Soviet Union should champion cultural values and human dignity in the face of fascism. Bukharin, amongst the first to take alarm at its emergence in Italy in the early 1920s, interpreted the phenomenon as a new social and economic offensive by the bourgeois class which required 'a kind of instrument, an extraordinary means that would give it an extra fist to smash the working class'.[40] He warned the Seventeenth Party Congress of the menace by citations from *Mein Kampf*.[41]

---

[37] J. G. Crowther, *Fifty Years with Science* (London, 1970), 77; N. I. Bukharin, Theory and Practice from the Standpoint of Dialectical Materialism', in N. I. Bukharin *et al.* (eds.), *Science at the Cross Roads* (London, 1931; 2nd edn. 1971), 1–33, and a re-evaluation of the meeting by S. Schaffer, 'Newton at the Crossroads', *Radical Philosophy*, 37 (1984), 23–8. See also V. Dusek, 'The Bukharin Delegation on Science and Society', in N. N. Kozlov and E. D. Weitz (eds.), *Nikolai Ivanovich Bukharin: A Centenary Appraisal* (New York and London, 1990), 129–47.

[38] *Literaturnaya gazeta*, 9 July 1934.

[39] This was a dress rehearsal for Bukharin's speech to the First Writers' Congress in August. See A. Kemp-Welch, *Stalin and the Literary Intelligentsia, 1928–39* (London and New York, 1991), 181–8.

[40] Speech to Twelfth Party Congress (1923), quoted, with approval, by A. G. Latyshev, 'Bukharin—izvestnyy i neizvestnyy', *Nedelya*, 21 Dec. 1987.

[41] *Semnadtsatyy s"yezd VKP(b): sten. otchet* (Moscow, 1934), 127–9.

Later in 1934 he wrote a series of articles on the 'Crisis of
Capitalist Culture and Cultural Problems of the USSR'.[42] The
none-too-hidden implication was that Stalinism should be
moderated to reduce the similarities between itself and the
Nazi regime. M. Gefter refers to the chance of an 'anti-Fascist
democratization in the Soviet Union', noting that 'Stalin had
a choice: he could have become the leader of a process of
normalization',[43] but, he argues, Stalin rejected it and launched
the Terror instead.

A third set of remedies was sought in the economic sphere.
Just as, under NEP, Bukharin had been willing to sanction a
considerable relaxation in retail trade, to the extent of permit-
ting, at least covertly, profiteering activity, so too in the mid-
1930s he took part in similar discussions behind the scenes. He
published an article on economic prospects in mid-1934 which
made a guarded defence of the market in a socialist economy.
Socialism, he argued, had substantially mitigated its earlier
'problematics' and had now become 'a relationship of organized
state, semi-state, and co-operative units, behind which stands
a unified, organized centralized will'.[44] To the rejoinder that
central control might seem to vitiate what remained of market
forces, Bukharin had two responses. First, the market could
not be eliminated in agriculture, either from individual farms
or from the industrial economy of collective farms, 'which must
not be despised in any case'. It was also necessary in retail
trade, not as 'the anarchic market of the past' but as 'the
correct regulator of its movements through utilization of the
market form', in which the state would continue to control
prices.[45] Even his tentative defence caused alarm in high places.
Stalin, we now learn, circulated a critique of the article to the
Politburo, denying Bukharin's statement that 'extremely high'
investment in industry over the recent period had been at
the expense of agriculture.[46] Soviet commentators have also
drawn attention to other of Bukharin's economic articles, on
the abolition of rationing, and on developing trade through

---

[42] N. I. Bukharin, *Culture in Two Worlds* (New York, 1934).
[43] See Gefter, 'Stalin umer vchera'.
[44] I am indebted in this paragraph to Professor R. W. Davies.
[45] N. I. Bukharin, 'Ekonomika Sovetskoy strany', *Izvestiya*, 12 May 1934.
[46] Published, in summary form only, in *Kommunist*, 13 (1988), 106–7.

market forces, thereby attaining a 'stable and genuine basis for correct financing and cost-accounting'.[47] As *Soviet Weekly* put it, 'his ideas on co-operatives and individual entrepreneurs, on money relations in the Soviet economy, on cost-accounting and on trade are as topical as ever before'.[48]

There is, of course, a methodological dilemma. The notion of historical alternatives presupposes that other, potential, courses of action are present in a situation, though not adopted. The case for their advancement continues to be disparaged as empty by empirical historians: 'How can we tell what would have happened if it had?'[49] However, historiography cannot be restricted to a chronicle of events: rejected opportunities are often equally instructive. For instance, as Danilov puts it, the several versions (variants) for collectivization proposed in the late 1920s 'were a negation of collectivization in its Stalinist form, but not of collectivization as such'. He argues that 'the views of Bukharin and Chayanov were also based on the idea of realizing the collectivization of land tenure and land use, achieving that objective through different paths, such as Lenin's Co-operative Plan'.[50] A similar case may be made for Bukharin's analysis of the burgeoning Soviet state. In 1928 he warned: 'We have overcentralized everything too much. We must ask ourselves: should we not take a few steps in the direction of the Leninist commune state?'[51] This reversion to his anarcho-syndicalist ideas of 1916 was eloquent and touching, but how could it have become practical politics under the Stalinist regime?

Bukharin's programme of the late 1920s, which has been called 'the unrealized alternative strategy to the one adopted by Stalin',[52] retained the market as an element in planning and industrial growth. Taken with a range of ownership models, the co-operative, *artel*, and even private, the market was ex-

---

[47] e.g. article in *Izvestiya*, 22 Dec. 1934.

[48] *Soviet Weekly*, 5 Nov. 1988.

[49] A. Gerschenkron, *Economic Backwardness in Historical Perspective* (Cambridge, Mass, 1966), 31.

[50] Contribution to Round Table discussion, *Voprosy istorii*, 3 (1988), 21–4.

[51] Bukharin, 'Zametki ekonomista'.

[52] M. Lewin, 'Das "organisierte Chaos". Bucharin und das Problem der Burokratie', in T. Bergmann and G. Schafer (eds.), *'Liebling der Partei': Bucharin-Theoretiker des Sozialismus* (Hamburg, 1989), 297–313.

pected to continue as a countervailing force to the power of the state. But Bukharin's 'strategies' faced a formidable logical problem: Bukharin was warning against an alternative that did not yet exist. Thus, in 1930, Stalin could hypocritically maintain 'NEP is the basis of our policy and will remain so for a long historical period',[53] while actually abolishing the policy. Until Stalinism appeared, Bukharin was railing against a possibility, his prophecies were only premonitions. When they had materialized, it was too late.

This outcome took key actors by surprise. A fatal combination of political blindness, combined with Stalin's supreme political skill, overtook his contemporaries. Brought up to believe that social forces, rather than heroes, make history, the Old Bolsheviks were reluctant to attach too much importance to mere individuals. Lenin had to reassert his leadership at intervals by the normal political procedures of persuasion and argument, or simply by outmanœuvring those who stood against him. Stalin's rivals in the succession struggle were inhibited, by ideology, from using *ad hominem* arguments until they were sure they disagreed with him *ad rem* on policy issues. When, in 1928–9, they eventually did, and disagreed in public, Stalin was ready with his retort. Referring Central Committee members to his erstwhile friendship with Bukharin, he stated,

Comrades, I will not dwell on personal matters, even though the personal element played quite an impressive part in the speeches of some of Bukharin's group. I will not do this because the personal element is trivial and it is not worth dwelling on trivialities. Bukharin spoke of our personal correspondence. He read several letters from which it was plain that yesterday we were personal friends, and now we are parting company politically. I don't think all these complaints and wailings are worth a halfpenny.[54]

Yet this was an ideological amnesia that Bukharin never fully overcame. Speaking in mid-1928, with what seemed to his interlocutor, Kamenev, an 'understanding born of revelation', Bukharin called Stalin a 'Genghis Khan' who would 'drown the

---

[53] J. V. Stalin, *Sochineniya* (Moscow, 1946–52), xi. 4.
[54] Quoted in Volkogonov, *Stalin*, 174–5.

Revolution in a sea of blood'.[55] Yet there remained a constant
hope that Stalin could listen to reason. Hence the stream of
notes addressed 'Dear Koba', much to his wife's dismay.[56]
Their personal relations were not broken off and the defeated
Bukharin, initially with Rykov and Tomsky, was willing to
propose a reconciliation.[57]

However, as the 1930s proceeded, there was a growing realization that Lenin had been right all along. The question of
personality was a 'decisive trifle'[58] which his successors had
ignored at their peril. Bukharin began to reflect quite seriously
upon the problem of political leadership (*vozhdizm*).[59] At the
Congress of Writers he declared that the central problem
of contemporary culture was 'quality'. Departing from his
authorized subject, Soviet poetry, he declared: 'The problem
of quality is the problem of diversity, of the multiplicity of
differing approaches to a question, of individualization, of
attaining greater depth, and so on. It is the fundamental problem in science, in economics, in the sphere of leadership and in
ideas.'[60] Gorky, who had initiated a similar discussion in public
and had invited Bukharin to address the Congress, concurred.
He told his secretary, in the solitude of his dacha, that political
leadership could degenerate into leader-ism, 'an illness of the
psyche, in which the ego grows like a sarcoma and poisons or
deforms the mind'.[61] Such a disease was chronic, spreading
steadily. In this state 'the personal principle begins to hyper-
trophy and the collective to atrophy'. It became a pathological
condition.[62] Gorky referred only to distant leaders of the past:
to the Caesars, to Attila, and to Napoleon, but dropped a
single hint. He referred to Lenin's 'amusement' that his fiftieth

[55] T. 1978.

[56] Interview with Anna Larina, Moscow, Aug. 1988.

[57] For instance, their visit to Stalin on New Year's Day 1930 (R. Medvedev,
Nikolai Bukharin: The Last Years (New York, 1980), 25).

[58] R. C. Tucker, *Stalin as Revolutionary, 1879–1929* (London, 1974), ch. 12.

[59] See earlier reflections in N. I. Bukharin, *Tsezarizm pod maskoi revolyutsii*
(Moscow, 1925).

[60] N. I. Bukharin, speech in *Pervyy vsesoyuznyy s'yezd sovetskikh pisatelei: sten.
otchet* (Moscow, 1934), 479; trans. as 'Poetry, Poetics and Problems of Poetry in
the USSR', in *Soviet Writers' Congress, 1934* (London, 1977; first pub. in *Problems
of Soviet Literature*, London, 1935).

[61] I. Shkapa, *Sem'let s Gor'kim* (Moscow, 1964), 249–50.

[62] Ibid.

birthday should be a day of national celebration. No one could forget the fulsome displays at Stalin's fiftieth birthday, in 1929.

Bukharin's own analysis, preserved in the 'last testament' which his widow memorized and kept to herself for almost twenty-five years of camps and imprisonment,[63] speaks clearly enough of the 'personal equation'. Noting 'the working of a hellish machine which, probably by the use of medieval methods, has acquired gigantic power, fabricates organized slander, acts boldly and confidently',[64] he contrasts this with its former conduct. 'At present, the so-called organs of the People's Commisariat of Internal Affairs (NKVD) are a degenerate organization of bureaucrats, without ideas, rotten, well-paid, who use the Cheka's bygone authority to cater to Stalin's sick suspiciousness (I dare not say more).' He predicts that his destruction would lead to the deaths of countless supporters, and protests his innocence:

My one head, guilty of nothing, will drag down thousands of guiltless heads. For an organization must be created, a Bukharinite organization, which is in reality not only non-existent now, the seventh year that I have had not a shadow of disagreement with the Party, but was also non-existent then, in the years of the right opposition. About the secret organization of Ryutin[65] and Uglanov, I knew nothing. I expounded my views, together with Rykov and Tomsky, openly.

I have been in the Party since I was eighteen, and the purpose of my life has always been to fight for the interests of the working class, for the victory of socialism. These days the paper with the sacred name *Pravda* prints the filthiest lie, that I, Nikolai Bukharin, have wished to destroy the triumphs of October, to restore capitalism. That is unexampled insolence, that is a lie that could be equalled in insolence, in irresponsibility to the people, only by such a lie as this: it has been discovered that Nikolai Romanov devoted his whole life to the struggle against capitalism and monarchy, to the struggle for the achievement of a proletarian revolution. If, more than once, I was mistaken about the methods of building socialism, let posterity judge me no more harshly than Vladimir Il'ich did. We were moving toward a single goal for the first time, on a still-unblazed trail. Other times,

---

[63] See *Znamya*, 10–12 (1988).

[64] N. I. Bukharin, 'To a Future Generation of Party Leaders', in Medvedev, *Let History Judge*, 182–4.

[65] See A. Vaksberg, *Literaturnaya gazeta*, 20 June 1988, and Ryutin's text in *Yunost'* (1988), 2.

other customs. *Pravda* carried a discussion page, everyone argued, searched for ways and means, quarrelled and made up and moved on together.

I appeal to You, a future generation of Party leaders, whose historical mission will include the obligation to take apart the monstrous cloud of crimes that is growing ever huger in these frightful times, taking fire like a flame and suffocating the Party.

I appeal to all Party members! In these days, perhaps the last of my life, I am confident that sooner or later the filtre of history will inevitably sweep the filth from my head. I was never a traitor; without hesitation I would have given my life for Lenin's, I loved Kirov, started nothing against Stalin. I ask a new, young and honest generation of Party leaders to read my letter at a Party plenum, to exonerate me, and to reinstate me in the Party.[66]

After an interval of fifty years, this appeal has at last been answered.

Despite the above, Bukharin did not ever speak out against Stalinism. Rather, in his apparent—and sometimes explicit—acquiesence, he appeared to endorse some, though not every, element. For instance, he returned from touring famine-stricken regions of the south prostrated and on the point of psychological collapse. Larina tells us he had to be revived on the sofa with valerian water.[67] This very human reaction was no substitute for practical politics. If there were written protests to the authorities about the awesome consequences of the collectivization policies, which he had earlier opposed, then they have yet to be placed in the public domain. It is clear that Bukharin intended, even under Stalinism, to remain within the Party fold. We can only speculate as to his motivation. Did Bukharin discover, like Danton before him, the impossibility of retiring from revolutionary politics? Did he just persuade himself that, faced with Nazism, Stalinism would be a lesser evil? Was this the meaning of the statement, quoted above, that from 1920 to 1937 he had 'not a shadow of disagreement with the Party'?

Solzhenitzyn is most censorious of these final days:

---

[66] N. I. Bukharin, 'Pismo "Budushchemu pokoleniyu rukoroditelei partii"', first official publication, *Moskovskie novosti*, 6 Dec. 1987, 12.

[67] A. Larina, *Nezabyvaemoe* (Moscow, 1989).

What did Bukharin fear most in those months before his arrest? It is reliably known that above all he feared expulsion from the Party! Being deprived of the Party? Being left alive but outside the Party? And *Dear Koba* had played magnificently on this trait of his (as he had with them all) from the very moment he had himself become the Party. Bukharin (like all the rest of them) did not have his own *individual point of view*. They didn't have their own genuine ideology of opposition, on the strength of which they could step aside and on which they could take their stand. Before they became an opposition, Stalin declared them to be one, and by this move he rendered them powerless.[68]

He approves of Koestler's portrait of Bukharin, in *Darkness at Noon*, supposedly offering up his life in the 'show trial' as a 'last service to the Party'. We know that Bukharin may have turned to philosophical and ethical questions in his condemned cell.[69] But we also know his last request: to pencil a note to Stalin asking, 'Koba, Why do you need me to die?', kept in the dictator's desk until his own death.[70] This sad act is not convincing evidence that he ever fully comprehended the phenomenon that put him to death.

BEYOND BUKHARIN

Russian historians are still divided over Bukharin's contradictory legacy. Volkogonov's assessment is rather negative:

If Trotsky (rather than Stalin) had been in charge of the Party, even more burdensome experiences would have awaited it, involving the loss of our socialist achievements—all the more because Trotsky did not have a scientific and clear programme for the construction of socialism in the Soviet Union. Bukharin had such a programme, his own vision of the general aims of the Party. But, in spite of his great attractiveness as a person, his considerable intellect, his gentleness, and his humanity, Bukharin for a long time did not understand the necessity of a sharp leap by the country in the growth of its economic power.[71]

[68] A. Solzhenitsyn, *The GULag Archipelago, 1918–1956: An Experiment in Literary Investigation* (London, 1974), 1–11, 414.
[69] Suggested by J. Berger, *Shipwreck of a Generation* (London, 1971).
[70] Medvedev, *Nikolai Bukharin: The Last Years*, 161.
[71] D. A. Volkogonov, 'Fenomen Stalina', *Literaturnaya gazeta*, 9 Dec. 1987.

R. W. Davies, who also quotes this, observes that 'many, though not all, of the defenders of the Bukharin position in the USSR manage to avoid discussing the question of urgent military needs altogether'.[72] This may be, but how pressing were 'military needs' in 1928–9? At least, one wonders whether Bukharin's supposed neglect of this requirement would have had less catastrophic consequences than Stalin's alleged recognition. It is at least arguable that a more planned, balanced, and less forced programme of industrial development would have prepared the Soviet Union more adequately for the Second World War.[73]

A second approach to Bukharin is less critical.[74] Its best exponents, such as the economist Otto Latsis, try to puzzle out why other, potentially possible, avenues were not taken. His answers are political and social: that there were alternatives to Stalinism; that they could have achieved respectable or greater rates of industrial development. To understand the reasons why Stalin's 'adventurist' and violent policies were adopted, the composition of the top Party leadership should be examined 'Stalin won organizationally, but not socially, or psychologically.' For final victory, terror was needed. But, Latsis suggests, Stalinism also prevailed over Bukharinism, because it was more closely allied to a backward and immature country which lacked 'an age-old democratic culture'.[75]

This sombre thought was echoed by Alexander Yakovlev in the autumn of 1990. Surveying the prospects for perestroika, of which he had been a principal architect, Yakovlev noted the dead weight of the past. Soviet society had yet to overcome the legacy of authoritarianism. To break through into democracy it was necessary to dispense with conservative practices of the

---

[72] R. W. Davies, *Soviet History in the Gorbachev Revolution* (London, 1989), 47, and *Détente*, 1 (1988).

[73] See, e.g., the case made by T. Shanin, 'Which road leads to the temple?', *Détente*, 11 (1988).

[74] For instance, the defence of Bukharin's 'alternative': G. I. Shmelev, *Oktyabr*, 2 (1988). Several critiques also appeared: e.g. V. V. Gorbunov, 'Kniga V. I. Lenina "Gosudarstvo i revolyutsiya" i ee istoricheskoe znachenie', *Voprosy istorii KPSS*, 4 (1988), 111–24, emphasizing his differences with Lenin before the Revolution, and G. A Bordyugov and V. A. Kozlov, 'Povorot 1929 goda i al'ternativa Bukharina', *Voprosy istorii KPSS*, 8 (1988), 15–33.

[75] O. Latsis, *Znamya*, 6 (1988).

Stalinist, and the even earlier, past. Democracy entailed the primacy of the individual over the state, law over arbitrariness, social and moral norms over wilful behaviour. The achievement of such a democratic condition would be the task of generations.[76] At the heart of this debate is Bukharin's dual legacy, which contradicts the arbitrary authoritarianism of Stalinism, through its advocacy and acceptance of a plural society, culture, and economy, while, simultaneously, seeking to remain faithful to the strongly autocratic spirit of Leninism. It could be said, in objection to Medvedev's title, *Let History Judge*, that history has no court. However, the jury on Bukharin is still out. It seems fairly certain that, as they review the future in the light of its past, the successors to Soviet Communism will contend the aptness of at least two elements of Bukharin's intellectual contribution. Sooner than most within the Party he foresaw and fought against two terrible features of the 'third revolution' of 1929, which lay like a deadly curse across subsequent development. He warned of the fatal consequences of forcible collectivization, and of the tyranny which would befall society under a planned and totally centralized economy. To say that his remedies fell short of his diagnosis is perhaps to identify the ultimate inadequacy of human intellectual endeavour. One wonders whether Bukharin would agree.

[76] A. Yakovlev, *Moskovskie novosti*, 21 Oct. 1990.

Select Bibliography

PRIMARY SOURCES

A. A. Bogdanov

Elementy proletarskoy kul'tury v razvitii rabochego klassa (Moscow, 1920).
Nachal'nyy kurs politicheskoy ekonomii (9th edn., Moscow and Petrograd, 1923).
O proletarskoy kul'ture, 1904–1924 (Moscow and Leningrad, 1925).
'O tendentsiyakh proletarskoy kul'tury (otvet Gastevu)', *Proletarskaya kul'tura*, 9–10 (1919).
Tektologiya: Vseobschaya organizatsionnaya nauka (Berlin, Petrograd, and Moscow, 1922; 2nd edn., 2 vols. Moscow, 1989).
Voprosy sotsializma (Moscow, 1918).
Vseobshchaya organizatsionnaya nauka (Tektologiya) 2 vols.; Moscow, 1917).

N. I. Bukharin

(a) Editions

Izbrannye proizvedeniya, ed. G. L. Smirnov (Moscow, 1988).
Izbrannye trudy: Istoriya i organizatsiya nauki i tekhniki (Leningrad, 1988).
K novomu pokoleniyu: Doklady, vystupleniya i stat'i posvyashchennye problemam molodezhi (Moscow, 1990).
Komintern, ed. F. I. Firsov (Moscow, 1989).
Metodologiya i planirovanie nauki i tekhniki, ed. P. B. Volobuyev (Moscow, 1989).
Problemy teorii i praktiki sotsializma, ed. G. L. Smirnov (Moscow, 1989).
Put' k sotsializmu v Rossii: Izbrannye proizvedeniya N. I. Bukharina, ed. S. Heitman (New York, 1967).
Selected Writings on the State and the Transition to Socialism, ed. R. B. Day (New York, 1982).

(b) Books and articles in Russian

'A. A. Bogdanov' (obituary), *Pravda*, 8 Apr. 1928.
Ataka: Sbornik teoreticheskikh statei (Moscow, 1924).
Azbuka kommunizma (with E. A. Preobrazhensky) (Moscow, 1919).
'Burzhuaznaya revolyutsiya i revolyutsiya proletarskaya', *Pod znamenem marksizma*, 7–8 (1922), 61–82.

'Diskussiya po voprosu o postanovke kul'turnoy problemy', *Sputnik kommunista*, 19 (1923).

'Doklad. Vsesoyuznoe soveshchanie s-kh. kollektivov', *Pravda*, 6 Mar. 1925.

Ekonomika perekhodnogo perioda, i. *Obshchaya teoriya transformatsionnogo protsessa* (Moscow, 1920).

'Ekonomika sovetskoy strany', *Izvestiya*, 12 May 1934.

Etyudy (Moscow and Leningrad, 1932).

'Itogi plenuma IKKI', *Pravda*, 28 June 1927, 3.

'K teorii imperialisticheskogo gosudarstva' (1915), in *Revolyutsiya prava*, i (Moscow, 1925).

'K postanovke problem teorii istoricheskogo materializma (Beglye zametki)' (1923), in *Ataka: Sbornik teoreticheskikh statei* (Moscow, 1924).

'Krizis kapitalisticheskoy kul'turi i problemy kul'tury v SSSR', *Izvestiya*, 6, 18 Mar. 1934.

'Kul'turnye zadachi i bor'ba s byurokratizmom', *Revolyutsiya i kul'tura*, 2 (5 Dec. 1927), 5–12.

K voprosu o trotskizme (Moscow and Leningrad, 1925).

'Lenin kak marksist', *Vestnik Kommunisticheskoy akademii*, vii (1924), 22–68.

'Leninizm i problema kul'turnoy revolyutsii', *Pravda*, 27 Jan. 1928, 4–5.

Mezhdunarodnoe polozhenie i zadachi Kominterna (Moscow, 1928).

Mirovoe khozyaystvo i imperializm (Moscow, 1918) (written 1915).

'Nauka i SSSR', *Bol'shevik*, 17 (1927).

'Ob itogakh ob"yedinennogo plenuma TsK i TsKK VKP(b)', *Pravda*, 4 Nov. 1927, 5–7.

'Obshchie itogi nashego razvitiya i ego perspektivy', *Pravda*, 24 Oct. 1924, 5.

Ocherednie zadachi partii. Doklad na XVI Moskovskoy gubernskoy partkonferentsii 20 noyabrya 1927 g. (Moscow and Leningrad, 1928).

'O kharaktere nashei revolyutsii', *Bol'shevik*, 19–20 (1926), 28–59.

'O likvidatorstve nashikh dney', *Bol'shevik*, 2 (1924), 3–9.

'O mezhdunarodnom i vnutrennem polozhenii SSSR', *Pravda*, 13 Jan. 1927, 2–4.

'O politike partii v khudozhestvennoy literature', *K voprosy o politike RKP(b) v khudozhestvennoy literature* (Moscow, 1924).

O rabkore i sel'kore: Stat'i i rechi (2nd edn., Moscow, 1926).

'Pismo "Budushchemu pokoleniyu rukovoditelei partii"', *Moskovskie novosti*, 6 Dec. 1987.

Politicheskaya ekonomika rant'e. Teoriya tsennosti i pribyli Avstriyskoy shkoly (Moscow, 1919).

'Politicheskoe zaveshchanie Lenina', *Pravda*, 24 Jan. 1929; repr. *Kommunist*, 2 (1988).

'Problema kul'tury v epokhu rabochei revolyutsii', *Pravda*, 11 Oct. 1922.

'Proletariat i voprosy khudozhestvennoy politiki', *Krasnaya nov'*, 4 (1925).

Proletarskaya revolyutsiya i kul'tura (Petrograd, 1923).

Put' k sotsializmu i raboche-krest'yanskiy soyuz (Moscow and Leningrad, 1925; 4th edn., 1927).

'Tekhnicheskaya rekonstruktsiya i tekushchie problemy nauchno-issledovatel'skoy raboty', *Sotsialisticheskaya rekonstruktsiya i nauka*, 1 (1933).

Teoriya istoricheskogo materializma: Populyarnyy uchebnik marksistskoy sotsiologii (Moscow, 1921).

'Teoriya "organizovannoy bezkhozyaystvennosti"', *Pravda*, 30 June 1929, 3–5.

Tsezarizm pod maskoy revolyutsii. Po povodi knigi N. Ustryalova 'Pod znakom revolyutsii' (Moscow, 1925).

'Vliyanie NEPa i "uklony" v rabochem dvizhenii', *Pravda*, 25 Mar. 1923, 2.

'Zadachi vypusknika-Sverdlovtsa', *Zapiski Kommunisticheskogo universiteta imeni Ya. M. Sverdlova*, ii (Moscow, 1924).

'Zametki ekonomista (K nachalu novogo khozyaystvennogo goda)', *Pravda*, 30 Sept. 1928, 2–3.

'Zheleznaya kogorta revolyutsii', *Za pyat' let, 1917–1922: Sbornik* (Moscow, 1922).

'Znachenie agrarno-krestyanskoy problemy', *Bol'shevik*, 3–4 (1925), 3–17.

(c) *Works in translation*

The ABC of Communism (with E. A. Preobrazhensky), trans. E. and C. Paul (London, 1922; repr. London, 1969; also Ann Arbor, Mich., 1966).

Building up Socialism (London, 1926).

Culture in Two Worlds (New York, 1934).

Die kapitalistische Stabilisierung und die proletarische Revolution (Moscow, 1926).

The Economic Theory of the Leisure Class (New York, 1927).

Economics of the Transformation Period (New York, 1971).

Historical Materialism: A System of Sociology (New York, 1925; London, 1926).

Imperialism and World Economy (New York, 1929).

Les Instituteurs et la jeunesse communiste (Paris, 1925).

'Poetry, Poetics and Problems of Poetry in the USSR', in *Soviet Writers' Congress, 1934*) (London, 1977; first pub. in *Problems of Soviet Literature*, London, 1935).

'Theory and Practice from the Standpoint of Dialectical Materialism', in N. I. Bukharin *et al.*, *Science at the Cross Roads* (London, 1931; 2nd edn., 1971).

'To a Future Generation of Party Leaders' (1937), in R. Medvedev, *Let History Judge* (New York, 1971).

A. V. Chayanov

Osnovnye idei i formi organizatsii krest'yanskoy kooperatsii (Moscow, 1919).
Osnovnye idei i formi organizatsii sel'skokhozyaistvennoy kooperatsii (rev. and enlarged 2nd edn., Moscow, 1927).
The Theory of the Peasant Economy (Manchester, 1989) rev. edn. of *A. V. Chayanov on the theory of peasant economy* (Homewood, Ill. 1966).

V. I. Lenin

Collected Works (45 vols.; London, 1960–70).
Imperialism (Moscow, 1917); rep. in *Collected Works*, 22, (1964).
Leninskiy sbornik ed. L. B. Kamenev *et al.* (40 vols.; Moscow, 1924–85).
New Economic Developments in Russian Peasant Life (1893; first pub. 1923).
'On Co-operation' (1923). in *Collected Works*, xxxiii (1966).
Polnoe sobranie sochinenii, 5th edn., 55 vols.; (Moscow, 1958–65).
State and Revolution (1917), in *Collected Works*, 25 (1965).

J. V. Stalin

'Concerning Questions of Leninism', (1926), *Works*, viii (1954).
Economic Problems of Socialism in the USSR (Moscow, 1952).
'The Foundations of Leninism' (1924), *Works*, vi (1953).
Sochineniya (vols. i–xiii, Moscow, 1946–52; vols. xiv–xvi (1–3), ed. R. H. McNeal, Stanford, Calif., 1967).
Works (13 vols., Moscow, 1952–5).
'A Year of Great Change' (1929), *Works, xii* (1955).

L. D. Trotsky

Novyy kurs (Moscow, 1924) trans. as *The New Course* (Ann Arbor, Mich., 1965).

OFFICIAL PROCEEDINGS AND RESOLUTIONS

Kommunisticheskiy nternatsional v dokumentakh (Moscow, 1933).
KPSS v rezolyutsiykh, iii–iv (Moscow, 1970).
Protokoll. Erweitert Exekutive der kommunistischen Internationale. Moskau, 22 November–16 Dezember 1926 (Hamburg and Berlin, 1927).
Protokoll. Fünfter Kongreß der kommunistischen Internationale (Hamburg, 1924).
Pyatnadtsataya konferentsiya VKP(b) (Moscow and Leningrad, 1927).
Pyatnadtsatyy s"yezd VKP(b): sten. otchet (Moscow, 1962).
Semnadtsatyy s"yezd VKP(b): sten. otchet (Moscow, 1934).
Shestnadtsatyy s"yezd VKP(b): sten. otchet (Moscow, 1930).
Trinadtsatyy s"yezd VKP(b). Mai 1924 g.: sten. otchet (Moscow, 1924; repr. 1963).

SECONDARY WORKS

ABRAMSKY, C. (ed.), *Essays in Honour of E. H. Carr* (London, 1974).
ANTONOV-OVSEENKO, A., *The Time of Stalin* (New York, 1983).
ASTROV, V. N., *Krucha* (Moscow and Leningrad, 1966).
AVINERI, S., *The Social and Political Thought of Karl Marx* (Cambridge, 1968).
AYKHENVAL'D, A., *Sovetskaya ekonomika (ekonomika i ekonomicheskaya politika SSSR)* (Moscow and Leningrad, 1927; 2nd edn., 1928).
BAILES, K. E., 'Alexei Gastev and the Soviet Controversy over Taylorism, 1918–1924', *Soviet Studies,* 3 (1977).
—— *Technology and Society under Lenin and Stalin: Origins of the Soviet Technical Intelligentsia, 1917–1941* (Princeton, NJ, 1978).
BAUMGOLD, D., *Hobbes's Political Theory* (Cambridge, 1988).
BAZAROV, V., *Na puti k sotsializmu* (Kharkov, 1919).
BENVENUTI, F., 'Kirov in Soviet Politics, 1933–1934' (CREES Discussion Papers, 8; University of Birmingham, 1977).
BERGMANN, T. and SCHAFER, G. (eds.) *'Liebling der Partei': Bucharin— Theoretiker des Sozialismus* (Hamburg, 1989).
BERLIN, I., *Four Essays on Liberty* (Oxford, 1969).
BETTELHEIM, C, *Les Luttes de classes en URSS* (Paris, 1977).
CARR, E. H., *A History of Soviet Russia: Socialism in One Country, 1924–1926* (3 vols.; London, 1958–64).
—— *What is History?* (London, 1961).
CLAUDIN-URONDO, C., *Lenin and the Cultural Revolution* (Sussex, 1977).
COATES, K., *The Case of Nikolai Bukharin* (Nottingham, 1978).
COHEN, S. F., *Bukharin and the Bolshevik Revolution: A Political Biography, 1888–1938* (New York, 1973; 2nd. edn., Oxford, 1980).

—— *Rethinking the Soviet Experience: Politics and History since 1917* (Oxford, 1986).

CROWTHER, J. G., *Fifty Years with Science* (London, 1970).

DANIELS, R. V., *The Conscience of the Revolution: Communist Opposition in Soviet Russia, 1917–1929* (Cambridge, Mass., 1960).

DAVIES, R. W., *Soviet History in the Gorbachev Revolution* (London, 1989).

DIACONOFF, P. A., 'Gosplan and the Politics of Soviet Planning', Ph.D. thesis (Indiana Univ., 1973).

ERLICH, A., *The Soviet Industrialization Debate, 1924–1928* (Cambridge, Mass., 1960).

FERDINAND, P., 'The Bukharin Group of Political Theoreticians' D.Phil. thesis (Oxford, 1984).

FITZPATRICK, S. (ed.), *The Cultural Revolution in Russia, 1928–1931* (Bloomington, Ind., 1978).

—— *Education and Social Mobility in the Soviet Union, 1921–1934* (Cambridge, 1979).

GEFTER, M., 'Stalin umer vchera', *Rabochiy klass i sovremennyy mir*, ɪ (1988).

GETTY, J. Arch., *Origins of the Great Purges: The Soviet Communist Party Reconsidered, 1933–1938* (Cambridge, 1985).

GORBUNOV, N. P., *V. I. Lenin vo glave velikogo stroitel'stva* (Moscow, 1960).

GOR'KY, A. M., *O russkom krest'yanstve* (Berlin, 1922).

GORI, F. (ed.), *Il XX Congresso del PCUS* (Milan, 1988).

GORZKA, G., *A. Bogdanov und der russische Proletkult* (Frankfurt and New York, 1980).

GOUDOEVER, A. VAN, *The Limits of Destalinization in the Soviet Union: Political Rehabilitations in the Soviet Union since Stalin*, trans. F. Hijkoop, (London, 1986).

GORELOV, I. E., *Nikolay Bukharin* (Moscow, 1988).

GRAHAM, L., 'Bukharin and the Planning of Science', *Russian Review*, 23/2 (1964).

GRAMSCI, A., *Selections from the Prison Notebooks*, ed. Q. Hoare and G. Smith (London, 1971).

HARDING, N., *Lenin's Political Thought* (2 vols.; London and New York, 1977–81).

HEITMAN, S., *Nikolai I. Bukharin: A Bibliography* (Stanford, Calif., 1969).

HUGHES, J., *Stalin, Siberia and the Crisis of the New Economic Policy* (Cambridge, 1991).

JOLL, J., *Three Intellectuals in Politics: Rathenau, Blum, Marinetti* (London, 1960).

KATKOV, G., *The Trial of Bukharin* (London, 1969).

KEMP-WELCH, A , *Stalin and the Literary Intelligentsia, 1928–1939* (London and New York, 1991).

KERSHAW, I., *The Nazi Dictatorship: Problems and Perspectives of Interpretation* (London, 1985).

KHRUSHCHEV REMEMBERS, trans. S. Talbott (London, 1971).

KNIRSCH, P., *Die ökonomischen Anschauungen Nikolaj I. Bucharins* (Berlin, 1959).

KOLAKOWSKI, L., *Main Currents of Marxism*, trans. P. S. Falla, (3 vols.; Oxford, 1978).

KNEI-PAZ, B., *The Social and Political Thought of Leon Trotsky* (Oxford, 1978).

KOZLOV, N. N , and Weitz, E. D., *Nikolai Ivanovich Bukharin: A Centenary Appraisal* (New York and London, 1990).

KRAMISH, A., *Atomic Energy in the Soviet Union* (Stanford, Calif., 1959).

KUN, M., *Buharin* (Budapest, 1988).

LABEDZ, L., (ed.), *Revisionism: Essays on the History of Marxist Ideas* (London, 1962).

LARINA, A., *Nezabyvaemoe* (Moscow, 1989).

LATYSHEV, A. G., 'Bukharin—izvestnyy i neizvestnyy', *Nedelya*, 21 Dec. 1987.

LEWIN, M., *Le Dernier Combat de Lénine* (Paris, 1967), trans. as *Lenin's Last Struggle* (London, 1975).

—— *Political Undercurrents in Soviet Economic Debates: From Bukharin to the Modern Reformers* (London, 1975).

LEWIS, R., *Science and Industrialisation in the USSR* (London, 1979).

LOWY, A. G., *Die Weltgeschichte ist das Weltgericht. Bucharin: Vision des Kommunismus* (Vienna, 1969).

LUXEMBURG, L., *Die Akkumulation des Kapitals* (Berlin, 1913); trans. as *The Accumulation of Capital* (London, 1951).

MALLY, L., *Culture of the Future: The Proletkult Movement in Revolutionary Russia* (Berkeley, Calif., and Oxford, 1990).

MANDELSTAM N., *Hope Abandoned: A Memoir*, trans. M. Hayward (London, 1974).

MÄNICKE-GYÖNGYÖSI, K., *'Proletarische Wissenschaft' und 'sozialistische Menscheitsreligion' als Modelle proletarischer Kultur* (Berlin, 1982).

MEDVEDEV, F., *Khrushchev* (Oxford, 1982).

—— *Let History Judge: The Origins and Consequences of Stalinism* (New York, 1971).

—— *Nikolai Bukharin: The Last Years* (New York, 1980).

NETTL, J. P., *Rosa Luxemburg* (abriged edn., Oxford, 1969).

NICOLAEVSKY, B., *Power and the Soviet Elite: 'The Letter of an "Old Bolshevik"' and Other Essays* (New York, 1965).

NOVE, A., *An Economic History of the USSR* (London, 1989).

—— *Glasnost' in Action: Cultural Rennaissance in Russia* (London, 1989).

—— and Nuti, D. M. (eds.), *Socialist Economics* (London, 1972).

PREOBRAZHENSKY, E. A., *The Crisis of Soviet Industrialization*, trans. D. A. Filtzer (London, 1980).

—— *Novaya ekonomika* (2nd edn., Moscow, 1926); trans. B. Pearce, *The New Economics* (Oxford, 1965).

REIMAN, M., *The Birth of Stalinism: The USSR on the Eve of the Second Revolution*, trans. G. Saunders (London, 1987).

RIGBY, T. H., Brown, A. H., and Reddaway, P. (eds.), *Authority, Power and Policy in the USSR: Essays Dedicated to Leonard Schapiro* (London, 1980).

SAWER, M. (ed.), *Socialism and the New Class: Towards the Analysis of Structural Inequality within Socialist Societies* (Sydney, 1978).

SCHAPIRO, L., *Russian Studies* (London, 1986).

SHANIN, T., 'Which Road Leads to the Temple?', *Détente*, 11 (1988).

SHKAPA, I., *Sem' let s Gor'kim* (Moscow, 1964).

SHUKMAN, H. (ed.), *The Blackwell Encyclopedia of the Russian Revolution* (Oxford, 1988).

SOCHOR, Z., *Revolution and Culture: The Bogdanov–Lenin Controversy* (Ithaca, NY, and London, 1988).

SOLZHENITSYN, A., *The GULag Archipelago, 1918–1956: An Experiment in Literary Investigation* (London, 1974).

SPRING, D. (ed.), *The Impact of Gorbachev: The First Phase, 1985–90* (London, 1991).

STEHR, U., *Vom Kapitalismus zum Kommunismus: Bucharins Beitrag zur Entwicklung einer sozialistischen Theorie und Gesellschaft* (Hamburg, 1973).

SUSILUOTO, I., *The Origins and Development of Systems Thinking in the Soviet Union: Political and Philosophical Controversies from Bogdanov to Present-Day Re-Evaluations* (Helsinki, 1982).

SZAMUELY, L., *First Models of the Socialist Economic Systems* (Budapest, 1974).

TARBUCK, K. (ed.), *Rosa Luxemburg and Nikolai Bukharin: Imperialism and the Accumulation of Capital* (London, 1972).

TSIPKO, A. S., 'Istoki stalinizma', *Nauka i zhizn'*, 11 (1988)–2 (1989).

TUCKER, R. C., *Stalin as Revolutionary, 1879–1929* (London, 1974).

—— *Stalin in Power: The Revolution from Above, 1928–1941* (New York, 1990).

—— (ed.), *Stalinism: Essays in Historical Interpretation* (New York, 1977).

VAGANOV, F. M., 'Pravyy uklon v VKP(b) i ego razgrom', doctoral dissertation (Moscow, 1970).

VIOLA, L., *The Best Sons of the Fatherland: Workers in the Vanguard of Soviet Collectivization* (Oxford, 1987).

VOLKOGONOV, D., *Triumf i tragediya: Politicheskiy portret I. V., Stalina* (Moscow, 1989); trans. H. Shukman, as *Stalin: Triumph and Tragedy* (London, 1991 .

Index

Page numbers in italic indicate entries in the Bibliography.